Stewart Granger

Don Shiach has written several books on the cinema
including *The Films of Peter Weir*, *The Movie Book*, *The
Movies* and *Jack Nicholson*. He is also the author of
numerous textbooks in English and drama for schools and
colleagues. He lives in Brighton and London.

STEWART GRANGER

The Last of the Swashbucklers

Don Shiach

First published in Great Britain
2005 by Aurum Press Limited
25 Bedford Avenue
London WC1B 3AT
www.aurumpress.co.uk

This paperback edition published 2006

A catalogue record for this book is available from the
British Library.

ISBN-10 1 84513 167 3
ISBN-13 978 1 84513 167 8

A catalogue record for this book is available from the
British Library.

10 9 8 7 6 5 4 3 2 1
2010 2009 2008 2007 2006

Text design by Roger Hammond
Typeset in Minion by SX Composing DTP, Rayleigh,
Essex
Printed and bound in Great Britain by Bookmarque,
Croydon, Surrey

for Jean Woollard

ACKNOWLEDGEMENTS

My thanks to Dr Cedric Jones, Reverend Wulstan Hibberd, Ray Pollingon, Tony Sloman, R. Bryce Taylor and Graham Coster of Aurum Press

CONTENTS

Chapter 1

JIMMY STEWART

T HE TWO SWORDSMEN have been duelling for almost ten minutes, the longest fencing sequence in movie history. The setting is a Parisian theatre of the late eighteenth century. One of the duellists is a French aristocrat, bewigged and elegantly costumed, and the other an actor dressed in the theatrical costume of the period. Both the cinema audience and the movie's theatre audience watch as these two skilful exponents try to kill each other with thrusts and hacks and all the elaborate ploys of expert swords-manship. The duel swings one way and then the other. They fight on the edge of balconies and seats in the stalls, and in the spacious foyers of the theatre. Finally, they are on the stage itself and the increasingly desperate aristocrat, fast losing his glacial coolness, is reduced to panic-stricken defence. The actor, with consummate skill, manages to disarm his arrogant opponent, who is now defenceless and at the actor's complete mercy. The victor is poised to make the final fatal thrust to the heart of the vanquished aristocrat, but unaccountably he hesitates. He backs away, seemingly puzzled by his own reaction to this hated but now vulnerable opponent. He throws his sword to the floor, walks to the back of the stage and disappears. The aristocrat is as astounded by this, as are the theatre audience.

The actor is called Scaramouche and the real-life actor playing him in the eponymous movie is Stewart Granger. His opponent is the Marquis de Maynes played by Mel Ferrer. This duel sequence comprises perhaps the finest moments of Stewart Granger's movie career, and *Scaramouche* is one of the movies for which he will always be remembered. For many film-goers, it is simply the best swashbuckler ever made, outranking even *Captain Blood* or *The Adventures of Robin Hood*, which both starred the most famous swashbuckling star in movie history, Errol Flynn. Certainly, Granger will forever be associated with the role of Scaramouche. It encapsulates all of the appeal that he had as a movie star: an uncomplicated masculinity, athletic grace, a sense of fun, a romanticism, a playfulness, especially towards women, a kind of honour, courage and decency. Granger rarely played an intellectual or a man of ideas. He was essentially a man's man who had a strong appeal to many women of his era, as well as a man of action and an old-fashioned romantic hero, a handsome champion who avoided effeteness, and a star who acted out a type of unfettered male fantasy.

That was Stewart Granger's screen persona, his movie image. Those were the qualities that made him an icon of his generation. But did that persona match the real-life Granger? Did all the qualities that made him one of the top box-office draws, firstly in Britain and then internationally through the movies he made in Hollywood, stem from within himself or was all that just a result of the parts he played? All actors use something of themselves in their profession. With some, the divide between their stage or screen persona and their real selves is huge. With others, there is a merger of the two. And there are those whose screen roles interact with their private lives with less than happy results. Granger belongs in this category.

Movie stars are undoubtedly a kind of phenomenon. They reach a height of fame and wealth that speaks volumes about the celebrity culture we live in. Ever since the mass-market movie industry started at the beginning of the twentieth century, there has been the need to create stars to draw the paying customers into the cinemas. Very often that inevitable fame comes rather undeservedly to the so-called stars the movie industry creates. Frequently, it has to be said, movie stars are without much or even any discernible talent. Many have little or no acting ability. Put certain movie stars on a theatre stage and demand a performance that requires some depth and they would be found sadly wanting. Often individuals are chosen for stardom not for their histrionic talents but because they possess a particular kind of look, or because they embody a contemporary 'type', raw material that publicists can use to build a persona. There is something about these individuals that movie producers think will appeal to the mass audience. Sometimes, actors are merely in the right place at the right time. Reaching for movie stardom is like playing a game of chance: the odds are hugely against you, and only a very few are chosen to be the 'lucky' winners.

Most famous movie actors encapsulate certain values for us, which movie audiences learn to recognise in these individual stars. Once the star's persona and the values attached to this persona become familiar to audiences, the star's mere presence in a movie acquires a significant meaning.

For example, Gary Cooper exuded an uncomplicated honesty and integrity in movies such as *Mr Deeds Goes to Town*, *Sergeant York* and *High Noon*. When audiences watched Cooper on the screen, they paired him with the values of American honesty and simple decency, and they knew they could depend on Gary to sort out the bad guys and right wrongs. Never mind that in real life Cooper was only semi-literate and a simplistic reactionary who played a less than glorious part in the persecution of supposed communists in Hollywood during the forties and fifties. Never mind that if Cooper had been asked to perform a role of any complexity on a stage, he would very likely have been out of his depth. As the marshal in *High Noon*, however, he seemed to embody all that is best about the American character.

Similarly, when she was at her peak, Bette Davis manifested values connected with a woman determined to get her way in a man's world, a cultured, educated and intelligent female who would not be put down by male patronage, an icon for oppressed women everywhere. But Davis in reality was repeatedly unhappy in her private life, was thought to be a real monster by many who worked with her, went through long periods of unemployment in her chosen profession as a movie star and seemed to become increasingly bitter as she got older. She was Bette Davis and Bette Davis stood for, well, Bette Davis and all that that symbolised on the silver screen.

All over the world, there seems to be a fatal tendency to confuse a movie star's screen persona with his real self. Hence, likeable old Ronald Reagan could be elected President because a sizeable proportion of the American public fancied as their head of state that nice guy from *Kings Row* who had his legs sawn off. More recently, the 'Terminator' himself, Arnold Schwarzenegger, has been elected to the governorship of the largest state in the Union. These two glaring examples are evidence that movie stars do carry a set a values for audiences and that sometimes many people confuse the screen roles these individuals play with their strengths as human beings in everyday real life.

No single movie star can symbolise all the values of their era, but individual stars inevitably embody some of those principles. Perhaps we get the movie stars we deserve; certainly screen personas have changed from generation to generation. The Gary Coopers and the John Waynes of the forties and fifties were overtaken by the likes of James Dean, Montgomery Clift, Marlon Brando and Paul Newman. Joan Crawford and Bette Davis symbolised a different kind of woman from those impersonated by Audrey Hepburn, Jane Fonda or Sharon Stone. The movie industry serves up aspects of our society in the differing appeal and values of the movie stars we, as the audience, partly create. We want rebelliousness; they will give you Jack Nicholson or Russell Crowe. We want integrity; they will give you Robert Redford or Sally Field. We want sexiness; they will give you Sharon Stone or Jennifer Lopez. We want male arrogance; they will give you Ben Affleck. We want male angst; they will give you Ben Stiller or Woody Allen.

We want romantic heroes; they will give you Errol Flynn or Stewart Granger. The movie industry has a star on tap for all tastes, periods and sets of values.

At the peak of his movie star career, both in Britain and later in Hollywood, Stewart Granger signified certain values to the cinema audience. To discover what those values were, and what exactly his appeal as a star was, is a part of the task of this biography, as well as exploring how his screen persona interacted with Granger the man. Did his screen roles shape Granger's private life and vice versa? Movie stardom invests a kind of immortality on the favoured few who achieve the first rank of stardom. Great stage actors from the past such as Henry Irving or, more recently, John Barrymore, are only remembered largely by theatrical historians, but even the most limited of movie stars live on, preserved in a kind of celluloid aspic as their films are replayed on television, DVD, videos and in repertory cinemas. A star such as Greta Garbo, for example, although it is over sixty years since she made her last movie, is still instantly recognisable to a sizeable proportion of the world's population. Marilyn Monroe, who died in 1962, is still one of the most famous women in history. Almost fifty years after his death, Errol Flynn still has legions of devotees. Clark Gable, Charlie Chaplin, Tyrone Power, Bette Davis, Joan Crawford, Steve McQueen, James Dean, Audrey Hepburn – these are just some of the movie stars whose 'existence' has been immortalised by the medium of film. Death may end a movie star's life, but it does not end the relationship the star has with his or her admiring public.

Stewart Granger may not have achieved the level of enduring fame of those giants of the cinema, but for a comparatively brief period in the middle decades of the last century he was world-famous and a big box-office star. Even now he has a lasting fan base. His stardom was a phenomenon of the time and we can learn something not only about the man in this biography, but the process by which he became a star and what that stardom tells us about that era.

*

James Lablache Stewart was born on 6 May 1913, in the Old Brompton Road in West London. The Old Brompton Road in those days was a fairly well-heeled area, as it still is. James was named after his father, a Scot and a retired army major. Granger was proud of his Scottish ancestry, as we will see, and also proud of his father, who was an MBE. However, Granger's father was fifty-five when his son was born, a rather elderly age to be starting a family. Stewart Senior had spent many years serving in India and had been a very athletic fellow. From his son's autobiography, *Sparks Fly Upward*, published in 1981, we learn that James Senior clearly found this belated fatherhood a problem.

Granger's mother had been, and remained, a 'famous beauty'. According to Granger, she had married his father to escape from a repressive home background after she had eloped and married an aristocrat, who had died of tuberculosis not long afterwards. Granger is frank in his autobiography about his mother's 'flirtations' and her long-standing relationship with a man whom Granger thought of as his 'uncle' until the information that this man was his mother's lover was communicated to him. His father, by all accounts, was a complaisant husband, regarding this long-lasting arrangement as the price he had to pay for the privilege of remaining her husband.

To understand Stewart Granger and the demons that drove him throughout his life, we have to reflect on his family background and the social milieu into which he was born. First of all, he struck it lucky in the sense that he was born with, if not the proverbial silver spoon in his mouth, then at least a silver-plated one. His family were not rich, but they were comfortably well off. In the social class structure of Britain of that time, they would have been identified as upper-middle class, although just a few miles away from their house in the Old Brompton Road, in London's East End, many thousands of people were living lives of squalor in abject housing conditions and with scarcely enough food to keep themselves alive.

Granger, then, was not born into great wealth, but his family were much better off than the vast majority of his fellow citizens. But in any class structure – and all societies have them, however much some may deny it –

the pattern is to aspire to the class above you and to despise the class below you. Perhaps class aspirations play a part in Granger's story. Some people of that era would have regarded him as not quite 'top drawer', especially as his mother came from a theatrical family (her mother had been a member of Henry Irving's company) and there was Italian blood in the family, albeit very famous blood, that of the Luigi Lablache, a famous bass singer and Granger's great-great-grandfather.

Granger's formative years therefore took place in the 1920s when Britain's social structure had not yet been shaken up by the events of the 1930s and the Second World War. It is probable that Granger was consistently dogged by a feeling of being 'not quite good enough'. This might explain some of the conflict that was to occur throughout in his life. At times he seemed almost to be seeking it out. Additionally, although his family background was reasonably wealthy, he would later mix with people from much more affluent surroundings. He undoubtedly felt the need to aspire to a certain level of material wealth, and this would have a huge impact on his movie career.

It is safe to say that the peculiar circumstances of his parents' marriage must have had a lasting effect on Granger. His sympathies seemed to lie with his father and he has some harsh words to say about his mother in his autobiography. He also wrote that he wanted to be close to his father, but he was never able to achieve this. In a *Photoplay* interview he gave to Ruth Waterbury in the 1950s, he said: 'We were always two generations apart in views and habits. We never had any intimacy at all.' He refers to his father as emasculated and a 'ghost in our home'. It is his mother who bears the brunt of his blame for this and it is hard to avoid the conclusion that Granger's ambivalent attitudes to women in later life were largely formed by his dismay at the state of his parents' marriage: separate bedrooms, his mother's devotion to her lover and his father's lasting unhappiness with this arrangement, although he complied with it. Upper-middle-class English chaps growing up in 1920s and 1930s would have quickly learnt that decent fellows didn't dwell too much on that kind of thing, certainly did not talk about their feelings and would never seek help to deal with the emotional problems that such a childhood trauma had created. In other words, chaps weren't expected to whine, but just to get on with it. If he had been born fifty years later, Granger might, once he reached adulthood, have sought therapeutic aid to help rid himself of negative feelings and a lasting sense of hurt arising from these childhood problems. As it was, it seems that he never really came to terms with the scars left by these family dramas, although he frequently referred to them much later in life in newspaper interviews and in his autobiography. He clung onto this sense of hurt, and never divested himself of it. His childhood experiences almost certainly made him wary of true intimacy with people, whom he grew to dislike and distrust more and more as he became older.

As was quite usual for upper-middle-class families like the Stewarts in that era, the children (young James soon had a younger sister Iris) were left in the control of a nanny, whom Granger refers to as 'a trouble-making cow'. Indeed his first relationships with females were seemingly fraught: he says war was declared early on between him and his sister, he hated the nanny and he was disappointed in his mother, who was causing his father such pain. He tried to get the attention of his father and his 'uncle' but they seemed uninterested. Any discipline imposed on the young Granger was at the hands of women and this he deeply resented.

Granger writes fondly of the family holidays they used to enjoy in Cornwall, although female fussing and controlling had to be circumvented if he were to enjoy the company of the fishermen and farmers he admired. A pattern was already developing: Granger wanted freedom from all shackles, especially female ones, was showing early signs of being an outdoors man's man and was rebellious.

However, his mother was a movie fan, so he was allowed to go the cinema frequently. It was the great days of the silent era and among the movies he saw were the silent versions of *Scaramouche* and *The Prisoner of Zenda*, which were to be important landmarks in his own career. Granger records that he got so excited while watching these movies that he had to leave the cinema to be sick from the stomach upsets that already beset him. Throughout his life, this romantic hero, the dare-devil adventurer of the silver screen, would suffer from chronic ailments, and these stomach problems would interfere with his life in a very important way when he was in his twenties.

Granger, because of his class background, was destined to be educated in private rather than state schools. As was usual for someone of his background, he attended a prep school, which he hated. He was subjected to bullying (who isn't at these establishments?) and this made him scared, which made him wonder whether or not he was cowardly. 'I was constantly trying to prove to myself that I wasn't a coward, so I went looking for trouble. This apparent belligerent attitude affected my whole life,' he later wrote. This comment from his autobiography shows a certain level of self-awareness. Individuals who have been bullied in their youth often acquire a kind of antagonistic camouflage as a warning to potential bullies. To help defend himself against these attacks, the young Granger became quite a skilled boxer and this, and the other sports he played with enthusiasm, helped him to develop a good physique.

It is interesting that Granger ascribes his 'belligerent attitude' in life to the bullying he received at school. This undoubtedly contributed to his aggression, but whether the level of bullying he endured at school was excessive by the standards of his time, it is difficult to know. Certainly, he considered it significant enough to dwell on it in his autobiography. However, a more likely and important motivation for his belligerence is the anger he felt about his family. He undoubtedly saw himself as ignored, unloved and in the midst of a family situation he could not really understand. This produces anger in a child, which has to be channelled in some direction. The school bullies were useful, then, as substitute targets for his fury. The bullying was doubtless real enough, but it seems there was a degree of displacement in operation as well. Boarding schools are a uniquely British institution. Middle-class and upper-class families in Britain will make all kinds of financial sacrifices to be able to send their children, some as young as seven, to be educated in public schools, which are in fact the opposite of the usual meaning of 'public' in that entry to them is restricted largely to those few in society who can afford their fees. For the higher economic groups in Britain, it is still a badge of social esteem to be able to pay these substantial fees for the privilege of making their children endure years of education away from the comforts of home and family support. However miserable they themselves may have been at their own boarding schools, and many people confess that they detested the experience, it seems they have to put their own children through the same system in order to give them a 'good start in life'. The old school tie syndrome still functioned in the 1920s when Granger first went to public school and many would say that its importance has not declined to this day. In attending Epsom College (which he did after leaving his prep school), then, as a boarding student in Wilson House, young Stewart was following a conventional path for a youngster of his class background.

Epsom College, situated in Epsom, a small town on the edges of London and famous for its racecourse where the English Derby is run every year, had been his 'uncle's' own school so his mother's lover clearly was central to the decision to send his 'nephew' to endure the same fate as he had done. It was surely indicative of the power struggle within the Stewart family that the son was sent to this particular school.

According to Granger's own testimony, it was not a happy match. In the ranking order of English public schools, Epsom College would not be considered among the most prestigious, such as Eton, Harrow, Winchester, Westminster or Rugby. Its status as a public school more or less matched the Stewart family's rank in British society. Epsom College was, and is, a 'respectable' public school of the middle rank and many people would have perceived Granger as having indeed 'a good start in life' by attending it. At Epsom he eventually joined the 'pre-med' class for those whose intention it was to train to become doctors when they left school.

Again, according to Granger's own testimony, he encountered bullying at his new school and the inevitable loneliness of a boy separated from his family and forced to live in close proximity with other boys. He became a target because he shone at reciting poetry and singing. Perhaps the fact that he was developing 'good looks' also made him the subject of envy. Granger said he took out his aggression on the rugby field and he generally did well at sports, but he has almost nothing positive to say about his secondary education. A good start in life it may have been, but his years at Epsom College did not seem to make Granger more amenable or fonder of his fellow human beings. Many people sentimentalise their schooldays, especially those who have attended public schools. They choose to forget the horrors and recall through rose-tinted spectacles the so-called school ethos and camaraderie. Granger was not one of those people.

The Reverend Wulstan Hibberd was a contemporary of James Stewart at Epsom: 'The only memory I have of him is not a pleasant one. He made, in a contemptuous tone, a rather unpleasant personal remark. To offset the idea that I bear a grudge, I may add that I thought of writing him on the occasion of his eightieth birthday. I did not do so partly because he might not welcome hearing from such a strange source. I rather wish I had – he might have sent a kind reply. He was rather arrogant.'

Dr J. Cedric Jones, another contemporary, also recalls him: 'I doubt if I would remember him if he had not been such a prominent member of the Rugby Fifteen for two or three seasons. He and a boy called Watkins were the wing-forwards in that team and a tough pair they were. I remember him as a flamboyant character, but I was surprised when I learnt that he had gone into films. I understand that our then headmaster [Arnold Powell] when he was asked about what memories he had of Stewart could only offer: "He used too much hair oil."'

Schoolboys are notoriously unpleasant at times to one another, so too much cannot be read into these recollections, but it is interesting that the same adjectives used about Granger in later life crop up when his schoolboy persona is described: 'contemptuous', 'arrogant', 'tough' and 'flamboyant'. The headmaster's comment about 'too much hair oil' may reflect a dated schoolmasterly criticism, but it points to a budding narcissism.

It was while he was at Epsom College, during a visit from his mother and 'uncle', that the emotional bombshell about his mother's real relationship with this man finally exploded in his face. Over tea at a local teashop, his mother told him that his 'uncle' was not really his father's brother but only 'a very special friend'. It can only be imagined how this affected the teenage Granger. It probably helped him understand why his mother seemed much fonder of his uncle than his father and why the latter was such a remote figure within the family circle, but it must also have instigated guilt and, no doubt, deep resentments. Granger wrote that up to this point he had felt fonder of his uncle than his father. Now that he knew the whole story, however, it was perhaps natural that he would feel remorse about his 'abandoned' father. It was an almost *Hamlet* scenario: the father has been displaced by the 'brother' and the son, once he knows the truth, is beset by guilt and resentment. Granger also wrote later that it was years before his mother, remaining true to the stiff upper-lip ethos of the English middle classes, even alluded to this family drama again. It seems amazing that there was this ongoing emotional and sexual tangle within the Stewart family and that no one talked about it at all. The young Granger was learning the harsh lesson that one didn't talk about these things; emotions had to be bottled up and family skeletons ignored. One just had to get on with life.

Schooldays came to an end and a decision about James's future education had to be made, now that he had passed his school exams. Stewart Senior told his son that he had been having financial problems and that, although he would probably be able to pay for him to go to train as a doctor, it would have to be with the aim of being a general practitioner rather than as a specialist consultant, which his son had set his heart on becoming. Young James, sensing probably that even to send him through university would be a severe financial strain on his father, opted to give up the idea of becoming a doctor and decided to look for a job. Much later in life, in a newspaper interview, Granger, despite all the fame and wealth that had come his way from being a world-famous film star, stated he still wished he had become a doctor. It is difficult to gauge the depths of young Granger's disappointment at the time, but it must have been something of a blow to a young man. Characteristically, however, he determined to make the best of things.

It seemed to be his decision to make his way in the world without formal education after school. Perhaps his reasons were mixed: he wanted to save his father the financial burden of putting him through years of university and hospital training, but also he may have been anxious to get out into the 'real' world in order to test himself against it. At this stage in his life, it seems, acting as a possible profession had not crossed his mind, despite his maternal family's ancestors. His mother, however, whose grandfather had been the famous Italian bass and whose father had also been a professional singer, had at one time nourished hopes that Jimmy would follow in their footsteps. She sought the advice of a singing maestro who pronounced: 'He has a fine voice – for two notes. After that, he's a frog.' So a singing career was out of the question.

There was always something of the gambler and the adventurer about Granger, as we shall see from his legal tussles and business ventures later in his life. He seemed to need to inject excitement into his life, even when that excitement brought him at times to the brink of ruin. This was another aspect of his trying to prove his courage, to test the fates and to extend himself, even at this very young age.

His first participation in the job market was not successful. He started working for the Bell Punch Company, which made ticket machines for bus conductors, but was sacked after clearly showing little enthusiasm for the mundane work. This was a young man making his way in the world without any clear direction, but very few young people in their late teens have established set goals, especially those who choose not to go on to higher education. Something had to turn up for the young Stewart if he were to make his, and eventually it did.

Film extra work is a 'profession' that people drift into and out of, but for Granger it was going to be an extremely important step. Life is full of random events that can shape the course of a life. Thus, when a friend recommended to Granger that he should register with an agent for film extra work, he did. On his index card, the agency wrote 'young upper-class playboy type'. That is an interesting description in this rather tawdry world. There was perhaps something slightly vulgar about Granger's looks and style, which suggested the playboy aspect, but his public school accent and background marked him as the movie world's idea of 'upper class', although it is safe to say that the real upper classes would not have recognised him as one of their own.

For a young man anxious to prove his courage and manliness, as Granger confesses he was prone to, it is probable that he considered being an actor rather a 'pansy' thing to become. Perhaps that is why, despite his family antecedents, he had never shown any interest in being an actor. But soon he was earning some kind of living in the movies. For someone without a strong sense of direction, it was a means of making some money and filling his time.

By Granger's own account, however, he quickly ran into problems with second assistant directors who were in charge of the extras: they expected a kickback if they put an extra on call for the next day's shooting or for the next film and they tended to yell. Granger's hackles inevitably rose and he became unpopular with the little Hitlers who misused their power in this way. Nevertheless, among the films he can be glimpsed fleetingly in as an extra are *Southern Maid* (1933), *I Spy* (1934), in which he also acted as stand-in for the star Ben Lyon, and *Give Her A Ring* (1934).

Among the people he met during this period in his life was the young Michael Wilding, who was also doing extra work at this time. Wilding would go on to be a star in his own right and later marry Elizabeth Taylor. Granger and he would remain firm friends until Wilding's premature death in 1979.

Around this time, Granger's 'uncle', his mother's lover, died in the family home, where he had moved, with Stewart Senior's consent, when he had fallen ill. This death clearly upset his mother very much, but it did not resolve in any way the chasm between Granger's parents. Granger wrote, ' I thought to myself, poor Daddy. He hasn't really got her to himself even now.' The death of this man whom Granger had known as his uncle until the truth was revealed to him and whom, by his own admission, he had preferred to his own remote and 'castrated' father, must have also affected Granger and left him with unresolved and confused feelings.

However, life had to continue and he had to make an income. During one of his stints as an extra, he injured his thumb and had to go to the doctor's surgery. It was another of life's seemingly random events that was to have important repercussions. The doctor's wife, a former actress called Susan Richmond, who had been part of the touring company that Granger's grandfather had run, recognised his name, made the connection with his theatrical antecedents and recommended that he go along to the Webber Douglas Academy of Dramatic Art. Granger, without any serious intent of following through on this, presented himself at the drama school, read a bit of Shakespeare very badly and, to his amazement, was offered a place. According to Granger, he laughed off the idea at first, but came round later. After all, he reasoned, there wasn't much, or anything, on the horizon at that time, so he might as well give this acting thing a go.

When you consider how difficult it is nowadays to gain entry to drama schools in London, Granger's comparatively easy acceptance at Webber Douglas seems remarkable. This undoubtedly was heavily influenced by his theatrical lineage; the people at the drama school knew the names of his theatrical ancestors by reputation and were obviously impressed. Thus, his family connections undoubtedly eased his way. Perhaps they recognised his potential as well – his looks, his air of confidence and his physical presence – but no one could describe his entry into drama school as difficult. Granger might have taken the whole thing a bit more seriously later in life if he had had to struggle to be accepted as a drama student, like many others. As it was, he walked into a profession that he had never seriously considered before.

Granger described his two years at Webber Douglas as 'what you might laughingly call study'. Certainly all the evidence points to the fact that drama schools in those distant days were not as professional and demanding as they are nowadays. Principally, students were taught how to enunciate clearly, project their voice, smoke cigarettes on stage, move around so they did not bump into the stage furniture and generally to become recognisable and acceptable West End actors. In other words, they were trained to be 'theatrical' actors, mannered, 'well-spoken' and inhibited. There would have been no training for screen acting, because sound movies had only been in existence for a few years and, anyway, the theatre people looked down on movies as second-rate. When you consider the rather shoddy state of British theatre in the 1920s and 1930s, the theatre people did not deserve to give themselves such airs, but this patronising attitude to screen-acting and cinema in general persisted for several decades until a new breed of British actor such as Trevor Howard, Albert Finney, Tom Courtenay and others appeared on the scene.

Thus, despite his experience of the movies as an extra, it was as a theatre actor that Granger was launched properly into the acting profession. At the age of twenty-two, circumstances had conspired to take this seemingly directionless young man and turn him into an actor. He sufficiently impressed someone who saw him act in his end-of-term show at Webber Douglas to be offered three pounds a week to play second leads at Hull Repertory theatre in Yorkshire.

Repertory theatre as such has all but vanished from Britain. During this era, however, there were many weekly repertory companies round the country offering regular work to actors who signed up for seasons of plays. They would generally act in a play for one week, while rehearsing during the day for the next production. It could be vital training for young actors because it allowed them to flex their muscles playing sometimes demanding parts and initiated them into the hard work that putting on a theatrical production can be. Very often, however, the productions and the plays were third-rate, the actors under-rehearsed and not prepared to take risks, and the whole experience less than exciting. Television may have helped to kill off repertory theatre companies, but they contributed to their own demise as well.

Hull in the 1930s was one of the major fishing ports of Britain, but it has never been known particularly for its culture or its beauty, so this first apprenticeship in the professional theatre could hardly be counted a glamorous start, but it gave Granger a chance to play leading roles in the kind of play (whodunits, light comedies, melodramas) that were the staple of that kind of repertory theatre. He quickly prospered and, perhaps characteristically, was soon knocking on the manager's door asking for a raise. When he was turned down, again perhaps characteristically, he gave in his notice and stated grandly that he was going to join the premier repertory company then operating, the Birmingham Repertory Theatre. That company was run by Sir Barry Jackson, a well-known actor of the era.

It is an old adage in the theatre that it's not the talent you are endowed with but the people you know that get you the good jobs. In Granger's case, this was borne out because, once more, the woman who had used her influence to ease his way into drama school now came through for him again. Susan Richmond knew Jackson, contacted him and recommended Granger. Fortunately, there was a vacancy for a leading man and, after a meeting with Jackson, Granger was offered a contract at double the salary he had earned at Hull. No doubt Jackson saw something in the young actor that impressed him, but it could not have done Granger any harm that he came with the personal imprimatur of someone Jackson knew well. How many doors in all professions are opened by personal recommendation and often at crucial junctures in someone's career? This would work for Granger on several occasions during his career, but just as often personal hostility towards him would work against him. Even in these early stages of his career, a pattern is beginning to emerge: there were people who were willing to bat for him, but there were as many whom he had managed to antagonise and who would, at the very least, not go out of their way to help him.

If Hull had been challenging, Birmingham Rep was one step up, and Granger felt the pressure. Although the plays were changed every two weeks rather than weekly, it meant that he would be acting in one play in the evenings, rehearsing the next play due for production in the mornings and 'blocking' a third play in the afternoon. Too much can be made of the trials and tribulations of professional actors, but this must have been hard work. However, it was not toiling down a mine or nursing in a large city hospital or teaching in a tough inner-city school. To his credit, Granger was always conscious that acting was in many ways a 'soft option' compared to the reality of many people's working lives. Most intelligent actors count themselves lucky to be paid to do the work they do and don't whine about the burden of it all; it is only a minority of self-pitying luvvies who complain about the difficulties of their profession.

Granger gained vital experience at Birmingham by acting in Restoration comedy and contemporary plays. Because it was one of the leading theatrical companies of its time, Birmingham gave the young actor the chance to meet important people in the theatre, including Bernard Shaw himself, who visited Granger in his dressing-room after a performance of Shaw's *The Apple Cart* in which he had played the character of Magnus. Shaw somewhat damned him with faint praise, but this incident reflects the fact that Granger was now rubbing elbows with some of the cream of the British theatre.

Birmingham was to be a very important shop-window for Granger. He also did a season at the Malvern Festival Theatre in 1937. Among the other roles he played during this period were Warwick in *St Joan*, Sir Broadfoot Basham in *The Clandestine Marriage*, St John Rivers in *Jane Eyre*, General Su in *Lady Precious Stream*, Alastair in *The Millionairess*, Charles Surface in *The School for Scandal* and Glumdalca in *Tom Thumb the Great*. None of these roles demanded that he scale theatrical heights, but they were stepping-stones for a future leading man.

Not only was his career blossoming at Birmingham, but he had met the woman who was to become his first wife. Elspeth March, 'a tall, statuesque, beautiful girl with thick black hair', was a leading actress with the company and the two started a relationship. Granger describes her as temperamentally different from him in that she was immensely popular with the rest of the company and seemed to like everyone. This implies that he wasn't universally popular and certainly did not like all of his fellow actors. Again, this would be par for the course. Throughout his career, Granger had a talent for getting on the wrong side of people and he seemed unable to hide his dislike of anyone. This tendency could be described as honest and forthright or arrogant and insensitive, depending on how you viewed Granger. Certainly, the evidence is that March was the networker of the two, and worked ceaselessly to advance her future husband's career.

His performances, especially his role in *The Apple Cart*, had brought him to the attention of important players in the world of the British theatre and cinema. An agent who happened to handle Vivien Leigh signed him up as a client and this new backer arranged that Granger should sign a long-term contract with Basil Dean, a very well-known theatre and film director. Elspeth March was also signed up by Basil Dean, so the personal and professional lives of this couple were now entwined. They had both been a success in provincial Birmingham and now London theatre beckoned with its additional challenges, and beyond that the prospect of real film parts. Although Granger had already made brief appearances in some British films these appearances were fleeting indeed and little more substantial than work as an extra, but they added to his filming experience.

The play that Granger began rehearsing in London was an adaptation of *Sanders of the River* (made famous by Paul Robeson's role in the movie of the same name), called *The Sun Never Sets*. It was directed by Basil Dean, whom Granger found to be very unpleasant. In truth, there were not many directors that Granger had a good word to say about during his career. It does seem rather unlikely that he was more unfortunate than other actors in the directors he worked with, but he consistently had major problems with them, because he considered them to be sarcastic or patronising or sadistic or simply incompetent. Some of them may have been all of these things, but Granger found it difficult to take direction, and the directors he so disliked almost certainly considered him arrogant and troublesome as well.

The production of *The Sun Never Sets* was not a success, but it did Granger no harm because shortly afterwards Laurence Olivier, no less, cast him in a play he himself was directing, *Serena Blandish*, opposite his wife Vivien Leigh. The play was an adaptation by S.N. Behrman of an Enid Bagnold novel, *A Lady of Quality*. Three days before *Serena Blandish* opened in the West End, Granger married Elspeth March. Among the guests at their wedding were Olivier and Leigh, the latter not yet having been cast as Scarlett O'Hara in *Gone With the Wind*, although she had set her determined sights on it. In *Serena Blandish* Granger played Lord Ivor Cream under Olivier's direction, but Granger later complained about Olivier's tendency to tell the actors how to say the lines so that even Vivien Leigh began to sound as if Olivier himself were playing her role. As for Granger's part, the actor had this to say: 'I got the impression that Olivier would have liked to have played Cream rather than me.' It was, of course, a great compliment that Olivier had chosen Granger for the role, and his over-attentive directing may have been an expression of his frustration with an actor who was much less accomplished than himself playing a role that he could have brought off with effortless ease.

After *Serena Blandish*, Granger appeared in a play called *Autumn* with Flora Robson. For a young man who had stumbled into the profession, he was doing remarkably well. However, in the midst of this success, he was faced with the second major loss of his life: the death of his father, who had struggled against cancer and had been nursed with devotion by Granger's mother. His father's death clearly upset Granger, especially because there were unresolved conflicts arising from his mother's attachment to his 'uncle'. Granger felt the lack of attention from both his parents, which may account in part for his wayward behaviour later in life. The conflicts he had with authority figures during his career (studio executives, directors, agents, powerful men) may have stemmed from the unconscious need to challenge these father figures in order to test their masculinity and in addition to gain the attention his father had never given him. Perceiving his father as 'emasculated', he unconsciously determined never to suffer the same fate himself, which may explain why so often in later life he was accused of having to assert his masculinity so much. The peril of being metaphorically castrated by a woman was exaggerated by the young Granger and this affected his relationships with women throughout his life.

Although Granger had appeared in front of the film cameras several times, he was now cast in a small part in a film called *So This Is London* (1938). The film starred Alfred Drayton and farceur Robertson Hare, so the romantic elements went for almost nothing, but it was the start of his journey as a romantic movie hero. If he was to pursue a film career, however, the name James Stewart was going to be something of a problem because there was a young movie star in the States of the same name who had already made a name for himself. Thus, Granger made the decision to change his professional name to Stewart Granger. Granger was his Scottish grandmother's maiden name. Friends and colleagues would continue to call him Jimmy for the rest of his life, but to the general public he was to become Stewart Granger.

There was, therefore, a perfectly logical reason for the young actor to change his name; however, on some deeper level, perhaps Jimmy Stewart felt the need to reinvent himself and to launch himself into the world again with a new identity. It is significant that he took his father's surname as his first name and that the 'Granger' harked back to another Scottish connection in the family. All artists (actors, singers, writers, for example) who adopt a professional name instead of their given name are in some way inventing a new persona. They are, of course, still the same person, but the effect of literally taking on a new identity may be liberating or confusing, or both. Perhaps the actor who was now called Stewart Granger wanted to leave behind Jimmy Stewart, but this never really happened. It was perhaps Jimmy Stewart who had to live up to being Stewart Granger, that heroic figure on the silver screen, that world-famous movie star, and sometimes that was burdensome. But the die was cast: to the world at large this young man was now Stewart Granger; in himself he was still Jimmy Stewart with all those unresolved conflicts and needs.

The Second World War was looming, the appeasement of the Munich agreement of a year before having been shown to be the delaying ploy on Hitler's part that it was. Granger and his new wife had been engaged to do a ten-week season of plays with a repertory company in Aberdeen on the north-east coast of Scotland. However, before they fulfilled that contract, Tyrone Guthrie, at that time a rising star of the theatre world, asked Granger to join the Old Vic Company for a season of plays. The company was to include Robert Donat and Constance Cummings, who eventually played St Joan in Bernard Shaw's play with Granger as Dunois. The Old Vic rehearsals were not due to start for two months so the Grangers were able to fulfil their Aberdeen obligations. Granger writes warmly of his time there and the reception from Aberdeen audiences. He clearly relished his Scottish connections and enjoyed being popular with a Scottish audience.

In the middle of rehearsals for the Old Vic season war broke out and Granger's instinct was to rush to join the colours, but he was persuaded that as the Old Vic was a national institution his first duty was to continue acting. Eventually the season was wound up early and the productions were mothballed, never, as it happened, to be unwrapped again. Meanwhile, Granger won a small speaking role in an early British war movie *Convoy* (1940). He can be seen fleetingly on the deck of a convoy ship and he has a few lines to say. The stars of the movie were Clive Brook and John Clements, two rather stodgy stalwarts of the British cinema. A few years later, however, it would be Granger who became the major star while their movie careers declined.

The Old Vic season having collapsed, there was nothing to stop Granger from enlisting, and his choice was the famous Gordon Highlanders, a regiment largely based in Aberdeen, where he had so recently enjoyed a local success. He joined as a private. In his autobiography he writes of how appalled he was at having to live in such proximity with hundreds of strangers. Barrack room life clearly did not appeal, but he wanted to do his part for the war effort, although during the next few months it hardly seemed that war had actually started. This was the period known as the 'phoney war' when there was a lull before the storm and the antagonists eyed each other across the channel before Dunkirk and the Battle of Britain plunged Britain into a crisis of survival. Granger went through his army training and recalls firing at Luftwaffe planes off the Aberdeenshire coast, but this was hardly the stuff of heroics. Granger's desire to do 'his bit' may well have stemmed partly from his allegiance to his father's memory, as he had spent a good part of his professional life in the army. But if he was dreaming of military glory, a rude awakening awaited him.

His wife was able to rent accommodation to be near her husband at this time. Importantly, she was pregnant, but her pregnancy ran into difficulties and the first baby of their marriage died a few hours after birth. Elspeth March would suffer several miscarriages before the couple succeeded in becoming parents. Granger's attitude to these setbacks was ambivalent: naturally, he was emotionally upset by the loss of the babies, but it is clear that he became increasingly exasperated with what he perceived as his wife's obsessional need to have a baby. Dubbing himself a 'male chauvinist', he expresses the opinion that he felt he should have been enough for his wife. Her repeated attempts to produce a child that survived, involving as it did long periods of just lying down to avoid miscarriage, was proving a strain to her very active husband, and this may have helped to bring about the end of their marriage some years later.

Meanwhile, Granger completed his basic training. For a man of his temperament, army discipline and controls must have been a trying experience. He had leapt to join up and yet he was languishing in a remote part of Scotland. However, an upper-middle-class young man with his education and background was not going to be restricted to the other ranks for long and, sure enough, he was chosen to apply for a commission as an officer. He chose to transfer between Scottish regiments and joined another famous Scottish battalion, the Black Watch, with the rank of second lieutenant, 'the lowest form of life known to man', as he put it.

However, this elevation in rank, and its promise that he would at last be able to do something worthwhile in this war, would not prove to be what he had been looking for. Shortly after his commission, his army career came to an abrupt halt. He had suffered from stomach upsets for most of his young life and now he had developed serious and chronic stomach ulcers, a condition that was to dog him all his life. He was officially invalided out of the army. His wartime service was at an end and any dreams of military glory were doused. There is little doubt that Granger was humiliated by this: there he was, a young man of twenty-six, a seemingly healthy male with an impressive 6ft 2in physique, and he could not serve his country in its hour of need. Many people in the same position would have publicly bemoaned their lot and privately rejoiced at the release, but Granger does not give that impression at all. He may not have been a team player as such, but he had an instinctive patriotism, a rally-round-the-flag impulse, a desire to prove himself in this most male of spheres and an identification with his father, the army major, which must have made this rejection a difficult pill to swallow.

Of course, Granger had absolutely nothing to reproach himself with. He had not waited for conscription, but had abandoned a very promising career in the theatre to join his Scottish regiment. Other famous actors and movie stars were not so impressive in their desire to 'do their bit'. If a comparison with John Wayne, with whom he would later co-star in *North to Alaska*, is made, it can be concluded that Granger acted with considerable honour. Wayne, who always expressed a kind of simplistic patriotism and constantly attacked 'anti-Americanism', 'commies' and liberals, and became an icon of American heroism on the screen, not only in westerns, but in war movie after war movie, in which he performed countless heroic deeds, actually asked to be deferred from military service in 1943 on the grounds that he had four children and a wife to support and that he was, at the age of thirty-four, just below the admissible age for men to join the US forces. The real reason was probably that Wayne had just had a huge success in movies such as *Stagecoach* and wanted to cash in on this new success. This would be acceptable enough in its way if Wayne had not spent the rest of his life pursuing 'shirkers' and supporting American military ventures such as the Vietnam War with the utmost vigour. Wayne could be accused of being an armchair general, like many men who advocate wars and have never participated in one themselves, but Stewart Granger certainly cannot be.

Granger's rejection on the grounds of physical ill-health by the army he had rushed to join can be seen as one of the shaping influences of his life. It clearly meant a great deal to him, and, as the war progressed, he had to sit on the sidelines while his former regiments went into battle and some of his former comrades sacrificed their lives in fighting the enemy. For this 'manly man' with his often-stated desire to prove his courage, it must have been galling and shaming. Back in civvy street, he was free to pursue his acting career, but what kind of profession was that? To many people, it wasn't a very manly way of spending your life and this was probably Granger's opinion as well. Some famous movie stars such as Spencer Tracy, Marlon Brando, Rod Steiger and Humphrey Bogart are on record as having ambivalent, at best, attitudes to being an actor. Errol Flynn was another major star to whom acting in the movies seemed scarcely 'masculine', and this attitude certainly helped to bring about his self-destruction through various excesses, almost always connected with living out a male fantasy of indulgence in drink, sexual promiscuity and reckless behaviour of all kinds. The idea that acting was a kind of 'pansy' thing for a grown man to spend his life doing may well have been an aspect of the gender politics of the period, but Granger almost certainly shared some of those attitudes with those overtly masculine movie stars.

Thus, Jimmy Stewart had failed to emulate the army career of his beloved, if remote, father, the army major who had had a distinguished military career. If Granger's rush to join the colours may have been in part a payment of an emotional debt he owed his dead father, then he had failed, through no fault of his own, to see off the debt. Jimmy Stewart had always, in prep and public school and in his early forays in the film and theatre worlds, tried to prove his courage, had bowed to no man or boy, had always stood up for himself in an attempt to prove his masculinity, and now the army had dumped him for the inglorious reason that he had a chronic ailment usually associated with much older men in sedentary jobs. His courage in his country's hour of need had remained untested.

So what could this other person, this Stewart Granger whom he had become, do in the world to prove he was a man, to test that courage he knew he had? The acting profession was not war, but in some ways it could require a different kind of courage. There were tests and challenges to be faced even in that profession; there were bullies to be trounced and markers to be set down. He was not going to be pushed around; he was going to control his life and other people. He was going to prove to the world that he could make it. One door had closed behind him – indeed, it had been slammed in his face. Another door was about to open and Jimmy Stewart was to blossom into Stewart Granger who would become world-famous. He had a lot to prove to himself and to the whole world.

Chapter 2

THE RELUCTANT MOVIE STAR

Britain was at war, but the British were still flocking in their millions to the theatres and cinemas of Blitz-torn London and the rest of the country. After the initial decision at the start of the war to close theatres and cinemas on the grounds of public safety, the government allowed places of entertainment to re-open and placed remarkably few restrictions on the entertainment industry, probably in the belief that the morale of the population would be better sustained if they were able to take their minds off the war for a few hours watching a play or a movie.

Indeed, the film industry in both Britain and the United States had a stupendous boom time during the war years. There was scarcely a movie made, however mediocre, that did not find a huge audience because of the pressing need of the general public to escape the reality of war in the escapist dreams served up by the movie-makers. Cinemas were known as dream palaces and, during the Second World War years, that was more or less an exact description for them. If movies had been an important part of people's lives before the war, they became even more important during the long years of the conflict when separation for prolonged periods from family members and loved ones was normal for much of the population. Prime Minister Winston Churchill offered only 'blood, sweat and tears', but the movies made up for some of that grimness with their resolute good cheer and determination to entertain, their romanticised representation of wartime problems and optimistic view of the future. The cinema offered an alternative reality to the grimness of war with its shortages, blackouts, bombing raids, separations and dislocation.

Granger's theatrical career was kick-started again after his brief wartime service when he acted with the famous movie star of the time, Robert Donat, in a play called *To Dream Again*. It does an actor's status and confidence no harm when a highly successful and respected actor becomes a backer, and Donat was a significant figure in Granger's early career. Olivier and now Donat had 'chosen' Granger: not that bad a track record for a guy who had stumbled into acting.

After *To Dream Again* Granger was cast as Maxim de Winter in the stage version of Daphne du Maurier's *Rebecca*, which had been a huge success as a Hollywood movie directed by Alfred Hitchcock (in his first American film) and starring Laurence Olivier as de Winter. Olivier had received very good notices for his performance (deservedly) and this opportunity to follow in Olivier's footsteps could only benefit Granger – if he was up to the task.

Although the reviews were not outstanding, they were generally favourable, so Granger had proved he could make it in 'matinée idol' parts, despite the inevitable comparisons with Olivier, and that he could carry a play on his shoulders. Both *To Dream Again* and *Rebecca* were important to Granger: the former because he was approved of by Robert Donat – who would later make a recommendation that would change the course of Granger's career forever – and the latter because Maxim de Winter was the kind of showy part that could earn an actor a reputation. Olivier in Hitchcock's movie had made something genuinely sinister out of the part, and, although it is hard to imagine that Granger had 'sinister' in his acting locker, he matched up to the romantic aspect of the character.

His stage career had resumed and now films beckoned again. He played a German officer in *Secret Mission* (1942), another war movie about intelligence officers landing in occupied France to spy on German defences. Among the leading actors was James Mason, who would very soon become a friend and a rival. Michael Wilding, his buddy from film extra days, also had a featured role.

At this point, therefore, Granger was lagging behind some of his contemporaries in the film world. If he were to become a leading man in the movies, he would have to make a rapid jump to stardom because by 1943 he was already thirty, which was considered old to be entering for the romantic hero stakes. However, he was becoming slightly better known as a film actor. Proof of that was when he was cast as the second male lead in *Thursday's Child*, directed by the playwright Rodney Ackland. Described as a domestic drama, this film was praised at the time, but it gained a limited release (although it was re-released in 1946), but it has been long forgotten and is very rarely shown nowadays. The story of the film hinges on the effect on a suburban London family of their young daughter (played by Sally Ann Howes) becoming a child star. The casting was completed at the last moment for the part that Granger eventually played, that of a handsome film star, a role that demanded youthful idealism from the actor playing it. Rodney Ackland knew that Granger was far from ideal casting for this role, but he was pleased that he 'seemed to be a cooperative chap who would do his best and take direction without argument'. However, Ackland in his book *The Celluloid Muse* also noted that Granger was generally resented, perhaps because he was so tall and handsome: 'The moment he came on the set for the first day's shooting, Granger, without being in any way rude or aggressive but through some extraordinary quality for which he has since become famous, succeeded in putting everybody's back up. I have never known any other actor to inspire such unanimous antagonism – yet he was perfectly easy to work with and, as far as I saw, never did anything specific that one could accept as a reasonable cause for dislike.'

Equally revealing is Ackland's analysis that it was the male technicians who disliked Granger; the reactions of the women on the set were very different. When the male studios workers made disparaging comments about him, Ackland reports that 'all masculine comment was drowned in a flood of passionate protest and a further upsurge of hysterical rapture from Stewart Granger's first film fans'. This pattern would repeat itself throughout Granger's career. There is no doubt that, whatever arrogance or conceit he himself conveyed, he was the target of much male envy.

However, it was not *Thursday's Child* that would be the launching pad for Granger to gain his first real opportunity in films, although having played a second male lead in any film was in itself a bonus. Instead it was the personal recommendation of his friend and colleague, Robert Donat, with whom Granger had also acted in an Old Vic season before he had gone to Aberdeen. Donat was a very big star in those days, not only in the theatre but in the movies, having starred in Hitchcock's *The Thirty-Nine Steps* and MGM's original version of *Goodbye, Mr Chips*, for which he had won an Oscar.

Gainsborough Studios had embarked on making what would prove to be a highly successful series of costume melodramas, correctly assuming that high production values, home-grown stars, a heady mixture of period romance, sex and unlikely tales of revenge ending in the triumph of virtue would ring bells at the box-office during the grim days of the war. The stars of their next movie, eventually called *The Man in Grey*, were already cast: James Mason, who would play the dastardly villain, Margaret Lockwood and Phyllis Calvert. A fourth lead was required and Donat, probably because he had acted with him on the stage and had been impressed, recommended Granger for the part.

Leslie Arliss was the director, a man Granger would soon come to detest. But, presumably with Arliss's approval, Granger was cast as the romantic interest in this picture, which was to transform his fortunes and change his life for ever. Three actors tested for the role in a scene with Margaret Lockwood, and the actress enthusiastically put her vote behind Granger. Hilton Tims in his biography of Lockwood, *Once a Wicked Lady*, noted the actress's enthusiasm for Granger: 'There was no question in her mind which of them deserved it; a dark, handsome, ebullient fellow called Stewart Granger.'

Granger would be acting with the current biggest stars of the British screen, and this association could scarcely do him much harm. Doubtless his previous screen parts and his role in *Rebecca* helped him to get the role, but there is little doubt that it was Donat's backing and Lockwood's enthusiasm that clinched it for him. Yes, Granger, throughout his career, would manage to antagonise and alienate many of his colleagues, but at the same time it cannot be gainsaid that at times friends and supporters would rally to his cause and put their own reputations on the line by personal recommendation. So, if Granger at times provoked hostility by his perceived arrogance and temper, that has to be balanced by the fact that he seemed to earn the loyalty of people who could do him some good. That is not to say that Granger exploited friendships and professional contacts (at least, no more than anyone else did). Some people liked him, others, it appears from the available evidence, cordially detested him. In terms of gains or losses for Granger's career, it may have averaged out. Granger is quite frank in his autobiography about his debt to Robert Donat.

In *The Man in Grey*, Granger played the love interest for the second female star of the movie, Phyllis Calvert, a dull suburban type of British film star who was not really a convincing love match for Granger on screen. Margaret Lockwood was much more Granger's style with her striking dark looks and feisty persona, but he had to make love on screen to Calvert, who was not in the romantic mould. Granger plays Adam Rokeby, a dispossessed young Jamaican landowner, who leaves for Jamaica so that he can claim the inheritance that will enable him to marry Lady Clarissa Rohan (Calvert). James Mason has the plum part in the movie playing one of his surly villains, Lord Rohan, who has not one redeeming feature, the kind of role that the

British cinema asked him to play repeatedly and which would eventually drive him to Hollywood to find better parts in better movies. Granger complained about Mason's scene-stealing ploys in their scenes together, but the fact is that Mason had much the better part and did not need to stoop to cheap scene-stealing tricks to gain the audience's attention. If the film's success was to make Granger a star, so it also firmly established Mason as the top British box-office actor.

Calvert plays the wife of the brutish Mason; Lockwood plays her socially inferior friend whom Calvert helps out. Lockwood sets out to capture Mason as her own, while the real lovers are seen to be Calvert and Granger. It all ends in an excess of melodrama with Lockwood killing Calvert and Mason killing Lockwood. As is usual in movies, the 'good' characters are certainly less interesting than the 'bad lots', so Granger deserves credit for attracting good notices for himself in such a straightforward, one-dimensional part. Of course, it is a costume drama and Granger, with his theatrical training and physicality, could wear period costume well. Female audiences, in particular, responded strongly to his screen persona.

The Man in Grey was a huge success when it was first released in 1943; wartime audiences warmed to its melodramatic tale of love, betrayal and villainy. The costumes were elaborate and the sets as fine as wartime restrictions would allow. It is the screen equivalent of a literary 'bodice-ripper', although, naturally, no bodices were ripped, as this was 1943 and sex had to be suggested rather than represented. The *Monthly Film Bulletin* claimed at the time that 'acting, settings, camerawork and direction all reach the highest technical standards', which was perhaps a way of saying the movie was well-made rubbish.

Viewed nowadays, it is an enjoyable enough piece of melodramatic frippery, the kind of movie made for television on a wet afternoon. It also has a certain historical interest, not only in terms of the British film industry, but as evidence of the mood of the nation in that pivotal year of the war. The prospects for survival and final victory had taken a decided turn for the better and there was already talk of opening up a Second Front through an invasion of France. However, rationing, the blackout, family separations, bombing raids and casualties in the armed forces were still harsh facts of life. In those circumstances, movies like *The Man in Grey* served a purpose in turning people's minds away from wartime reality to a bygone age of elegant costumes (like everything else, clothes were rationed in Britain during the war), grand houses and romantic intrigues. There was also something slightly racy about these Gainsborough melodramas, which may have reflected in some way the relaxation of strict sexual codes in society, as people took the attitude that they might as well live for the day because they did not know what the morrow would bring. The strong female roles also reflected the changing roles of women in wartime Britain as millions were employed in factories and other places to take the place of the men in the armed forces.

Not everyone was impressed with the film, however. James Agate, the American film critic, wrote: 'There was not a moment when I would not have gladly dived for my hat.' *Time* magazine said merely that the Gainsborough mix included 'all the time-tested materials: gypsy fortune-teller, scowling black-browed villain; gushy diary kept by a doe-eyed girl who munches candied violets; a fire-eating adventuress who dotes on discord and low-cut gowns.' All this is very fair comment, but the movie is enjoyable nonsense in the final analysis. Audiences in Britain flocked to it in great numbers.

Granger was at last in a movie that was a major hit, and even though his part was not as showy as Mason's ('the scowling black-browed villain') or Lockwood's ('the fire-eating adventuress'), audiences noticed this handsome, tall actor who looked good in period costume. Stewart Granger had arrived. However, during the making of the movie, Granger, despite the fact that this was his first big chance in films, managed to antagonise his fellow cast members with his behaviour, including a liberal use of profanities and abuse of his colleagues. It was a troubled production from the beginning with James Mason actually hitting director Leslie Arliss at one stage.

Margaret Lockwood's view of Granger is insightful: 'Stewart Granger, the new boy, was inevitably something of an outsider and compensated by being the life and soul of the unit, but the combination of boisterous self-assurance, a certain degree of nervousness over handling a part he realised could make him a star, and a short fuse didn't always endear him to his colleagues. On one occasion he kept fluffing his lines and fired off a fusillade of expletives.' Lockwood and rest of the unit were not amused by this behaviour. Her explanation for his conduct was this: 'He had what seemed to be an enormous inferiority complex which came out sometimes in a flow of bad language and in abuse of everybody because he hadn't done his piece as well as he wanted.' So upset were his colleagues, however, that they penned a letter of complaint to Granger's agent asking him to lean on this upstart to curb his behaviour and 'cloak his feelings a little more ably'.

Whatever the rights and wrongs of the situation, it does seem astonishing that Granger in his first really important screen role should manage to provoke some of his fellow professionals sufficiently for them to take such a step. For Granger the new boy, there was no curbing of his usual language or boisterous behaviour, no acknowledgement that he was new to this movie star world and no deference to the more established stars. He was to be his own man and that was bound to rile some of his co-workers, as he came over as arrogant, insensitive and foul-mouthed to many of them. This aspect of his personality would manifest itself in almost all the movies he made. Lockwood, in homing in on his sense of inferiority as an explanation for his behaviour, was almost certainly correct.

But the wider picture was that Robert Donat's recommendation and Lockwood's initial endorsement had paid off big-time. Granger was now a film star. However, he was never entirely comfortable with this status. Yes, he wanted to succeed at what he did but he disliked, according to his own frequent testimony, what was attached to the privilege of being a film star: the unwanted attentions of fans and the press, the public appearances that his film bosses demanded of him, the intrusions into his private life, the long-term contracts under which he laboured, and the lack of control he had over the parts he was offered. He particularly disliked being referred to as a 'heart-throb', as he was in the fan magazines and newspapers, even though it was almost inevitable.

James Mason in his autobiography, *Before I Forget*, described attending the press showing of *The Man in Grey* when C.A. Lejeune, film critic of the *Observer*, said to the company at large, 'It's not often we have the privilege of attending the birth of a great new star. This young man, Stewart Granger, isn't he marvellous?' Mason states he had no illusions about his own contribution to the film, but somehow he failed to enjoy Miss Lejeune's little talk. In short, it seemed he was rather put out that his co-star was getting all the critical and public attention. The praise of a female fan, albeit a critic, and the envy of a male colleague: it was to become a familiar pattern for Granger.

In 1945, for example, two years after his success in *The Man in Grey*, the magazine *Picture Show* ran a feature article about his 'life story': 'In 1943 this brilliant newcomer took the hearts of the film-going public by storm in the romantic Gainsborough film *The Man in Grey*. Since then he has become the idol of fans all over the country.' The words 'romantic', 'idol' and 'heart-throb' were seldom absent from the many features written about Granger throughout his career. The article went on to say that Granger hated the tendency to make a heart-throb out of any romantic lead in films and that he personally hated the thought of being a matinée idol. Despite this protestation by the subject of the feature, it concluded that Granger was 'handsome, devil-may-care, with a laughing glint in his eye'. Granger may have hated this kind of fan magazine feature, but it is possible that this persona of the 'devil-may-care' adventurer may have stuck to him, not just in his screen roles, but in his off-screen life as well. How many times can an actor play that role on screen and be written up in those terms in countless articles before some part of him or her begins to believe it and start living it?

Were Granger's complaints about the tribulations of being a movie star just the complaints of a spoilt actor who should have counted his blessings and his cash? Perhaps he can be given the benefit of the doubt about this. His dislike of the publicity associated with being a film star seems to have been genuine. He wanted to be popular with film-goers, but he did not want to be the centre of attention all the time. It clearly bored him, and he needed to be Jimmy Stewart as well as Stewart Granger. Other stars of the entertainment world faced the same dilemmas, and many continue to do so. They struggle to achieve success and fame, then find that they have created a kind of prison for themselves. They begin to wish for anonymity. There are other stars who have a constant craving for the oxygen of publicity and public adoration, and they only seem to exist as the star persona that has been created for them. Granger definitely did not belong in that category.

Thus, Jimmy Stewart, after his success in *The Man in Grey*, had already proved something to himself, his family and the world at large. He was somebody now, a famous movie star, albeit a domestic British one. But would this turn out to be what he really wanted? He had stumbled into the acting profession and now found himself burdened with the obligations of stardom.

Meanwhile, Granger's former regiments were fighting in North Africa and part of him was obviously with the fighting soldiers. He must have heard the reports of their exploits with mixed feelings. Some part of him must have been enjoying the fruits of his success, but that enjoyment may well have been laced with guilt that he was not doing his bit for the war effort. No doubt motivated in part by these feelings of guilt, Granger made an attempt to use his new-found fame to help the propaganda war. In doing so he showed he was already aspiring to something more than just being a film star.

He had been working on a film script, *The Ladies from Hell*, about a Scottish regiment during the First World War. The title refers to the name that the Germans gave the kilted Scots soldiers. Granger, proud not only of his Scottish ancestry but of his service with the Gordons and the Black Watch, clearly wanted to be part of a film that would boost morale and pay tribute to the fighting spirit of the Scottish regiments. If he couldn't be in the war himself, then he could make his contribution by promoting a movie in praise of the fighting forces, in particular a Scottish regiment. So he hawked the script around and tried his best to get it made into a movie. There were no takers. This must have been a major disappointment to him on more than one count: if his script had been accepted and a film had followed, it might well have led to his being involved in the creative aspect of movie-making other than appearing in front of the camera and, then, importantly, the 'propaganda' movie might have helped him to feel less guilty about missing out on war action.

However, another movie part had now to be fulfilled. This time he would be directed by Leslie Howard, the famous British actor who played the wan Ashley Wilkes in *Gone With the Wind*. The film was *The Lamp Still Burns*, a worthy and rather pious tear-jerker about noble nurses and doctors in a wartime hospital. It was meant to be a morale-booster for wartime audiences, extolling the sacrifice that the brave medical profession was making for all the population, but it suffers from an excess of gentility, sentimentality and inhibition. Granger's role is unmemorable and the main focus of the movie is the nurse played by Rosamund John. She has to choose between her devotion to the noble calling of nursing and marriage to Granger, a factory owner, who is a patient in the hospital known as the Punctured Lung. As this was wartime, the message that sacrifices had to be made is firmly entrenched in the movie; she chooses her chosen career over love, but the audience is left with the impression that everything will end well.

The film was adapted from Monica Dickens's novel *One Pair of Feet* and it is a modest achievement by any standards. If Granger had appeared in this before *The Man in Grey*, it is hard to see how anyone would have noticed him in this role; however, he was now a star so his screen appearances attracted more attention. One related fact is of interest: director Leslie Howard died shortly after completing the film when the plane he was travelling in was shot down by the Germans in mysterious circumstances. C.A. Lejeune, the female critic who had so admired Granger in *The Man in Grey*, added another dollop of hero-worship by describing his part in this movie as 'everything a probationer might dream of'. Lejeune considered

Granger to be 'still quite brilliantly bad', but, she added, 'I don't know any British actor I would sooner sign as a prospect.' Bosley Crowther noted in his *New York Times* review of *The Lamp Still Burns* that Granger had 'a ravishing dental smile'.

Elspeth March was still determined to become pregnant, despite the diagnosis of a tilted cervix. One expert told her that if she really wanted to sustain a pregnancy, she would have to lie still for seven months. Granger tried to persuade her that they could adopt a child, but she persevered and finally managed to give birth to a son, whom they called James. Granger had finally become a father. He proclaimed himself delighted and was determined 'to be a good father', and that James 'wouldn't make the mistakes I'd made, that I would guide his life and love, advise and protect him'. Granger and March would have a second child two years later when their daughter Lindsay was born.

There is no doubt that Granger was proud of his children and very fond of them, but the comment in his autobiography that he became increasingly alienated by his wife's obsession with having a child is very revealing. This is more than the rather insensitive and churlish attitude of a confirmed male chauvinist; it is an unconscious acknowledgement that he needed to be the centre of attention of those closest to him, especially women. Neither of his parents had given him sufficient love or attention, his father had felt alienated from the family because of his wife's relationship with the uncle figure, and most of his mother's emotions, it appears, were used up by this relationship. As a child, Granger, by his own testimony, felt left out and emotionally under-nourished. For the rest of his life, it appears he craved the attention and love that his childhood had lacked. Actors often become actors because of this need, thinking that the adoration of the audience will make up for earlier emotional deprivations. It certainly seems that, to an extent, Granger looked to public attention to satisfy this emotional gap, as well as for approval, but it is in his relationships with women that he particularly expressed this need.

Granger reluctantly now signed a seven-year contract with Gainsborough Studios, which now, in effect, belonged to the Rank Organisation. He was indeed hesitant to sign away seven years of his life to a production company who would be able to choose roles for him, demand public appearances and, to an extent, control his private life. Granger was always restless for freedom, so why would he tie himself down in this way when he so loathed this kind of servitude? But what he was dealing with here were the hard facts of the film industry. Gainsborough/Rank were offering Granger the status of film star and a continuous supply of film parts. As one of their stars he would be well paid, and their publicity machine would ensure that he was always in the public eye. Was there an alternative? Were he to turn down such a contract, could he hope to further his film career by other means? The answer is clear: if he wanted to continue on this path and earn the kind of money and status that *The Man in Grey* had won for him, then he had to sign, however reluctantly. But there is no doubt that such servitude was a constant irritation to him.

Now, it has to be said that the degree of sympathy that a highly paid film star should be granted is limited, but individuals can feel themselves trapped by all sorts of different circumstances, however favourable they may appear to other people. Many other actors, and members of the general public, would have envied Granger's position, but then they were not living his life nor experiencing its frustrations day to day.

One of the advantages of being a movie star was that he was inevitably mixing with very attractive women. Granger was married and was now a father. He was also very famous and everything he did would be subjected to public scrutiny, although it has to be stressed that the paparazzi of those days were not nearly as numerous or as intrusive as they are in our contemporary celebrity-mad culture. Nevertheless, it was about this time that, according to his own testimony, he began to 'fall out of love' with his wife and started having affairs.

One serious affair was conducted with Deborah Kerr, who at that time was making a name for herself in British movies. Also of Scottish extraction,

Kerr was a beautiful red-haired young woman in her early twenties when Granger first met her on a blind date. She had made her film debut in the 1940 movie of Shaw's *Major Barbara* and would follow this up with roles in *Love on the Dole, Hatter's Castle,* and Powell and Pressburger's *The Life and Death of Colonel Blimp.* Here she was poised on the brink of world stardom, an extremely attractive and vivacious young woman, and there was Granger, equally famous now and also, it seemed, destined to become very successful indeed. Perhaps it was not so surprising that they found each other attractive. Each of them reflected back to the other their own attractiveness and success. They were equals in terms of professional potential and sexual status. They probably felt they deserved each other, despite Granger's marital status.

Given their early fame and the spotlight in which they both lived, it must have been very difficult for them to disguise the fact that they were having an affair. Even though the intrusiveness of the press had not nearly reached the proportions that it has nowadays, there would still have been an overwhelming need for secrecy. If their affair had become news, then there would have been quite a scandal, so both were playing risky games, but then the element of risk in sexual affairs is a potent aphrodisiac. The affair would continue over a period of years, affecting Granger's marriage and feelings in a serious way.

Granger's next movie, *Fanny by Gaslight,* was another Gainsborough melodrama with distinct resemblances to *The Man in Grey.* Having found a winning formula, Gainsborough eschewed experimentation and went for the tried-and-tested box office success: a period costume drama with lustful lords and innocent virgins, lots of elaborate frocks and a story of virtue rewarded and villainy thwarted. They cast three of the principals from *The Man in Grey:* James Mason, Phyllis Calvert and Granger. Mason again had the showy part of the villain and performed it well within its stereotypical limitations. Calvert is the illegitimate daughter of a Cabinet minister, who has to be saved from Mason's lustful advances. Granger plays the agent of salvation, a role which, again, did not demand too much of him, apart from looking handsome in Victorian costumes.

The film was directed by the well-known British director, Anthony Asquith, who made *The Way to the Stars*, *The Winslow Boy*, *The Browning Version* and *The Importance of Being Earnest*. In this movie, he seems to have let the melodrama take its course in that rather characteristically genteel Gainsborough manner. In the United States, the film was re-titled *Man of Evil*, in reference to the Mason character. James Mason was the British star audiences loved to hate and once more he had the plum part in this concoction. At any rate, despite the obvious limitations of the movie, Granger had another major film under his belt, albeit a not very memorable one. The film historian and critic Leonard Maltin describes it as 'an elaborate but ponderous costumer about a maniac who tries to run people's lives to suit his fancy; overdone and not effective.' It is another piece of enjoyable escapism, a fairly obvious sequel to *The Man in Grey*.

Granger was then forced, by the terms of his contract, to do another Gainsborough potboiler, which was again intended to be a wartime morale-booster. Released in 1944, *Love Story* is a saccharine romantic tale about two people who fall in love when time is running out for both of them. Margaret Lockwood is Lissa, a famous pianist-composer who is dying from some unnamed disease. As is customary in this kind of movie (think Bette Davis in *Dark Victory*), the heroine is not unduly handicapped by this fatal illness apart from feeling wan at times and having to lie down and clutch her head. Granger plays Kit, an ex-RAF fighter pilot who, while on active service, sustains a wound that will result in his going blind in a few months' time. Patricia Roc plays the other woman, the rival for Granger's favours, who, in the final reel, steps aside to let the dying Lockwood and shortly-to-be-blinded Granger be together to face whatever short-lived future they have.

The sub-text of the movie is clear: people in wartime Britain must grab what happiness they can because no one knows what tomorrow might bring. Again, Gainsborough was trying to key into that wartime feeling of making hay while the sun shone, but the plot lacks all plausibility. Lockwood will not tell Granger what is ailing her and that she is due to depart from this life very soon, and the character Granger plays inexplicably fails to mention that he has been invalided out of the RAF because he is going blind, so the local population, and the Lockwood character, take against him because they think he is a coward dodging active service.

Granger said he thought this film 'absolute crap' and in many ways his judgement was correct. However, the movie may have rung a few personal bells for him. After all, he had been invalided out of the armed forces like the character he played, albeit with a much less serious chronic complaint: duodenal ulcers. It would be surprising if he had not been aware of some nasty implications about his not being in the forces, given that he was, on the surface, a very fit young man. When so many people were making sacrifices during wartime, a successful, healthy movie star who was not putting his neck on the line would undoubtedly have suffered aspersions about his courage and his willingness to serve his country. That would have been most unfair, but since when was the world fair? Undoubtedly, Granger was very sensitive to this issue and it may be that he hated *Love Story* partly because of the parallels in his own experience to the character he played.

The film was directed by the detested Leslie Arliss, who, in one scene, asked Granger to dive from a Cornish cliff into the sea. Granger for once declined the challenge and said his stand-in should do it in long-shot. Arliss, whether by design or not, chose a short stand-in who also had bandy legs. Granger was most offended by this and absented himself from the dinner party that Arliss had laid on at the Savoy Hotel in London after the premiere of *Love Story*. Arliss reputedly commented it was Granger's revenge for his using the bandy-legged double.

However, *Love Story* was another huge box-office success in Britain – if not particularly so in the States where it was known as *The Lady Surrenders* – and cemented the status of Lockwood and Granger as top British stars along with James Mason, Patricia Roc and Phyllis Calvert. The theme music of the film became a huge hit as 'The Cornish Rhapsody', and the movie is frequently shown as afternoon matinée fodder on television, which is its appropriate level. C.A. Lejeune described it as 'a splendid, noble and fatuous piece', which seems rather generous in retrospect. Richard Winnington, the film critic for *Punch* magazine, wrote: 'In psychology and dialogue, this is straight out of *Mabel's Weekly*.' The movie was aimed at female audiences and it was intended that there would not be a dry eye in the house at the end when Granger and Lockwood face the very uncertain future together. The *Monthly Film Bulletin* praised Granger as 'attractively masculine as Kit', but also noted the 'incredible misunderstandings and misplaced nobility' of the plot.

Perhaps some of Granger's dislike of the role had something to do with his generally macho attitudes: there he was playing in a silly romantic melodrama, being fought over by two women and having nothing much more to do than looking rather peeved at times and deciding which woman he would finally choose. He must have known the movie was intended as a 'woman's picture' and this almost certainly did not sit well with him. Yet he was the male star that the two beauties of the British screen, Margaret Lockwood and Patricia Roc, were vying over so that must have fed his vanity and helped his box-office clout, but he probably partly despised that aspect of his appeal, considering that there was something rather unmanly about a man who was too attractive to women.

Granger and Kerr had a further opportunity to cement their relationship when they embarked on an ENSA European tour in 1945 in a production of scenes from that old potboiler *Gaslight*. The actors rehearsed at Drury Lane under the direction of John Fernald, a well-known man of the theatre who would later take charge at the Royal Academy of Dramatic Art. In Eric Braun's biography of Deborah Kerr, Fernald said he recalls his gratitude for Kerr's 'great good humour and professionalism, the chief factor in smoothing over some of the more intolerant patches of the leading man's behaviour.'

The *Gaslight* tour lasted eight weeks and played in Belgium, Holland and

France. It was by all accounts well received by the troops. Perhaps ironically, it was Granger who introduced Kerr to her future husband, Squadron-Leader Tony Bartley, who was at that time stationed near Brussels and was a friend of Granger's. Some time after this, Bartley approached Laurence Olivier to ask his advice about whether he should go ahead and marry Kerr, despite family opposition. Olivier advised him to do so and said her only fault was that she was 'unreasonably chaste'. So the Granger–Kerr affair had indeed been kept well under wraps if that was the general opinion of Kerr.

Granger's love life had become complicated and tense, therefore, but his dealings with agents and studio executives were always fraught. His attitude to agents, barring one later in his career, was largely contemptuous, believing that they were leeches and took too much of his money for very little effort. This is a fairly common attitude among those in the entertainment and arts world in general, but Granger's dislike and distrust of his agents is par for the course for a man who rebelled against any authority and control over him. Shades of the hated nanny whom Granger claims helped to blight his childhood? The powerless child seething with resentment about the injustice of being controlled by an unfair and judgemental adult becomes the rebellious adult with a chip on his shoulder.

As far as film executives were concerned, he saw them as envious of their attractive stars, in whose numbers he counted himself no doubt. To Granger, they were uniformly untrustworthy and conniving. It was not long before he was having problems with the Rank/Gainsborough executives, and their demands on him to play the film star game by making public appearances at premieres and giving newspaper and magazine interviews quickly chafed on his nerves. This frustration leaked its way into the press and soon he was being written up as being 'difficult', especially as he did not go out of his way to make friends with the show business reporters whose job it was to fill the pages of newspapers and movie magazines with vacuous slop about film stars. The epithet 'difficult' almost certainly simply meant he wanted to be his own man and he had enough self-respect not to genuflect to the press and jump every time a studio executive asked something of him.

If *Love Story* was a very silly movie, then Granger's next film would top it by several degrees of silliness. *Madonna of the Seven Moons* was another Gainsborough extravaganza, set in Italy this time, and full of such staple elements of melodrama as childhood traumas, gypsy curses, vile seducers, bad girls, split personality and illicit love. Phyllis Calvert plays a woman who suffers from a dual personality syndrome; from time to time she flees her respectable life as the wife of a rich wine merchant to be with her lover, Nino (Granger), a kind of Sicilian gangster. Granger plays the role with darkened hair and an earring. It all ends badly, as it must by the moral principles of the day. Even by the low standards of its genre, this movie is total nonsense. The Italy and Italians represented on screen never existed outside the pages of the worst kind of romantic fiction and the whole movie is as plausible a picture of Italy as *Finian's Rainbow* is as a picture of Ireland or *Brigadoon* as a representation of Scotland. However, those two musicals have certain redeeming features; it has to be said *Madonna of the Seven Moons* has none.

The critic Leslie Halliwell wrote of the movie: 'Novelettish balderdash killed stone dead by stilted presentation; but highly successful in its day.' The *Monthly Film Bulletin* commented on its 'crude melodramatics'. Yet, wartime audiences flocked to it in great numbers, warming to its outrageously camp evocation of Italian and gypsy life. Phyllis Calvert is about as sexy as the average Orpington matron, and is, again, decidedly miscast as Granger's lover. No spark existed on screen between this pair and, reading between the lines of Granger's autobiography, there was probably little love lost between them. 'You really have to feel love at the moment you are being photographed, otherwise that camera picks it up immediately,' Granger wrote. 'Eventually I got over this tricky situation by thinking of someone I really loved as I gazed adoringly into the face of someone I wasn't so mad about. However, quite soon there were a couple of scenes in the can with Miss Calvert.' Calvert, equally ungraciously, commented about her love scene with Granger in Matthew Sweet's book *Shepperton Babylon*: 'We shot it just after lunch and his breath smelled terribly of sardines.'

In addition Granger's character had to sing while strumming a guitar, and the producers chose to dub his voice with a falsetto tenor, which was a blow to Granger's manly pride. It was bad enough that he had to play this ridiculous part, but to be dubbed by a guy with a high-pitched voice? Granger's sense of himself, it seems, was constantly being offended.

Again, like *Love Story*, this film was obviously intended to be a 'woman's picture' with its fantasy about escaping from the mundane duties of a dull marriage to the arms of this exotic lover, Granger with an earring. It is a fair assumption that Granger was embarrassed at being seen in junk movies such as this, even though it was a great success. His fellow professionals would know what rubbish it was, although many of them would have been desperate to land starring roles like this. And again, Granger's sense of his own worth and masculinity would have been offended by the campness of the whole enterprise

Nevertheless, this part undoubtedly reinforced Granger's reputation as the male heart-throb of British movies in the 1940s. If you asked British film-going women in that decade which home-grown male star they swooned over all those years ago, then many choose Granger as the one they most remember. James Mason appealed to the more thinking woman, perhaps, because he radiated intelligence and suaveness. John Mills was the ideal husband in need of mothering, while Laurence Olivier, in his matinée idol persona, conveyed something dangerous. But for straightforward, uncomplicated masculine appeal, they chose Granger in their millions. With something of the exotic and caddish, he was the shop girls' delight.

For a man like Granger, with his need to show his courage and manliness at every turn, this appeal he had for millions of women must have created ambivalent feelings. Most actors want to be thought of as attractive to women, but being nothing but a male sex symbol soon becomes a prison. Twenty or thirty years later, Robert Redford would encounter the same difficulties as Granger, but he would fight his way out of that imprisoning categorisation via more challenging roles in superior films and through becoming a movie director. Granger would never really leave his early reputation behind him and this would become both a source of frustration to him and a barrier to his continuing his movie star career at the highest level.

In an article he wrote for the *Daily Mirror* in 1945, Granger again expressed his dislike of the heart-throb tag. After dispensing with the idea that the life of a movie star was at all glamorous, he described an average day for the so-called 'glamour boy' at the studio: 'He gets up at 6.30 a.m and has to be at work by 7.30 a.m. He gets dressed for the part, is made-up and is on the set by 9.00 a.m. – sharp.' Granger complains about the 'never-really-admiring eyes of the director' and 'the intervals of standing about and keeping out of the way of carpenters and electricians until 7.00 p.m.' Then, Granger writes, 'he drives home and works on his lines for the next day and says hello to his wife.' Granger also vigorously defends his right to a private life: 'Too many movie fans think an actor shouldn't be allowed to have a private life of his own. But that's not for me. My family and my home life are my business. When I'm not working, I'm off the scene with my wife, my small son and my friends.' There is a combative tone to this article and it is clearly heartfelt. Although it can also be interpreted as the whining of an overindulged movie star, this piece makes clear Granger's attitude that he owed nothing more to his fans than a good performance on the screen.

Once the Normandy landings of June 1944 had taken place, everyone knew that victory was in sight. The Rank Organisation would dominate British film-making and distribution for the next twenty years. However, Granger's attitude to J. Arthur Rank – who had made his money through flour mills and had distinctly narrow-minded views about contemporary issues – was hostile, and he utterly detested Rank's chief executive, John Davis. Rank and Davis expected their contracted stars to toe the moral line and to jump through the hoops that the company put in front of them. There was always going to be conflict between men like these and the types like Granger who resisted control and had never had an easy relationship with authority figures.

The working class of Britain rarely featured in British movies of this era except as comic relief or as servants pandering to the needs of stars such as Noel Coward, Anna Neagle and Michael Wilding. However, Granger's next movie, *Waterloo Road*, did attempt to represent working-class London life and the problems that wartime dislocation had sometimes caused. *Waterloo Road* tells the story of an ordinary cockney soldier (John Mills) who goes absent without leave to sort out his marital problems. His wife has obviously been having an affair with a spiv (played by Granger). Of course, given the censorship operating at this time, the wife's adultery has to be suggested, not spelt out. The film deals with the problems of wartime separation and what that can do to a marriage: the lonely wife prey to the predatory attentions of other men; the worried husband in the army wondering what his wife is getting up to. It would have been a very familiar scenario for many of the wartime audience. Additionally, the spiv figure (Granger) had become a familiar stereotype in the culture of the time. Undoubtedly, there existed a flourishing black market in all kinds of things that were either rationed or were in very short supply because of wartime shortages. The term 'spiv' had been coined to describe those who dealt in black market goods, thereby profiting from the deprivation of wartime. The press and the media in general had built up the spiv to be a figure of intense dislike and a danger to the morale of the population as a whole. A spiv was letting the side down, definitely not playing the game, and was seen as decidedly un-British.

Therefore, Granger's role as the spiv in *Waterloo Road* can be seen as a departure from the usual heroic role he had played in films so far. It is interesting to speculate why he was cast in the first place. Perhaps he was perceived as rather vulgar in his good looks, which were, after all, tinged with a Latin flavour, so the producers could see he would suit this part of the cocky, amoral opportunist. The opposition of John Mills and Granger spells out where the film's values lie. Mills is the salt of the earth, serving his country and trying to save his marriage. Audiences were accustomed to seeing Mills in heroic officer roles such as *In Which We Serve* and *We Dive at Dawn* or as the straightforward family man in Noel Coward's *This Happy*

Breed. Mills's screen persona signified respectability, honour, courage and loyalty to the cause. He was terribly, terribly British. Granger in this movie represented the opposing pole to Mills's patriotic and unselfish motivations. He was perceived as selfish, a shirker, immoral, in that he was taking up with the wife of a soldier away defending his country, and criminal in his taking advantage of wartime shortages. The clash of these opposing values is represented in an elongated fight between the two characters at the end of the movie, a fight that teeters on the edge of farce as the 6ft 2in Granger is licked by the diminutive John Mills.

If audiences of the time found that hard to accept, so did one of the participants of this screen scrap, Granger himself. Granger dwells on this in his autobiography and states how much he resented losing out to Mills in this fight, mentioning how vertically challenged Mills was. On one level, this seems incredibly petty; after all, Granger is referring not to a real fight but a fight that was enacted as the climax to the movie. It was not Jimmy Stewart/Stewart Granger who was being beaten by Johnny Mills but the character he was playing. Somehow, nevertheless, this got under Granger's skin, and once more his sense of his own masculinity was offended. There may have been another element to explain his outrage: he may have realised that audiences would find the fight ridiculous and he did not want to be the target of ridicule. But on some macho level, Granger was clearly peeved that he had to lose out to Mills within the story-line of the movie, even though the whole logic of the film leads up to the honest hero having to vanquish the shirker spiv.

One of the other problems with the movie, which sets out to create a realistic picture of wartime London around the Waterloo Road just south of the River Thames, is in the casting. John Mills was never at his best when playing chirpy cockneys – he adopted a standard RADA-trained impersonation of the lower orders – and Granger is not much better as the cockney wide-boy. It would be another twenty years or so before British actors from working-class origins, such as Albert Finney and Tom Courtenay, would convincingly portray working-class characters in British movies. Till then, audiences had to put up with reach-me-down, ready-made 'turns' from actors like Mills (admirable as he was in many other parts). Nevertheless, *Waterloo Road* has a certain historical interest for its portrayal of wartime London, and was certainly an advance on the *Madonna of the Seven Moons* type of meretricious fantasy. Indeed, the *Monthly Film Bulletin* praised the film for its 'remarkable degree of fidelity to background and character'. The Granger–Mills punch-up did not seem risible to the *Bulletin* and they described it 'one of the most convincing ever filmed'. Granger also comes in for praise for 'successfully rounding the most difficult role and putting over the showy artificialities of the conceited philanderer'.

Granger's standing as a leading British film star was no longer in any doubt. A *News Chronicle* feature of the time by their film critic gave the opinion that 'Stewart Granger is the most sensational discovery of the war – undoubtedly the No. 1 heart-throb of the moment.' The article mentions that the British public were standing in line to see *Waterloo Road* and *Madonna of the Seven Moons* and says that 'Wardour Street, the film headquarters, has been amazed by his box-office success'. Whatever Granger felt about the quality of the movies he was being forced to do, there is little doubt that they were hugely successful and had made him the most popular star in Britain next to James Mason.

During the making of Granger's next movie, the prestigious Rank production of Bernard Shaw's *Caesar and Cleopatra*, matters came to a head between Granger and his wife. His affair with Deborah Kerr had continued, and the strain on his marriage was now intense. Granger moved out of the family home and rented a flat. It cannot be easy when one of the partners in a marriage has become very successful and famous, and the other is stuck with domestic and child-minding duties. Granger was working in a sphere where there were bound to be many temptations and he was no monk.

Caesar and Cleopatra was Rank's attempt to rival expensive Hollywood productions, but with the extra kudos of literary respectability to give their production the kind of prestige most Hollywood extravaganzas lacked. Elaborate sets were built for the production and it quickly became Britain's costliest movie at £2.5 million, a great deal of money in 1945. No expense was spared on the costumes and art direction. It was over a year in production. A fine team of specialists were assembled to create this extravaganza: four of Britain's top cinematographers, Freddie Young, Robert Krasker, Jack Hildyard and Jack Cardiff, shared the honours of filming the action, such as it was; George Auric, the talented French composer, wrote the score; Oliver Messel designed the costumes and John Bryan the sets. The Technicolor picture looks good in rather a 'tasteful' way, but it is dull. George Bernard Shaw adapted his own stage play for the screen, but he did not seem to understand what was required for a motion picture. In fact, the dialogue Shaw wrote bears uncomfortable resemblance to the kind of inflated nonsense so-called Hollywood hacks wrote for vulgar American epics such as *Quo Vadis* and *Samson and Delilah*. There are some impressive sets, however, but the battle sequences are rather perfunctory and the whole enterprise seems much ado about very little, without point or much significance.

The cast was as prestigious as the writer, director and technicians. Vivien Leigh played Cleopatra, Claude Rains was Caesar, and, apart from Granger, the other players included Flora Robson, Cecil Parker, Basil Sydney, Stanley Holloway, Leo Genn and, interestingly, a fifteen-year-old Jean Simmons, who is seen briefly in a non-speaking part as a slave harpist. Gabriel Pascal, in searching for a young girl to play this role, went to a dancing school in Golders Green in North London. There he saw Jean Simmons and announced to the other girls in the class, 'You are witnessing the birth of a star.' This 'discovery' of Jean Simmons would have important repercussions for Granger.

Rodney Ackland, Granger's director on *Thursday's Child* who had been brought in to do some re-writing on *Caesar and Cleopatra*, saw Simmons as 'no more than a plump, jolly schoolgirl – and she seemed then to have no more than a schoolgirl crush on Stewart Granger'. Granger, Ackland noted, dealt with her with a 'fatherly interest', but deeply resented Gabriel Páscal stroking Simmons's hair and patting her cheeks. 'How dare he! She's only a child! It makes me sick to see him lay a finger on her!' Granger is reputed to have said.

Simmons's full name was Jean Merilyn Simmons. Born on 31 January 1929, she was the youngest of the four children of Charles and Winifred Simmons of London. Her father was a physical education teacher. Between 1939 and 1943, Jean was evacuated to Somerset because of the London Blitz, and when she returned to the capital in 1943, she was enrolled in the Aida Foster School of Dancing in Golders Green in North London, where Pascal 'discovered' her.

The director and distinguished cast of *Caesar and Cleopatra* could do little with the stilted, wordy script, and Granger as Apollodorus, a Sicilian artist who is meant to symbolise the love of life among the ancients, fares no better than the rest. James Mason had turned down the part, which may not have endeared Granger to the role, especially as in the annual popularity polls organised by the various British film magazines, such as *Picturegoer* and *Picture Show*, he regularly lagged behind Mason among the top British male stars. Granger plays the role in that characteristically bright and breezy manner of his, but he certainly does not 'disappear' into the part. In his autobiography Granger explains his failure in the role on the fact that Shaw obviously intended Apollodorus to be 'queer'.

Granger frequently makes homophobic allusions in his book and it has to be said he betrays a certain amount of anxiety about this issue, which manifests itself in bigoted remarks about homosexuals. Of course, this was another era and attitudes have changed, but he was working in a profession that also employed many gay people, so it could be expected that he might have shown more tolerance. However, because in the public mind, male actors were considered a bit effeminate, he often over-compensated and beat his manly chest on every occasion he could to make it clear there was nothing 'queer' about him. By stating that he was not convincing as Apollodorus because the author perceived the character as gay, Granger in effect is saying he was far too masculine and straight for the role. He was still, it seems, routing the bullies and projecting his manliness. His attitude is not that of a fully mature man, or even someone who was absolutely at ease with his own sexual identity. As it is, as Apollodorus, he does have action sequences including a sword fight with Roman soldiers, being hoisted up into the air by a crane and diving from a great height into the Nile. Perhaps it was the costumes designed for him by Oliver Messel that gave him concern; he wears a succession of brightly coloured togas and cloaks, and one earring. They are on the camp side of good taste, but he carries them off in his usual manner. In one scene, he is meant to be singing in a boat as he ferries Cleopatra wrapped in a carpet across the Nile and the film-makers again gave him a high tenor voice, which probably increased his anxiety about the effeminacy of the character.

Apollodorus is not a large part; apart from Leigh and Rains as Cleopatra and Caesar, Flora Robson, Basil Sydney and Francis L. Sullivan are on screen much more than Granger, yet in the credits, Granger comes third with a 'page' to himself and before Robson and Sydney. This is a tribute to his star status rather than the importance of his role. Yet Granger need not have worried about the impact his Apollodorus would have on his career: his adoring fans must have loved him in the part.

The production itself, however, acquired a lasting notoriety for its extravagant waste and put paid to Gabriel Pascal's producing and directing career. It was made amidst wartime restrictions and the British press were quick to pounce on tales of profligacy. Delays occurred during shooting, including when Vivien Leigh suffered a miscarriage and subsequently had a nervous breakdown, which meant she was absent from the shoot for five weeks. The press criticised Pascal for moving the production to Egypt to shoot some of the desert sequences, ridiculing the fact that they transported a papier-mâché Sphinx all that way when the actual Sphinx was there in the desert. An M.P. even made a speech in the House of Commons attacking the extravagances of this movie production at a time when resources needed to be focused on the war effort. However, when the film was premiered, Queen

Mary attended and the film entered the mythology of the British film industry as a 'grande folie', a failed attempt to rival Hollywood grandiosity. The *Daily Sketch* review sums up the gist of the response to the film: 'The direction is so completely uninspired, so heavy-handed (to the point of 'ham') that the film falls flat as a pancake.' It is hard to disagree with that verdict.

In 1945, the war ended. Granger did not have a 'good war' in the sense of military achievements or recognition. Many of his contemporaries, men of his class and education, would come back from the war with distinguished war records and some with military decorations. Others whom he would have known personally would not be returning at all. While the war had been fought, Granger's career and life had been irrevocably changed. Money, success and fame had flowed into his life. He was by then one of the top stars of British movies, but how much that compensated for Granger's sense of loss and guilt about not 'doing his bit' is difficult to say.

He could tell himself that by helping to entertain people during the grim war years, he was performing a very important task in maintaining morale, and no doubt he was told that again and again by people in the theatre and film, but all his references to his lack of active service are negative and full of a sense of personal disappointment. He was, first of all, disappointed in himself for being such a 'weakling'. He had set himself this goal of being a 'man' and had fallen short by his own standards.

His next movie was guaranteed not to make him feel any better about himself or the Rank Organisation. *Caravan* is another Gainsborough piece of exotica, set in Spain this time. Once more Granger is cast as a 'Latin type', Richard Darrell, son of a country doctor and a Spanish mother. His two female co-stars were Jean Kent and Anne Crawford.

Kent was a distinct improvement on the suburban Phyllis Calvert and an appropriately sensuous foil for Granger's maleness, but the whole film sinks under the weight of its unlikely plot and clichéd evocation of Spain. Adapted from a bodice-ripper by Lady Eleanor Smith, no less, the plot has Granger as a poor author attacked by his rival in love and left for dead. He is cared for by a gypsy girl (Kent), who falls in love with him. Gypsies were a familiar element in Gainsborough melodramas, but the hero only dallies with them before returning to the arms of his more suitable intended, in this case the character played by Anne Crawford. Another famous 'gypsy' movie of this period was *Golden Earrings* starring Marlene Dietrich. Gypsy women on screen were sexy and immoral, a contrast to the more demure and 'moral' heroines. *Caravan* is another junk movie which has a certain period interest, but is laughable in its phoney romanticism and absurd melodramatic ploys.

Granger hated every moment of the shooting of this movie, probably because he knew it was going to be very bad and because he was once more saddled with an impossible part. Yet the movie, like all his other films to this point, apart from the prestigious *Caesar and Cleopatra*, made a lot of money and enhanced his position as a top box-office star. However, he would have read the dismissive reviews and doubtless been the target of barbs from his fellow thespians, many of whom, again, would have loved to have starred even in such a bad movie. The *New York Times* review mentioned the actors 'grappling with stilted lines and an embarrassingly archaic situation with neither the players nor the plot making much entertainment while *Caravan* moves with the speed of an oxcart'. Granger wanted to have worthwhile parts in better movies, but those executives who controlled his career kept putting him into third-rate pictures, when he saw himself quite differently as a man of action, not some milksop heart-throb for women to swoon over.

Thus, his dissatisfaction with his career and the Rank Organisation was growing. His marriage was in trouble and he disliked many of the appurtenances of being famous. In a short period of five years, Jimmy Stewart had become Stewart Granger, the movie star, but this transformation had not made Jimmy feel much better about himself or his life. In the eyes of many of the acting profession, his success would have been enviable, but he had not had a '*succès d'estime*'. He needed a serious role to challenge him and a series of movies that could be taken seriously. He was tired of appearing in silly romances and playing parts that risked making him look just a little ridiculous. Something had to change not only in his personal life, but in his professional career as well. It would not be long before dramatic changes in both spheres would sweep him along and wider horizons would beckon.

Chapter 3

SUCCESS AND FAILURE

T HE WAR HAD ended, but Britain was still undergoing the shortages of basic creature comforts that we (or most of us in the rich countries of the world) can take for granted nowadays: food, such as meat, eggs, milk and fruit; clothes, fuel and decent housing. Rationing would continue well into the 1950s. The 1945 General Election had given the electorate, including those still in the Forces and already demobbed soldiers, sailors and airmen, the opportunity to reject the policies of the Depression years. Winston Churchill, the Conservative Prime Minister during 'our finest hour', was unceremoniously turfed out of office. The majority of the people had made sacrifices during the war and they did not want to return to the deprivations and poverty of the 1930s. The Conservative Party was perceived as the uncaring party of the well-to-do, whereas the Labour Party promised a Welfare State that would take care of every citizen 'from the cradle to the grave' and full employment.

Cinema's boom would continue for a short period, until the effects of the spread of television sets and radical changes in the Hollywood studio system would halve the number of cinema tickets sold. The days of the big studios were numbered and the Rank Organisation, Granger's employer, would not be immune to the decline in the movie market over the next twenty years. These changes would affect Granger's career directly, as they did almost every movie star in Britain and Hollywood, but things seemed to be set fair in career terms for now, although his private life was still in turmoil.

As for the transformation in British politics that the 1945 election heralded, Granger never made any direct party political comments in his autobiography, but his general attitudes can be pieced together from odd statements here and there in the book and from other public pronouncements: he was a traditional man, a product of his class and educational background, and he would not have welcomed the changes in British society that the election of a radical Labour Party would bring about. It may have even hastened his departure to Hollywood in 1949, especially as tax rates for higher earners were very high in the post-war years.

His affair with Deborah Kerr having been terminated by mutual agreement, Granger now decided to return to his family in an attempt to patch up his differences with his wife and restart his marriage. In Eric Braun's 1977 biography of Kerr, which had the full co-operation of Kerr herself, as well as her family and friends, and was published five years before Granger's appeared, there is no mention of the affair, although Granger was quite happy to spill the beans in his autobiography. It is worthy of note that Granger was not one of those interviewed for Braun's book, despite having made several movies with the subject. There is no record of any comment by Kerr when Granger revealed their affair.

Granger now bought an Elizabethan manor house near Stoke Poges in Surrey, a particularly beautiful part of south-east England and an hour from London. The house had once belonged to the late Leslie Howard, one of the stars in *Gone With the Wind*. There seemed to be quite a vogue for famous English actors to buy period houses in the country; the Oliviers had also bought a rural home, in their case a medieval abbey. Granger's purchase perhaps tells us about his real aspiration to live the life of a country gentleman. Actors at that time were not generally perceived as being completely sociably acceptable by the upper classes, especially a fellow who appeared 'in the films'. Granger's decision to buy this expensive and highly desirable property was undoubtedly his attempt to prove himself in the eyes of his 'betters' and to acquire respectability.

Not only did he buy this period house with its overtones of country squiredom, he proceeded to venture into the business of breeding pheasants to provide shooting for himself and his friends. Hunting, shooting, fishing and riding were, and are, badges of social status and accomplishment among the British upper classes. Granger's attempt to breed pheasant on his land adjoining the Elizabethan manor house must be seen not only as a business venture that went almost inevitably wrong but as an attempt to raise his social status.

Jimmy Stewart had not been born into wealth, but Stewart Granger wanted to become rich: this much is pretty obvious from his various business ventures in which he risked the money he made as a movie star. Genteel impoverishment often leaves its mark on the offspring of middle-class families so that they in later life have a strong drive to make up for that impoverishment, especially if they have been educated with other people from much more comfortable circumstances. It has to be remembered that his father had not been able to send him through medical school and he had had to take a fairly menial job as his first step to making his way in the world. Now that he was a highly paid film star, he seemed determined to compensate for the perceived impoverishment he had suffered from by rather conspicuous consumption (the Elizabethan house) and the trappings of the landed gentry (the pheasant shooting). There were 2,000 acres of land so he could fairly claim to have joined the landowning classes. There was also a stable and he was to become an expert horseman, something that would stand him in good stead during his Hollywood career. He employed two gamekeepers for the pheasants, three gardeners for the extensive grounds, two maids, a cook, a nanny for the children (despite his own bad experiences of nannies as a child), a private secretary and a chauffeur. In other words, he had acquired most of the accoutrements of the social class to which he clearly aspired. However, all these employees meant he had to meet substantial weekly wage bills, and so he had to keep earning at a high rate from his film work.

However, the shooting was not to be a successful venture. Something went wrong with the breeding of the pheasants and the venture was a costly failure. It would be the first of numerous business ventures that would prove expensive. His choices about where he invested the money he was making as a film star were not always wise, but they do tell us a lot about his values. Buying the Elizabethan house was also an attempt to create a pleasant and permanent home for his wife and children in the vain hope that somehow the ashes of his marriage could be rekindled. It seems he was sincere in this attempt: Granger was at heart a quite conventional man in moral matters. He certainly was not a reckless seducer and wanted to make his relationships with his lovers and wives work.

If his business venture was a failure, so was his next film, at least artistically. To his dismay, Gainsborough and Rank decided to cast him as the violinist virtuoso Paganini. Now if you were looking around in the 1940s in England for an actor to play a composer and violinist, it would not seem very likely that you would come up with the name of Stewart Granger, but that is exactly what his employers did. Granger was to play Paganini in *The Magic Bow*, another period costume melodrama in colour, a tale supposedly based on the colourful life of the Italian musician.

Granger duly and inevitably confronted the studio executives, thrust his hands in front of them and told them those were the hands of a boxer, not a virtuoso violinist. Again, it seems as though his sense of his own masculinity was offended by the notion that they wanted him to play a sensitive artist: the implication is that he would much have preferred to play a boxer. In this instance, of course, he was absolutely right to be angry because he was indeed woefully miscast as Paganini. It ranks with the casting of Cornel Wilde as Chopin in the 1944 *A Song to Remember* or Robert

Walker as Brahms in the 1947 *Song of Love* as infamous casting blunders. A *News Chronicle* report from December 1945 hints at the ridicule that Granger probably feared for having this role foisted on him: 'In the film *Paganini*, Stewart Granger will shed his glamour and hide "the torso" in an elongated Lord Fauntleroy suit. A professional violinist is constantly on the set to put Mr Granger's fingers in the right place while he is supposed to be playing: what one will hear will be the playing of Yehudi Menuhin.' Clearly, the knives were already being sharpened to give the film and Granger a critical mauling.

James Mason had had the good sense to turn down the part before Granger was dragooned into it, so once again he must have had the feeling that he was getting Mason's leftovers. Indeed, none of the Gainsborough stars were keen to appear in this movie. Margaret Lockwood turned it down (according to Hilton Tims's biography), partly because she was not particularly keen to work with Granger again after her experience of him on *The Man in Grey*. The same went for Phyllis Calvert, who phoned Granger to find out what he thought about being in the film: 'After three films we did get rather bored with each other. I remember ringing Granger and saying, "Do you think we ought to do it?" And he said, "If you're talking about personal feelings, no. But if you're talking about Our Public, yes."' Thus, despite his protests to the studio bosses, Granger realised that however awful *The Magic Bow* would be artistically, there was a good chance of it turning out to be another box-office smash for him and that would consolidate his star status. After all, the *Daily Mail* had conducted a readership poll to find out what the most popular films of the war years had been and the result had been *The Way to the Stars*, *The Man in Grey* and *Madonna of the Seven Moons*. *Love Story*, *Waterloo Road*, and *Fanny by Gaslight* were also on the list. 'Populist trash' seemed to pay off in terms of mass audience popularity and Granger had starred in two of the three most popular British films of the war years.

However, whether or not Granger was being honest with Calvert over his feelings about making *The Magic Bow*, he could only register his protest at this crass piece of casting. He was under a seven-year contract and he had just invested heavily in the manor house and pheasant-shooting venture. If he had refused to accept the part, he would have probably been suspended and the money would have stopped flowing in. He was, in essence, a wage slave, like most people, although his wages were far in excess of what most people could even dream of earning. In addition, income tax was soon to hit nineteen shillings and ninepence in the pound for the very highest earners, which included Granger. It would hasten his departure from Britain.

This turned out to be a pattern in Granger's film star career: he had to go on making a lot of money through his films in order to subsidise his business ventures, where most of his energies and hopes were focused. Although he would grumble about being in thrall to his movie employers, in some ways he made a rod for his own back by investing his money unwisely and overspending, so that when something like his being cast as Paganini came up, he was left with little or no room to manoeuvre because of the financial imperatives weighing on him.

As with most biopics about famous composers, *The Magic Bow* bore little or no relation to the actual facts of Paganini's life, but then that was not the point of the picture. Paganini is portrayed as an adventurer, a gambler, a lover and a duellist. If the producers had wanted to make a serious film about the violinist's life, then they would not have cast Granger in the first place. It was an excuse to make another period costume drama with some 'serious' music thrown in to give the film some dubious class. They hired a real virtuoso to dub the violin-playing, the young Yehudi Menuhin, who taught Granger the elaborate fingerwork he would have to employ during close shots when he was supposedly playing the violin. To help him negotiate the fingering, the technicians put butter on the violin strings. To give him due credit, he seemed to manage that aspect of this unwanted role with panache, so his 'boxer's hands' did not appear to have been too much of a handicap. However, not everyone gave him credit for his 'playing'. The *Daily Graphic* review opined that Granger 'appears to be sawing wood with one hand and milking a cow with the other'.

In truth, the movie is a turgid fiction of love and betrayals. His female co-stars were Jean Kent and Phyllis Calvert. Not only was he being continually cast in bad movies by Gainsborough, but he was always, it seems, being cast opposite the same female stars. But then, Gainsborough was like a film repertory company, a miniature MGM with its huge roster of contracted stars, so he was bound to be repeatedly starring with the same actresses. The *Monthly Film Bulletin* considered Granger was 'sadly miscast' and commented that 'his penniless fiddler never seems to be any other than a well-fed, rather aristocratic musician whose appearance refutes all suggestion of poverty'. In other words, the costumes won out yet again.

His next movie, *Captain Boycott*, was not a Gainsborough production, but again it was a period historical drama, this time set in west of Ireland in 1880, a time of great upheaval when Charles Parnell was the charismatic leader of Irish hopes for home rule. However, it is a movie of reasonable quality, although Granger as Hugh Davin, a young Irishman who opposes the rascally English landowner, played by Cecil Parker, is again not ideal casting. Granger struggles with an Irish accent, which comes and goes during the film. The fact that he was mostly acting with seasoned Irish actors did not help his cause, but one can be too critical about this kind of thing. A kind comment would be that he struggles manfully with the difficulty of playing an Irish farmer from County Mayo.

In the same year, 1947, another film about the Irish troubles, *Odd Man Out*, directed by Carol Reed, would be released. It was a much better film and Granger's rival James Mason gave an outstanding performance in it. However, Granger had been offered the part of the IRA man before Mason and, quite unbelievably, had turned it down. According to the journals kept by Richard Burton (and quoted in Melvyn Bragg's biography of Burton), Granger had been sent the script by Carol Reed. Granger had 'flipped through the pages where he had dialogue before deciding that the part wasn't long enough'. Burton comments that *Odd Man Out* was the best movie Mason made 'while poor Granger has never been in a good classic film. You could have a James Mason Festival, but you couldn't have a Stewart Granger one except as a joke.'

'Poor Granger' had committed that worst sin of all vain actors: reading a script on the basis of how large his part would be, and in the process had turned down the chance of being in one of the great British movies of all time. It is, however, difficult to envisage Granger making as much of the part as Mason did, but the opportunity had been there and it beggars belief that his judgement was so faulty.

Although the setting of *Captain Boycott* is more realistic and the narrative much more plausible than what had been served up in *Madonna of the Seven Moons* and *Caravan*, the film is little more than an action melodrama with little interest in examining in any real depth the 'Irish question' and the role of the British state in the oppression or otherwise of the Irish peasants. The problem of the strife-torn relations between the Irish people and the British is laid at the door of individual profiteering landowners such as the one played by Cecil Parker, the Captain Boycott of the movie's title. The specific historical interest of the film is the fact that the term 'to boycott' stemmed from the actions of the Irish farmers who shunned or 'boycotted' the avaricious Boycott for evicting them when they did not pay him the exorbitant rents and for moving other tenants onto to the land of those evicted.

Granger plays a figure of reconciliation in the drama of opposing factions. At the start of the movie, he is shown to be in favour of violence and armed resistance to the evictions and high rents. However, he is won over to the cause of peaceful resistance after hearing Charles Parnell speak at a public meeting, which he and his fellow activists have gone to disrupt. Parnell gives the farmers the idea of boycotting the Captain, forcing him to bring in outside labour to gather his crops and to ask for the protection of British troops. Although some 'hotheads' among the farmers advocate violent action, Granger heads them off and wins the day for compromise and peaceful solutions. The rascally landowner, apparently undergoing an unlikely change of heart, is forced to return to England. The final speech of the movie endorsing peaceful actions is given by the local Catholic priest played by Alastair Sim.

Granger's love interest in the film is played by Kathleen Ryan, who also appeared in *Odd Man Out*. She was a much more interesting actress than some Granger had been teamed with. Her dramatic function in the screenplay is that of a calming influence on the volatile Davin (Granger) and another voice for moderation and peace. Other parts were played by members of the Abbey Theatre in Dublin. Granger's former mentor, Robert Donat, played a cameo role as Parnell, the doomed Irish nationalist leader. Granger's role has no complexity, but he displays his usual screen presence and carries the hero's role convincingly within its limitations. He has an opportunity to show his riding skills and is involved in numerous action sequences.

Captain Boycott is not a masterpiece of the British cinema but it was several steps up from the last three movies Granger had made. It certainly is of some historical interest and is in some ways propagandist for a 'balanced' approach to the Irish question: it is sympathetic to the wrongs endured by Irish peasants at the hands of greedy British landowners, but warns against taking arms against the British State. One of the less convincing aspects of the movie is when the commander of the British troops tells Boycott that they are unwilling to carry out orders because of the injustice the Irish are suffering. This is one of the methods by which the makers of the film let the British State off the hook. In addition, the casting of Cecil Parker, an actor usually associated with comic roles of pompous and bumbling upper-class English gentlemen, softens the Boycott character.

After this, Granger was cast in another Gainsborough-type period melodrama, *Blanche Fury*, although the production company this time was Cineguild. Set in Victorian times in the marshlands of Kent (it was based on a notorious murder case known as the 'Rush murders'), the only real interest is that Granger plays a murderer who is out to inherit the property for which he has been the steward. Once more, then, Granger wears period costume and plays a dispossessed aspiring gentleman. Only three of the movies he had made since *The Man in Grey* had been contemporary in theme and allowed him to wear modern clothes. In a way, he had become a kind of 'clothes-horse' star because it was considered – with some justification – that he could wear period costume well. Granger was cast opposite a rather chilly star of the British cinema of the period, Valerie Hobson (who would later marry the Tory Minister John Profumo, the man at the centre of the Profumo Scandal in the early 1960s). It is obvious why Hobson was cast in this role of a murderer who plots with Granger the death of her husband: she had a steely, cold quality and had played Estelle in David Lean's *Great Expectations*. Yet even she baulks at Granger's plans to kill off Lavinia, the young heir to the estate, and shops him to the police. Granger is hanged and Hobson dies giving birth to his baby, who will then inherit the estate.

Blanche Fury is a familiar melodramatic mix of illicit passions, intrigues, murder, revenge and the reconstitution of the established order of things. The Technicolor photography gives the film some visual quality, which makes up for the rather mechanical plot twists and conventional elements. Characterisation is on a very basic level. The story is told in flashback, a familiar technique in many 1940s movies, and especially in film noir. In some ways, *Blanche Fury* sets out to be a Victorian film noir, but it lacks the subtlety to raise it above its Victorian melodrama origins. *Variety* described it as a 'curious mixture of degenerate nobility with melodramatic staples'. Granger's best moments 'are those of passion'.

None of these films did Granger enjoy making, but he had to work to make money to maintain his family, property and lifestyle. By 1947, he was making £15,000 a picture, which was a lot of money for those days when the average wage was around £10 a week. But if he was indeed making money, Granger was not slow in spending it either. He had bought a custom-made green and black Bentley car, which cost £8,000, and later a sea-going yacht. His attempt to repair his marriage to Elspeth March, however, was not working out. In his autobiography, he is quite frank about some of the affairs he had during this period. He tells of a publicity jaunt to France that he was forced to make by Rank, during which he had an affair with a French woman, an escapade which left him with a dose of the 'clap'. As a movie star, he must have been propositioned by women all the time, especially as his film star reputation was as a heart-throb. Granger succumbed from time to time, and on this occasion he paid the price by contracting a social disease, which he had to tell his wife about for obvious reasons.

Granger's next movie would be undoubtedly one of the highlights of his screen career: *Saraband for Dead Lovers* was an Ealing Pictures production and reflected that studio's usually excellent technical, screenplay and direction standards. The screenplay was by John Dighton and Alexander MacKendrick, who would later direct some of Ealing's best comedies (*The Maggie, The Man in the White Suit* and *The Lady Killers*) as well as one of the best Hollywood movies of the 1950s, *Sweet Smell of Success*. The colour photography by Douglas Slocombe and the art direction are outstanding, contributing to the beautiful visual impact of the movie. However, the visuals and the excellence of the sets and costumes are not just there as a feast for the eye. They express the stifling and decadent nature of the Hanovarian court where the action is mostly set.

Granger plays Count Konigsmark, a military adventurer and gambler, who is in love with Sophie Dorothea. She, in turn, has been forced to marry Prince George Ludwig of Hanover, who later became George I of England. It is a story about naked power and how that power will stop at nothing to protect itself from interlopers such as Konigsmark, against whom the Hanovarian royals close ranks to prevent the lovers escaping together. The marriage between George and Sophie is loveless, but it has to be protected from harm because George's hopes of gaining the British throne would be ruined should there be a scandal involving his wife running off with an adventurer. In the end, Konigsmark/Granger is killed by his enemies and the princess spends the rest of her life shut up in a castle mourning her dead lover.

Once more, Granger is cast as the outsider, the handsome gambler who is perceived as 'not quite the thing' by the established order. In his own life, he had been trying to acquire the property and trappings of the landed gentry, but without much success as far as the land or the exploitation of it was concerned. Parallels between an actor's life and the roles he plays should not be over-cooked, but nevertheless Konigsmark is a typical Granger part, which may reflect something of the man himself. He had encountered this feeling of being an outsider at school and in the army, was finding it quite difficult to move upwards in British society, and this role somehow reflected his own position in real life.

Saraband for Dead Lovers was in a totally different league of film from any he had made so far. It is one of the most enduringly worthwhile British movies of the 1940s despite a certain stilted air arising from stodgy direction. It is perhaps in a sense too tasteful in its aesthetic appeal, thereby, to some extent, stifling spontaneity, vitality and passion. Joan Greenwood played Sophia and although she was effective in many roles, she is not the actress one would instinctively choose to play a doomed lover, and sparks do not really fly between her and Granger on screen, partly because of the inhibitions in the direction but also partly because the two actors did not fire each other.

Nevertheless, despite its faults, the film was greeted warmly. The *Monthly Film Bulletin* described it as having 'suspense, romance, interest and excitement in full measure'. The film displays some of the strengths of the British film industry: top-class cinematography, excellent art direction and costumes, superior musical scores (this one by Alan Rawsthorne) and painstaking attention to historical detail. Granger was working with some of the top people in the industry and it is a pity that for the sake of his career he was not in their company more often. Granger stated that this was one of few films he made of which he was proud. Nevertheless, it lost money and, according to Charles Drazin's book *British Cinema of the 1940s*, the losses were so heavy that Sir Michael Balcon, head of Ealing Studios, 'was not inclined to consider favourably any proposition in relation to Technicolor or period pictures'.

*

Granger's attempt to return to the domestic hearth and play the patriarch within a conventional marriage was failing. Once more, he moved out of the family home and this time it would be for the last time. The couple moved to divorce and, as was quite usual in those days, evidence of Granger's adultery was cooked up with Granger's connivance and lawyers' co-operation. Divorce laws in the late 1940s had not yet been liberalised (it would be another twenty years before reforms were introduced). No doubt Elspeth March could have provided proof of Granger's adultery with women she knew about, but they both wanted the marriage to end as amicably as possible and without involving third parties known to them. Granger in his autobiography tells of a weekend spent in Paris with a woman and co-operating with the private detective who came calling at their hotel room. The whole affair was a sham. No adultery took place on this occasion, the private detective knew it, the lawyers knew it and the judge who granted the divorce probably realised it, too, but this was what people who wanted to divorce were forced to do at that time.

It was about this time in his life that Granger became close to the young woman who was to become his second wife and the lady with whom he was mostly associated in the public mind: Jean Simmons. After her brief appearance in *Caesar and Cleopatra*, the career of this beautiful girl from Cricklewood in London had flourished. Soon she had had noteworthy parts in three of the best British movies of the decade: as the Indian servant girl in Powell and Pressburger's *Black Narcissus*, as the young Estelle in David Lean's *Great Expectations* and as Ophelia in Olivier's film version of *Hamlet*. Thus, by the time she was seventeen, Jean Simmons had notched up three significant screen roles. Of all the films Granger had made, only *Saraband for Dead Lovers* came anywhere near the quality of those three movies.

Of course, Granger was a major star of the British cinema at this time and no doubt the very young Simmons was attracted not only by the man himself but by his fame and success. Granger, for his part, would have realised that Simmons was going to be very, very successful. He became not only her closest friend but her adviser as well, now that she was under long-term contract to the Rank Organisation. Simmons was also a very fitting consort for a handsome star, although she was sixteen years younger than him. She had startlingly attractive dark looks, was very talented and mature beyond her years. The difference between a thirty-four-year-old man and an eighteen-year-old young woman, however, is more than an age gap; there is a disparity in maturity, life experience and emotional security. Simmons must have perceived Granger as a father figure to some extent and he no doubt had paternal feelings towards her.

Granger's attitudes to women can be categorised as fairly conventional, if not decidedly reactionary. If actors use parts of themselves in the roles they play, it is interesting how often Granger played roles that at the very least smacked of misogyny or a deep ambivalence towards women. Now the gender war was a staple element in many movies of this time, and arguably it still is; the hero and heroine have to conflict before they come together at the end of a movie. However, it is perhaps not stretching the evidence to say that Granger found himself playing on screen men who were at best patronising towards women and at worst hostile and distrustful.

Even those who dislike Granger as a movie star – and he was, and is, not universally popular – have to grant that he seemed to be very attractive to many women. Yet being attractive to women does not mean a man particularly likes them as a sex. Of the statements that Granger made about the female sex, the gist of them all is that he distrusted women in general and because of this sought to control them. This undoubtedly stemmed from his childhood experiences and his resentment towards his mother at her perceived treatment of his isolated father.

Thus, for Granger, part of Simmons's attractiveness might have been her youth. It would be surprising if in their relationship the much older man did not act as the guide and mentor, the father figure and controlling hand. Simmons, for all that she had packed a great deal into her young life, would have been pliable and anxious to have emotional guidance and security provided for her by this successful and mature man. For Granger, with his emotional history, she must have seemed to be one woman he would be able to control. His first wife had been equally as mature as he, was the mother of two children and had had, and was about to resume, a successful career. Simmons was quite a contrast. She was just embarking on a career that promised great things, had just obtained womanhood and had little experience of the world. If Granger wanted to be in charge of the most important relationship in his life, he could hardly have chosen a more suitable object of his affections than this beautiful eighteen-year-old. The power relations in the Granger–Simmons match would undoubtedly change over the next dozen years, much to Granger's despondency, but for now he would be in charge of both their lives.

Granger's divorce had been granted under his original name of James Stewart. This was done to avoid the press from latching onto the break-up of his marriage and is further evidence that he profoundly disliked the publicity attendant on being a famous movie star. But despite the fact that he was now divorced, Granger and Jean Simmons felt they had to disguise their close relationship from the world. Inevitably, however, it became obvious that they were now an 'item' and he was summoned in front of J. Arthur Rank himself and his chief executive John Davies, a dauntingly cold and authoritarian man. They were concerned that their rising young star Jean Simmons would be harmed by bad publicity if the press found out she was having an affair with a married man. Granger was able to contradict them by pointing out triumphantly that he was no longer married and that they need not worry about their young star being compromised.

But there was obviously more involved in this than their worry about Simmons's reputation. Granger's relationship with the Rank executives was continually fraught and he was seen as one of their troublesome stars. It has to be emphasised that the Rank Organisation was an authoritarian employer and treated their stars and starlets with a good deal of condescension and even something close to contempt. Thus, Granger's problems with them did not all stem from his intransigence or because he liked being awkward for the sake of it. Nevertheless, they did in fact originate partly from his aversion to the business of being a film star (premieres, personal appearances, interviews, various official junkets) and the basic fact that he was a spirited and perhaps rather headstrong man who did not take kindly to authority figures who tried to control him. In part, too, he must have felt trapped by his own responsibilities to his former wife and his children and the property he had bought, although that was sold shortly afterwards. Incidentally, Granger in his autobiography blamed the failure of the pheasant-breeding venture on the gamekeepers he had employed, who, he claimed, had cheated him. This would be a pattern in his business ventures: either he was very unlucky with the people with whom he did business or he was a bad judge of character. In Granger's overall life, however, he would always need someone other than himself to blame for misfortunes. In some ways, he expected to be let down and became increasingly paranoid.

The press did not find out that Granger had been divorced by his wife until months after the event. The *Daily Mirror* reported in July 1948:

> The story of film star Stewart Granger's divorce had been one of the best-kept secrets of all time in movie business. When the undefended case of Stewart versus Stewart was heard in London on 13 April and Mrs Stewart was granted a decree nisi and custody of the two children, hardly anyone connected the case with Jimmy Granger. Granger never wanted any publicity about the divorce. When the rumours got very hot and it seemed certain that someone would stumble on the facts very soon, he and his buddy, Mike Wilding, took a trip in Jimmy's yacht to the South of France.

The press no doubt knew about Granger's relationship with Simmons, but in those distant days journalists merely gave heavy hints as in this 1948 newspaper article from the *Daily Mirror*, headlined: 'Jean (Ophelia) Simmons is Stewart Granger's Pin-up'. The report describes how Granger had bought a sketch of Simmons as Ophelia by the artist Roger Furse. According to the report, Granger also bought another Furse work and two by Augustus John from the same exhibition. 'I have always been interested in paintings,' Granger is quoted as saying, 'but I have never been able to afford them. I still can't.' A rueful comment from the actor on his own extravagance.

If misogyny was part of Granger's make-up, then it found an outlet in his next screen role in *Woman Hater*. A Rank production directed by Terence Young, this film has Granger as the woman-hating Lord Datchett who makes a wager in his club that he will seduce a famous theatre actress, who has said she wants nothing to do with men. Granger invites her to his country estate and passes himself off as Mr Dodds, the agent for the estate. The actress discovers his real identity and takes her revenge by making him fall in love with her then abandoning him. The plot is similar in many ways to Shakespeare's *Much Ado About Nothing*; the hero and heroine have to realise their true needs and feelings about one another. In the end Granger gives up his resistance to women, the Garbo-like actress who has stated she just wants to be left alone has to acknowledge her real feelings for him and the two are united.

It is in part a movie about the battle of the sexes and how mutual resentments can get in the way of healthy relationships between men and women, but it is too soft-centred about the hero's misogyny and the heroine's distrust of men. Because this is a commercial movie and Stewart Granger must always get the girl in the end, both their resistances have to melt away to make way for a conventional happy ending.

Granger's co-star was the famous French actress Edwige Feuillère, who was, like the character she played in this film, better known as an actor on the stage rather than in films. Made by the Two Cities company, it was clearly an attempt to attract audiences in both Britain and France by co-starring a major star from each country. It also represents a view of upper-class English life for the mass audience, replete with dotty dowagers, forelock-pulling tenants from the aristocrat's estate and eccentric servants. It reflects a view of English life that encompasses residence in a medieval castle, dressing in evening clothes every night for dinner, gentlemen's clubs, an existence that seems to have no burdensome duties other than attending christenings of the children of loyal retainers, opening the local village fête and quaffing lots of wine and brandy. The film makes no critique at all of the social hierarchy it represents and indeed endorses it. The film must have appeared dated even in 1947 in its social attitudes and its representation of British society.

It is probably not an accident that Granger was cast as this 'woman hater'. He had a rather patronising tone towards women in many of his movies, comes over too often as cocky about his own attractiveness, tends to tease women as though they are errant children and plays immature games in his dealings with the opposite sex. That these kinds of attitudes were replicated in his own life is hardly surprising. As an English aristocrat, however, Granger is less than convincing. There is too much of the smooth Mayfair car salesman about him.

Leslie Halliwell describes this movie as 'incredibly slight material', which is 'interminably stretched out well beyond an excellent cast's ability to help'. The *Monthly Film Bulletin* was relieved, however, 'to see Stewart Granger out of period clothes'. Granger was never at his best in comedy and although this was intended to be sophisticated comedy rather than of the broader variety, he struggles with the rest of the cast to make the material anything other than clichéd and mechanical. He mugs, he hams it up, he does slapstick, yet he remains resolutely uncomic. *The People* asked the question: 'Does Mr Granger make me roar with laughter?' then answers it with an emphatic, 'No, he doesn't!' *Woman Hater* was not a hit movie and is seldom shown nowadays, even on cable. Granger's reputation was not enhanced by it. Indeed, the critics generally felt that his participation in the film was a major error.

Certainly, Granger was no happier with movies like *Woman Hater* than his critics were. The press reported that the star 'No. 1 British screen heart-throb' was 'fed up' with his film roles. 'I am certainly not going to do any more films like *Woman Hater*,' he is quoted as saying, 'that got spat at.' He added, 'In my contract with Rank I have the right to choose my own scripts and if I don't like what's offered, I can make films for other companies.

Apart from the possibility of my making a film for Korda, or perhaps MGM, negotiations are going on for me to go into a play.' Public pronouncements like these about his most recently released movie could scarcely have endeared him to his Rank bosses and by this time it is clear that there was little prospect of the parties negotiating a new contract. Behind Granger's public bravado, it is likely that he was secretly worried about his longer-term prospects. It is noteworthy that he mentions MGM specifically in this report; he may have already had wind that the studio was considering him for an important MGM production.

In a 1948 *Picturegoer* article entitled 'Are They Doing Right By Our Jimmy?' the writer contends that British movies, and by inference the star's bosses, were letting Granger down and not exploiting his talents sufficiently. The writer mentions his 'irresistible magnetism' for women, his 'magnificent physique and vitality' and his 'undoubted and proven acting ability'. However, his movies were not matching up to those talents: *The Magic Bow* had been 'one of those awful mistakes', *Blanche Fury* was 'out of key with the times' and *Saraband* had been drained of life. In a robust defence of the star's supposed 'temperament', the writer describes how he had been present when Granger had 'blown up' because a journalist had poked fun at him when he had had to dive into a muddy ditch while on location for *Woman Hater*. Granger had insisted on being padded with cushions and had sworn profusely when he emerged from the mud. His defender pointed out that it had been Granger who had insisted on doing the stunt himself and he had been aggrieved by the follow-up story the journalist had written. He describes Granger as a man who 'has the courage of his convictions and will stand up for himself wholeheartedly, even against the tycoons, when he believes himself to be in the right'. The feature sums up many of the traits that people recognised in Granger at this time and it is interesting that although he had his many detractors who loathed his apparent arrogance and rudeness, he also had his enthusiastic proponents. As evidence of that, Granger topped the *Kinematograph Weekly* poll for 1948 as the most popular British male star.

Another 'row' that Granger instigated at this time has him defending the rights of film-goers to see films in their entirety. In a radio programme called *Picture Parade*, Granger told the story of a projectionist near his home in Haslemere, Surrey, who in order to keep his dates with his girlfriend, regularly used to put one reel of film to the side and show the film without it. More seriously, Granger stated, 'I have seen my own movies cut about and I've seen American pictures cut.' He said he was speaking as a film fan who went regularly to the cinema in his neighbourhood. The headline of the newspaper report is 'Granger Starts a Row', which obviously fitted the image that the press had created of Granger as a troublemaker, but on this occasion, it appears that he was speaking up to help stop a practice that robbed cinema-goers of the right to see films as they were intended to be shown. He might have often been dismissive of his films and movies in general, but he seemed to care enough to speak out about this unlicensed cutting.

Also around this time, Granger had an encounter with Hedy Lamarr, the famous Hollywood beauty, who was one of the current sirens of the screen. Granger tells how he met her in Paris while on a publicity tour and they went back to her hotel room together. According to him, she wanted him to make love to her and lay naked in bed waiting for him. However, she issued such explicit instructions about how he should go about it that Granger's courage wilted and he left her without consummating the relationship. This account is only of interest now to us because of what it might tell us about Granger's attitude to women. Granger's complaint about Lamarr was that she was far too bossy and mechanistic, and that this quite took the wind out of his sails, so to speak. This is, of course, his perspective on the encounter; no doubt Lamarr would have told a different story. But Granger's account fits in with this idea of his needing to feel in control of women and his resentment when women tried to tell him what to do, especially, it seems, in bed. However, years later Granger felt the need to recount this episode in his autobiography in some detail, when chivalry might have demanded he keep quiet about it. The fact is that he probably felt very flattered by Lamarr's attentions, as she certainly was one of the most beautiful stars of her era, and even thirty years later, he was vain enough to tell the story.

Granger now put his attention on finding vehicles that would star Simmons and himself in tandem. This can be interpreted as a benevolent act on his part, the older man and a successful film star guiding the relative newcomer in this minefield world of the entertainment business. Less charitable observers might have thought unworthy thoughts along the lines of control and exploiting her new-found fame to make his own star shine even brighter. People's motives are often very mixed: his attempts to take control of Simmons's career in the short term at least may have been motivated by his conflicting needs.

It is surely not accidental, though, that the first of the two vehicles he found for them was a story about a much older man and a teenager whom he gradually realises is no longer a child but a mature young woman with emotions and sexuality. The film is *Adam and Evelyne* and, although the screenplay was written by four writers, including Noel Langley and Lesley Storm, it was Granger himself who initiated the project and created the story-line. He would later claim that he 'wrote' *Adam and Evelyne*, but that 'they' would not give him a screen credit for the screenplay.

The story of *Adam and Evelyne* concerns Adam (Granger) whose best friend dies suddenly, leaving a daughter, Evelyne (Simmons). Adam has promised to adopt her and the girl thinks he is her real father. She is sent to a finishing school in Switzerland, while Adam resumes his former life of gambling and society life. When she returns, however, she has changed into a beautiful young woman, which Adam chooses to ignore until their feelings for each other become clear and he perceives her not as his adopted daughter but as the woman he loves.

The parallels to Granger and Simmons's own lives could scarcely be closer. Granger had first met the very young Jean Simmons when they both worked on *Caesar and Cleopatra* three years previously. Those three years had seen the fifteen-year-old Simmons transformed from a promising newcomer into a fully fledged star and also a very attractive young woman. Granger had been married when he met her first, which parallels the character's quasi-fatherly role in the movie. Now with the passing of the years, and Granger's 'freedom', he realises that this female is a child no longer and has strong feelings towards him. Perhaps Granger, like his character in the movie, had to overcome feelings of guilt about her youth and the yawning gap in their ages before he could acknowledge his feelings for her and defend them to himself. Perhaps, indeed, *Adam and Evelyne* is an unconscious attempt on Granger's part to justify his relationship with the very young Simmons to himself and to the wider world.

It is a *Daddy Long Legs* story; in fact, it seems very derivative of that novel by Jean Webster (the Astaire–Caron movie version of it would be made in 1955). The film offers light entertainment and is intended to pass a pleasant hour and a half in the cinema without challenging the brain cells too severely. It skirts any awkward questions about teenage sexuality and older men, except on the most superficial of levels, and the elegant Mayfair settings represent a kind of lifestyle that the vast majority of the film's intended audience could not hope to afford, but that was one of the functions of the British cinema at this time in particular: to take the mass audience's mind off their own rather less affluent existences and to bring some glamour and elegance into 'their humdrum lives'. When most British people were struggling with continuing rationing of basic items, low wages, poor housing, power cuts and high unemployment rates, the function of the British cinema was, in part, to represent an alternative reality.

Granger and Simmons provide some sparks on the screen and they do communicate real feelings for one another within the limitations and inhibitions of the script. At eighteen Simmons comes over as remarkably mature and Granger is his usual bright and breezy self, although he shows more tenderness and sincerity in his love scenes with Simmons than he does with some of his other screen partners. *Adam and Evelyne* is not at all a memorable movie in its own right – indeed, it is very lightweight and seems dated now – but it may throw some light for us on Granger's attitudes at the time and his need to reflect on his relationship with Simmons through the medium of this film. The *New York Times* review by critic Bosley Crowther considered Granger 'perhaps a bit stiff' but 'adequate on the whole', which was not the kind of review to have an actor dancing the streets. The *Monthly Film Bulletin* commented that the love scenes between Granger and Simmons were 'discreetly acted'.

The other venture intended to provide a vehicle for the new lovers involved Granger risking more than his professional reputation. It was his financial backing that enabled a stage production of Tolstoy's *The Power of Darkness* to be financed; indeed, Granger had to guarantee half the production costs, which were considerable, and he would not get his money back unless the play recouped its production costs at the box-office. Again, this was an interesting choice for Granger. If he had wanted to fund a stage vehicle for Simmons and himself, he could have chosen something more commercial and less grim than the Tolstoy piece, with its brutish Russian peasants. His decision to back *The Power of Darkness* must have reflected his wish to be involved with something more worthwhile than the majority of the movies he had been making. It is his attempt to aspire to 'seriousness' in his acting career, and if he could not find that in the movies he was being offered, then he would turn to the theatre. Simmons had already appeared in several 'serious' movies, and part of his reason for choosing the Tolstoy was no doubt to showcase his future wife's acting credentials in serious parts.

The production toured the big cities in the provinces including Manchester, where it broke box office records, before coming into the West End of London, the heart of British theatre. The provincial reviews were generally warm, but when it opened in London at the Lyric Theatre on Shaftesbury Avenue on 25 April 1949, the critics slaughtered it. *The Times* review of 29 April summed up the general feeling: 'The disastrous weakness of the present performance is that throughout it is namby-pamby. None of the principals can conceal the tell-tale marks of civilisation. While Mr Stewart Granger is being goaded by the farmyard Lady Macbeth to kill his illegitimate baby with a spade, it is the actor rather than the man who tremblingly approaches a situation which he clearly feels to be rather too strong for his audience.' Later in the same review, however, Granger is described as 'a striking figure of sullen, sensual masculine pride'.

However, not even the fact that two film stars were co-starring in the production could help the box-office, although Granger claimed he financed out of his own pocket a run of several weeks so that the cast and crew would not be deprived of their jobs. He lost all his investment, which was clearly a deep disappointment to Granger, not only in terms of the financial disaster, but his hopes of becoming a theatrical producer.

Thus, with the failure of his pheasant-breeding scheme, the subsequent divorce and sale of the Elizabethan manor, and now this crushing loss on *The Power of Darkness,* Granger's finances were not in a healthy state. He was making, by most people's standards, a great deal of money from his Rank contract, but he had this pattern of over-extending himself and risking too much without really knowing enough about the business he was getting into. This was probably true of his investment in the pheasants and the manor house, and it appears to be an accurate assessment of his backing of the Tolstoy production. After all, Granger's experience in the theatre had been fairly limited up to this point. He had never before been involved in the financing of stage productions, yet suddenly he was taking on a large share of the costs of a major production, the commercial potential of which must have been in doubt from the start. His initiative can be admired on one level, but was it a kind of hubris that led him into this losing gamble? He was a gambler, perhaps even a rather reckless one, and this gamble had certainly failed. Part of the London critics' reaction to the production may have stemmed from an attitude about these film stars daring to venture onto the London stage with this 'serious play'. Theatre critics' attitudes to films in those days were notoriously parochial and patronising (that attitude has certainly not disappeared entirely) and they must have got their knives out for Granger in particular, who would have been perceived as this upstart matinée idol, the adored icon of millions of shop girls, and not really an actor at all. Granger was aware of this prejudice, and it would undoubtedly have increased his resentment at his lot and his inability to break free from the constraints of being a romantic hero of the flicks.

His continuing dissatisfaction with the Rank Organisation and his rejection by the London critics undoubtedly influenced him in turning his thoughts towards Hollywood. Granger in his autobiography also recalls a telling incident during a boating holiday in the Mediterranean he and Simmons took with Tyrone Power and Power's then wife Linda Christian. At the time Power was at the peak of his fame and box-office clout. When the boat's anchor got caught in Portofino harbour, and crowds gathered to gawp at the stars, Granger noticed with some resentment how 'Ty Power nonchalantly continued to sip his drink, waving to all the laughing fans'. However, he also noted: 'One thing this slight balls-up had taught me was that to be an international star you had to go to Hollywood. All the fans had been screaming out Ty's name and no one had noticed me and I had starred in about twenty British films.'

The fact that Granger gives a detailed account of this memory from the late 1940s reflects how much impact it had on him. It also tells us that, for all his supposed indifference to the trappings of stardom, on some level he was envious of Power's fame and fortune, and wanted some of this for himself. He realised that to become that kind of international star, he would have to make it in Hollywood. It would not need much persuasion for him to quit England and Rank in order to test his fortunes in Tinsel Town. After all, he had been mostly forced by his British employers to make movies he despised and when he had tried to do something worthwhile on the British stage, he had been cut down to size by the critics. Well, he would show them on the other side of the pond, where at least they appreciated get-up-and-go and British class.

Before that, however, he was given the chance for another stage appearance, which, if he had accepted the challenge, might have dramatically affected the direction of his career. Margaret Selznick, the ex-wife of David Selznick, the famous producer of *Gone With the Wind* and numerous other box-office successes, and the daughter of the head of MGM Louis B. Mayer, had seen Granger in *The Power of Darkness* and thought he would be ideal for the part of Stanley Kowalski in a forthcoming London production of Tennessee Williams's *A Streetcar Named Desire*. This was the role that had made Marlon Brando a star on Broadway. The London production was to star Vivien Leigh and be directed by Laurence Olivier. For any actor, this offer would have been not only very flattering, but an incredible opportunity and challenge. However, Granger turned it down and his chance to take on a heavyweight part in the theatre was gone forever. In retrospect, it seems a pivotal moment in Granger's career. However, it is hard to see how Granger could have convincingly played the loud-mouthed American working-class Kowalski, a role that Brando had made his own. It may be that Granger knew his own limitations and, having been badly bruised by the critical roasting dished out to the Tolstoy, decided to refuse the challenge in order to avoid another mauling. The opportunity was bypassed and his career took quite another direction. Bonar Colleano, the American actor based in Britain and a familiar face in British movies of the period – such as *Pool of London* and *The Sea Shall Not Have Them* – was eventually cast by Olivier, but the role did not catapult him into major stardom before his early death in 1958. Vivien Leigh, by contrast, won the part of Blanche Dubois opposite Brando in the 1951 Hollywood version of the play directed by Elia Kazan.

MGM was looking for someone to play Rider Haggard's hero, Allan Quatermain, in the film version of Haggard's *King Solomon's Mines*. They needed an Englishman who could be convincing as a big-game hunter and guide and who already had some kind of movie pedigree and star status. Stewart Granger fitted the bill and soon the offer came through from Hollywood. Granger's need to become an international star was about to be fulfilled and he was heading for the most glamorous of all the major Hollywood studios.

When rumours of Granger's impending departure for Hollywood broke in the press, the Rank Organisation was quoted as saying, 'We know Stewart

Granger is leaving us, but no one knows when.' It was clear there was no love lost between Granger and Rank, but when Granger was asked whether there had been any difference between himself and Mr Rank, he replied diplomatically, if rather inaccurately, 'There has never been any difference of opinion between myself and anyone with whom I work.' His tongue must have been firmly in his cheek and this quote must have produced many a guffaw among those in the know. But all that was shortly to be behind him. The film Hollywood wanted him for was a tale of adventure and Granger was about to begin his own Hollywood odyssey. Fame and wealth beckoned.

Chapter 4

MGM, KSM AND HH

THE HOLLYWOOD GRANGER was bound for in 1949 was undergoing substantial changes in its structure, production plans and attitude to employing a roster of stars and other key personnel such as directors and cameramen. The peak year for movie tickets bought in the USA had been 1946, when the domestic market alone produced 90 million ticket sales per week. Even in those days, American movies were dominating the world market, because ticket sales in the rest of the world were equally healthy. However, in the next ten years, sales would be reduced by 50 per cent and, because of this economic imperative, the studio system that had been born in the 1920s and 1930s was about to change. It would have dramatic impacts on the way movies were set up, how film stars were employed and, very importantly, the number of movies the studios in their new form made each year.

The economic downturn in the fortunes of the Hollywood studios in the late 1940s and 1950s is usually laid at the door of television. The Second

World War had temporarily halted the introduction of television services to a mass audience, but now that the war was over, television quickly became the major source of cheap entertainment for the masses, displacing not only the cinema but radio as well. Soon, most American homes would possess a television set and the major television companies would be competing directly with the movie studios for audiences. The spread of television in the UK and Europe was slower and it would not be till the mid-fifties that almost every household in Britain, for example, would boast a set, but a similar downward trend in audience figures as in the US forced domestic film industries to draw in their horns.

However, there was another very important factor in bringing about these dramatic changes in the Hollywood film industry, a factor that is often overlooked. A piece of anti-trust legislation in 1948, which became known as the Paramount Decree, forced the major studios to divest themselves of the exhibition side of their business. Basically, there are three aspects to the film industry: production, distribution and exhibition. Until the 1948 Paramount Decree, the majors (MGM, Warners, Paramount, 20th Century Fox and RKO) were allowed not only to make films themselves, but to distribute the actual celluloid to the cinemas on the prime city centre sites that they owned as well. What was in operation was in fact an oligopoly, a system of vertical integration and a monopolistic structure shared among several top players, which also included Columbia, Universal and United Artists. Before the Second World War, the American government had started its attempts to dismantle this oligopoly, because, rightly, they considered it a restraint on free enterprise. It was not a healthy situation when the major film-producing studios controlled what was shown in the biggest and best-placed movie cinemas in the land. It meant they had a virtual stranglehold on the business and it was very difficult for anyone outside the magic circle to break it. If an independent producer managed to make a movie, he or she still had to find cinemas in which to show it. The major studios wanted their own products in their own cinemas so it was, in essence, a shut-out, which was why the US government passed the

Paramount Decree into law.

Faced with the competition of television and now the forcible sale of the most profitable arm of their business – the exhibition of the movies they made in the cinemas they themselves owned – the studios made an objective judgment and decided there had to be cutbacks. In the course of the next ten years these would be substantial. The golden era of the old Hollywood studio system, then, was in the process of being dismantled when Stewart Granger arrived in Tinsel Town to discuss starring in *King Solomon's Mines*.

It was also a time of tremendous strife and tension in Hollywood because while the industry was retracting in scale, it was also under attack by the McCarthyite House Un-American Activities Committee (known as HUAC), which had been set up by the Senate to investigate the influence of Communists and Communist propaganda in Hollywood movies. There had been the notorious case of the Hollywood Ten, a group of writers and directors, who had been charged with using the films they had made to insert 'commie' propaganda. All of the ten were found guilty of contempt when they refused to co-operate with HUAC and sentenced to terms in prison. Other Hollywood notables had already cooperated with HUAC, clearing themselves of being tainted with the charge of being a 'red' by naming colleagues with whom they had attended Communist party meetings or who belonged to organisations which the Committee considered to be Communist fronts. HUAC would continue its investigations for almost ten years. It was a period of real fear among the Hollywood community, and many careers were ruined or put into temporary hold because of an unofficial black list that the studios quickly put into operation in order to be seen not to be soft on these 'commies'.

Granger would have been fully aware of what was going on in Hollywood during this period, as everyone working in the industry would have discussed the issues and known colleagues who were being persecuted for their supposed political beliefs. Yet not once in his autobiography does he allude to the HUAC hearings or mention anyone who suffered because of this persecution. Granger's omission is significant. He either did not care about what had happened, which marks him down as particularly limited and self-serving in his attitude, or he did not want to comment because of his previous approval of the witch-hunt that had gone on. Hardly anyone, even on the extreme right, would now seek to defend what went on during those so-called investigations. It was a disgraceful period in Hollywood history and Granger lived through it as a Hollywood star of that era, but he makes no comment at all on it. Perhaps this in itself speaks volumes. What political opinions Granger did voice were of a right-wing variety, supporting what he saw as American get-up-and-go free enterprise, the British monarchy and, later, Mrs Thatcher.

Rider Haggard is a favourite author of Conservatives and it was for an adaptation of the novelist's tale of African adventure, *King Solomon's Mines*, that Granger had come to Hollywood to film. He was not on a long-term contract with MGM yet; at a time when the studio was seeking to cut their overheads in a shrinking market, this was a one-picture deal. No doubt, MGM were wary of adding to their wage bill by offering the usual seven-year contract to this relatively untried British actor. Granger might have been near the top of popularity polls in Britain, but that did not necessarily cut any ice with the MGM supremos. Many a British star had tried to make the leap to Hollywood stardom from the basis of domestic stardom and had failed. Even James Mason, who had left for Hollywood about a year earlier, was struggling to find worthwhile roles and he never really won top star status in Hollywood at any time during his years there. Olivier had, but other British stars such as Alec Guinness and John Mills never made it as Hollywood stars. They were perhaps seen as too British and not quite macho enough for American tastes. Stewart Granger was a different 'product', however, and MGM probably considered they could sell this virile actor, now in his late thirties, to the American and international cinema-going public.

By 1950 American weekly ticket sales had shrunk to 60 million per week from an all-time high of 90 million in 1946. This shrinkage in domestic ticket sales meant that the Hollywood studios began to look to Europe for box-office revenues. One way of ensuring that European box-office returns did not suffer as badly as US sales had done was to increase the number of movies with a distinct European interest and subject matter. If this was to be the policy, then they needed British stars specifically; of the first seven MGM movies Granger would make, six would have a direct European connection. Another factor in luring Granger to Hollywood was that the leading swash-buckler of Hollywood, Errol Flynn, was on his last legs as a heroic leading man because of his self-destructive tendencies, and MGM thought Stewart Granger could fit the bill to replace him. Compton Bennett, the director assigned to *King Solomon's Mines*, had wanted to cast Flynn as Quatermain, but he had been overruled by Sam Zimbalist, the MGM producer. Granger knew that Bennett would have preferred Flynn in the role, so this undoubtedly added to the antagonism between star and director which was to be such a feature of the making of the film.

Granger had to fend off intrusions into his private life almost the minute he arrived in Hollywood. The British press reported his denial in Hollywood that there was a romance between Jean Simmons and himself: 'We are the greatest of friends, but she has never wanted to marry me, nor have I wanted to marry her.' In the same report, Granger is quoted as saying Britain 'was not a happy place at the moment' because it resented having to depend on American charity to survive: 'There is little for an Englishman to be proud of at the moment and an Englishman without pride is a sorry thing indeed.' Granger was to give Hollywood, and Americans in general, multifarious examples of an Englishman's pride over the next ten years. His hosts would not always warm to it.

King Solomon's Mines was clearly going to be a very important movie for Granger. If it were a success and audiences reacted favourably to him in particular, he must have known he would be offered a long-term contract by MGM. Then there was the issue of whether or not he would accept such servitude. He had chafed at the bit under the Rank contract, so why should anything be any better under MGM? However, there were the financial imperatives. He had lost a lot of money in his various ventures, had to pay alimony to his wife for the support of his children, owed the Inland Revenue £15,000 and had a certain lifestyle to maintain. Perhaps he was not in the best of positions to play too hard to get. MGM, with hindsight, got Granger very cheaply, paying him $25,000 in a one-picture deal. It would be a different ball-game once the movie was released, however.

First of all, of course, the picture had to be filmed, which meant five months of location shooting in Kenya. His co-star was Deborah Kerr, his ex-lover, the woman he had nearly left his wife for in years gone by. She had since married and her first husband, Tony Bartley, was with her during the shoot at MGM's expense. It is clear that Kerr and Granger were now good friends and they supported each other during the often arduous and strained shoot in the African bush.

In Eric Braun's 1977 biography of her, Kerr gave an account of how she came to be cast: 'I was invited to dinner at the home of Dore Schary and, having read *The African Queen*, I thought it an ideal moment to say, "I have read a marvellous book called *The African Queen*; it would make a marvellous film and I would love to go to Africa." "A-ha," said Mr Schary, "that property belongs to Warners and we already have an African script, *King Solomon's Mines*, and, as you say, you would love to go to Africa!" Need I say more! I was on my way to Nairobi before I knew it.'

King Solomon's Mines would be the first colour feature movie shot in an African location. Africa at that time was usually represented in movies by the jungles of Southern California, and if that background did not suffice, stock footage from documentaries or newsreels was interspersed. But MGM was to pull out all the stops on this production, despite some misgivings among some executives about the cost. MGM had acquired the rights over the Rider Haggard novel for $5,000 (the copyright had run out in the USA, but was still current in Britain). Granger, Kerr and Richard Carlson, who would play Kerr's brother in the movie, would be the only non-African cast members to be transported to Africa and the crew was to be kept as small as possible. When the crew landed in Nairobi in October 1949, it was supplemented by thirty Kenyans, almost all of British origin. Thirty-five

Wakamba tribesmen were also hired as porters and hunters. There were to be no lights used during the shooting because of the difficulty of transporting them. All the crew had were four reflectors. The emphasis was to be on portability and flexibility.

Granger devotes many words in his autobiography to telling the tale of the making of *King Solomon's Mines*, not only because it was a very important movie in his career, but also because it gave him the opportunity to test himself in 'manly' pursuits such as big-game hunting and exploration. He managed to shoot – according to a newspaper report that quoted Tony Bartley – four buffaloes and two rhinoceros, which, from today's perspective, seems indefensible, but this was the late forties and the preservation of endangered wild species was not the big issue it later became. While he was shooting one of these water buffaloes, Granger was struck in the ribs, so his quest for manly thrills cost him some pain.

There is little doubt that filming *King Solomon's Mines* was an exhausting task for the twenty-four people comprising the Hollywood unit. It took two and a half days to ship them from Culver City in Los Angeles to the film's headquarters in Nairobi. For the first scenes of the movie, they were driven for sixty miles every morning over poor roads to Machakos. Their travels would take them to Mount Kenya, Jinja on the shores of Lake Victoria, the Murchison Falls in Uganda, to Stanleyville in the Congo and the Serengeti Plain in Tanzania. An average day consisted of waking at 5.30 a.m., on the move by 7 a.m., start shooting at 9 a.m. and ending at 4.30 p.m. The Hollywood unit was supplemented by local technicians, carriers, labourers and cooks, comprising 150 in all. The preservation of the Technicolor film stock in the heat was a problem because it deteriorated quickly and had to be kept at a constant temperature of fifty degrees. The last major Hollywood production shot in Africa had been the 1929 *Trader Horn*. The complexity of the *King Solomon's Mines* production dwarfed the problems that that production unit had faced.

Granger suffered from dysentery while in Kenya, as did many of the crew and cast. He complained bitterly about MGM risking the health of their stars, including himself, which he saw as typical of the attitude of studio executives. Thus, nothing had changed about Granger with this change of employer. There was even a matter of a $10,000 bill for expenses he incurred during the shoot. He claimed he had been assured he could run up expenses while on location and that MGM would pick up the tab. Later he would be confronted with this large bill by MGM, which merely increased his paranoia about studio bosses and accountants. The cast and crew spent the Christmas of 1949 on location in Kenya, but MGM did try to make it as seasonal an event as possible. However, a few months after he signed with the studio, Granger was already disgruntled with his new employers and this dissatisfaction would continue throughout his eventual long-term MGM contract. How much this was due to Granger's general 'chip on his shoulder' attitude and how much it was the result of MGM's tough management style is difficult to say. Perhaps it was a mixture of the two. Certainly, as MGM drew in its financial horns in these straitened times, it was not prepared to pick up a $10,000 expenses tab for this 'one-off' British movie star.

It is very probable that Granger saw this 'expedition' as a chance to prove his manliness once more and certainly he was keen to do his own stunts. Throughout his Hollywood career, this was to be the pattern: he had to prove he was no weak limey who baulked at doing anything at all dangerous; indeed, at times, as we will see, he undertook unnecessarily risky exploits, driven, it seems, by this need to prove himself again and again. His role in *King Solomon's Mines* lent itself to derring-do. For example, he had a near miss with a cobra in a scene for the movie and in another scene he had to carry an African, which resulted in lasting back pains that troubled him throughout his life. Yet, he was so anxious to act the 'man' that it is hard to feel too much sympathy for him. He insisted on doing these stunts himself, so if injuries resulted, then he had himself to blame. In many ways, Stewart Granger was a driven man.

Once more, Granger had tremendous conflict with his director, Compton Bennett. Bennett's main claim to fame at this point was that he had directed the huge British hit, *The Seventh Veil*, although Granger states that James Mason, the star of the film, had virtually taken over the direction of the movie because Bennett was so incompetent. Bennett had also directed *The Forsyte Saga* (*That Forsyte Woman* in the US) with Greer Garson and Errol Flynn. Granger quickly grew to hate the rather 'superior' Bennett and was at daggers drawn with him throughout the making of the film, until he was influential, it appears, in having Bennett sacked by MGM before the movie was completed and his being replaced by Andrew Marton, a 'man's man' and much more to Granger's liking. Marton's comment on Granger was: 'He's got guts in proportion to his ego.'

When they got back to Culver City and the MGM studios, Marton re-shot some of the interior scenes and desert sequences which were now located in Death Valley, where the actors and crew had to work in temperatures in the hundreds. In March 1950, Granger was rushed to a Hollywood hospital from Death Valley suffering from pleurisy. It was a 230-mile trip and the illness was acute. Granger had not felt really well since his return from Africa. For such a strapping leading man, he seemed remarkably prone to illness of one kind or another.

The rights and wrongs of the director situation on *King Solomon's Mines* are impossible to untangle, but it is clear that Granger was still having difficulty in accepting the authority of directors, and if he took a dislike to one in particular, then he entered into a struggle with him from which he would not back down. Granger had a kind of 'for me or against me' relationship with many of his male colleagues. He inspired intense loyalty as well as deep loathing. It is clear that there was absolutely no love lost between Granger and Compton Bennett. His co-star Deborah Kerr, however, responded to the overtly masculine aspect of Granger's persona, as seen in this startling statement: 'Women sense there's a bit of a brute in him. A woman's intuition tells her that being a gentleman hasn't watered down his virility and that he would as soon as thwack her on the rear as not.' Richard Carlson, his other co-star on the film, hedges his opinions: 'Everything about him is on a huge scale. I often had the feeling he would have been happier as an Elizabethan.'

In his autobiography, Granger praised the way white farmers and planters, at the time *King Solomon's Mines* was made, treated their African workers. The film was shot in Kenya shortly before the Mau-Mau rebellion against British colonial rule and the subsequent victory of the freedom fighters. Granger remained unimpressed by this establishment of a new Kenya under an African government and asks whether the black Africans were any better off governing themselves without the British. This is further testimony that Granger was an old-fashioned unreconstructed Conservative who believed in the values and practices of the British Empire.

While on location, he took the opportunity to go on a safari at the foot of Mount Kenya with a white hunter, Eric Rundgren. He shot two buffaloes, but one was only wounded so the two hunters followed him into the bush. 'I suddenly looked up and saw him coming towards me,' Granger later told journalist Dick Richards. 'We kept pumping lead into him but nothing seemed to stop him. There was no way out. We had to take the charge. I was caught in the ribs and knocked stupid. The hunter was gored in the head, then turned round and dropped the buffalo before he could turn and make a second charge.' This reads like a scene from *King Solomon's Mines* itself, but there seems little reason to doubt his account. This is Granger acting out some Hemingwayesque male fantasy of man facing the ultimate test of courage, but in reality, it was a tale of a couple of guys with big guns shooting wild animals who were doing no harm at all. Granger was parading the hairs on his chest yet again.

King Solomon's Mines was a huge hit for MGM and Granger. It was even nominated for the Best Picture Oscar for 1950, although it lost out to *All About Eve*. The picture, however, did win two Oscars for colour cinematography (Robert Surtees) and editing. The photography is excellent and Surtees deserved his award, but it is difficult to see why the Academy thought so highly of the movie as a whole. Stunning locations expertly photographed do not a fine movie make. *King Solomon's Mines* has a curiously flat quality despite all the 'thrills' and adventures offered in this tale of the search for the mythical mines. The stars are attacked so often by snakes, lions, rhinos, giant spiders and sundry creepy-crawlies, not to mention the untrustworthy locals, that it is amazing they survived to reach their destination and to return in one piece. But this representation of the dangers of the African bush is a conventional and clichéd approach that, it was clearly hoped, would keep the audience on the edge of their seats. Television could not offer anything like this: exotic locations, major stars, genuine African tribal dancing and extras, a version of a famous adventure tale, and all in Technicolor and on a large screen. It was the kind of movie that clearly MGM executives hoped would entice people away from the second-rate entertainment being offered in their front rooms. If movies were to survive, then they had to be different from the anodyne family entertainment of American television. 'Make it big, make it good, give it class' was an unofficial motto of MGM, and in *King Solomon's Mines*, they had combined a certain level of literary prestige with the expense of sending a large crew and cast to Africa, and had produced an entertaining movie for a mass audience.

Granger (with his hair artificially silvered at the temples to add maturity) plays Allan Quatermain, the rather autocratic and bad-tempered big-game hunter and expert on all things African, who is employed by Kerr and her brother (Carlson) to embark on a trek to find Kerr's missing husband who has set out to find the mythical King Solomon's Mines. It is exactly the kind of action man, authoritative male role that Granger had been so lacking in Britain, where he had been cast too often as the romantic lead. Here the romance between him and Kerr takes a back seat to the mishaps and dangers of the trek. Again, Granger plays a misogynist character, whose wife had died six years before and who is unwilling to be employed by a woman and to take her along with him into the bush, because, in his opinion, she would be a liability on trek. 'Any woman who wants to go tramping through the jungle,' Quatermain/Granger opines, 'must have something wrong with her.' Kerr/Mrs Curtis responds by asking what his sickness was: 'Nothing to live for?' Naturally, as this is a Hollywood film, the tensions between the hero and the heroine are ironed out. The screenplay finds numerous opportunities for the hero and heroine to embrace when the latter stumbles in the bush or needs protection from whatever wild life is attacking her at any given point. Henry Curtis, the husband they are meant to be trying to find, turns out to have expired in the mines of King Solomon, so there is nothing to stop them from getting together in time-honoured movie fashion. However, the love story is subsumed by the adventures of the trek. Granger plays Quatermain in a bush hat with a leopard-skin band, a style that he seemingly helped to make fashionable in game-hunting spheres.

It has to be said that Granger is a success in the part, not that it makes great acting demands of him. He is believable as the misogynist and bullying hunter and guide. He has a natural authoritative air about him that borders on arrogance. Viewed from the perspective of today, however, the race politics of the movie are decidedly suspect. The African bearers are portrayed as basically dishonest and lazy, with a few exceptions, and their tribal culture as bloody and primitive. There are clichéd references to being cooked in pots, and members of the Watusi tribe are on hand to supply exotic local colour and perform tribal dances.

If Andrew Marton did indeed carry out a patchwork rescue of the movie after Compton Bennett was sacked, then it was only partially successful. The film is curiously one-paced and never really reaches a dramatic climax. It just kind of peters out. However, one interesting aspect of the film is that it uses no orchestral score, employing only the singing of African tribal music, which gives it some kind of authenticity. Yet for all these deficiencies of pacing and dramatic structure, it still has a certain interest and in 1950 when it was released, it is perhaps easy to understand why the film attracted such huge audiences. An earlier film version of Haggard's tale starring Cedric Hardwicke as Quatermain and Paul Robeson as the exiled African chief, made by Granger's former employers Gainsborough in 1937, had been more faithful to the original, but had been decidedly creaky, especially as Robeson sang several inappropriate songs at various intervals. This MGM version was much more striking in visual terms, having been filmed in colour, and its use of locations far outstripped the earlier film. Leslie

Halliwell called it a 'travelogue with the merest trimmings of a story', which is fair comment. It is not the story of the film that holds the audience but the background and the photography. *Variety* described it as a 'fancy package of screen entertainment earmarked for big box-office'. This journal of American show business gave Granger a pat on the back, too, stating that he 'scores highly as the African hunter'. The *Monthly Film Bulletin* described Granger as only 'adequate', however, and noted that the movie was 'a somewhat stilted epic strangely lacking in excitement'.

Despite these critical reservations about the movie's qualities, MGM had a hit on its hands and that was what counted for the beleaguered studio. Louis B. Mayer, the legendary head of production, was under attack for being out of touch with the times and would shortly be replaced by Dore Schary, who was seen to be more in touch with contemporary tastes. MGM could no longer be content to serve up glossy star vehicles consisting of tasteful literary adaptations, a tradition that had been started by Irving Thalberg in the 1930s. In some ways, *King Solomon's Mines* is in the tradition of the old MGM product: it was expensive and glossy in its own way.

The important thing for Granger, of course, was that his first American film was a success and a huge one at that. The Hollywood Stewart Granger screen persona had been established in this first movie: the adventurer, the loner, the man of action irresistible to women but who had combative relationships with them and had the need to dominate and control them. He now found himself in demand and the international stardom he had sought now definitely beckoned. However, he had not got off on exactly the right foot with MGM bosses and had certain financial problems to clear up, so he was not in the best negotiating position when the subject of a long-term contract came up.

Despite the fact he had not felt well since his return from location in Kenya, immediately work on the movie had ended, Granger headed back to Africa for an eight-week safari holiday. A newspaper report at the time said his 'bag' included a lioness and a leopard, and that Granger had had an encounter with a charging elephant that nearly reduced him to a 'vital statistic'. Granger is quoted as saying, 'I kept hitting him but he kept coming on. There wasn't much in it when I finally got him.' Newspaper reports like these only added to Granger's image as an outdoor, athletic he-man, which he probably welcomed to counter all the 'glamour boy' publicity he kept getting. However, from today's perspective, it is painful to read about this movie star 'bagging' lions, leopards and elephants. Before he left for Africa, he recorded a Lux Radio Theatre hour-long dramatisation of *B. F.'s Daughter* with Barbara Stanwyck as his co-star. He was now acting with Hollywood royalty, even if, so far, it was only on radio.

Granger, on the back of the huge success of *King Solomon's Mines*, was now offered a seven-year contract by MGM; this was the usual term for stars under contract to the studio. He always claimed he fought long-term servitude to his film employers, but the evidence points to the fact that he had narrowed down his options because of his extravagant ways and risky business ventures. Alimony, back taxes, financial losses, even the $10,000 bar tab, all these burdens meant he was more than a little anxious to conclude a deal. In theory, then, he may have wanted to escape a long-term contract; in practice, he had little choice if he were to clear up his debts and aspire to the international stardom that he believed would bring him not only wider fame but more rewards and opportunities.

MGM negotiators would have known about Granger's financial problems and these were hard-nosed executives used to the cut-and-thrust of Hollywood deals. They recognised that the success of *King Solomon's Mines* had made Granger a worldwide star, so they needed him under contract to make the kind of movie that British stars, in their eyes, were more suited to than many of their own domestic stars: historical dramas, period costumers, movies with a European background. Another factor in these negotiations was that the European market had become increasingly important to the Hollywood studios as the US domestic market shrank, so it made sense to sign up this British star who already had a following in his own country, and

Europe in general, and to star him in movies that were either set in Europe or had strong European associations.

After some hard negotiations Granger signed the seven-year contract. He would earn $1,500,000 during this contractual period, which, given that he only earned $25,000 for all those arduous months shooting *King's Solomon's Mines*, is testimony to how highly MGM rated their new British star. There would have been a six-month option clause embedded in the contract, meaning that every six months his employers could choose to end the contract or extend it for another six months. This 'option' clause was used as a kind of Sword of Damocles over the heads of MGM's stars; it was a way of keeping them in line and persuading them to do what they were told. If a recalcitrant star was told his or her option might not picked up next time the option time rolled around, then it might well have a sobering effect on an actor used to living high and enjoying the benefits of being at the studio which boasted that it had more stars than there were in heaven. The financial rewards were high, but along with these came a kind of fancy wage slavery. MGM liked to talk about themselves as a 'family', especially during Louis B. Mayer's period of tenure, but if it was a family, then the 'children' were treated with a firm hand by the patriarchal 'fathers'.

There were two interesting aspects to Granger's deal with MGM. As part of the package that was worked out, MGM agreed to buy Granger's London apartment, which they then used to lend to visiting executives and stars. This obviously suited Granger as he was about to move to Hollywood, but it is an illustration of how MGM could use a potential employee's financial needs for its own benefit. The other noteworthy aspect of the contract is that Granger insisted a film version of Sabatini's novel *Scaramouche*, starring himself in the title role, should be part of the overall deal.

Granger had admired the silent screen version of *Scaramouche* made by MGM and starring Ramon Novarro, and he clearly wanted the role for himself. It clearly was important to him because he insisted on making it an integral part of the deal. He saw himself as Scaramouche, the romantic tearaway who hides behind the actor's mask, before emerging to right wrongs, win the beautiful lady and discover he was really an aristocrat after all, not just a middle-class man with yearnings he cannot quite understand himself. It does seem particularly significant that this was the role he coveted most when he joined MGM. It is safe to venture that, whether consciously or unconsciously, he perceived Scaramouche as expressing something central to his own character and his view of himself as a film star and as an individual.

Granger was flushed with success. His personal reviews for *King Solomon's Mines* had been mainly warm. He was now on his way to being the international star he wanted to be. A British newspaper report at the end of March quoted Granger as saying he was looking for a house in Hollywood where he intended to settle. He called it 'a fine place to work and live'.

Then another article in the *Daily Mirror* at the beginning of October 1950 ran the headline, 'Stewart Granger says: "I love Jean"'. The reporter quotes a conversation he had had with Granger six months previously: 'Of course, I love Jean and I think she is very fond of me. But we know the snags of two people in the same profession marrying, particularly when there is such a disparity in ages. We decided to wait until Jean was really old enough to know her own mind. We agreed not to see each other for a year to see if our feelings would change. And now we find there is still nobody else.' The reporter comments that the only snag he can see is that their professional contracts would keep them apart for long spells.

Nevertheless, despite these perceived 'snags' to their marriage, Granger asked Jean Simmons to marry him when she was in Chicago promoting one of her British films, *Trio*. The announcement of their engagement was reported in the British press in October 1950: 'Granger, 37, says he has known Jean Simmons since she was 13,' stated the *Daily Express*. 'She is now 21.' For someone who valued his personal freedoms, Granger did not allow himself much time between his divorce from Elspeth March in 1948 and his engagement to Jean Simmons. Separated as they were by the Atlantic Ocean while she continued her film career in Britain and he was subject to MGM's regime, Granger may have been anxious to capture this beautiful young woman for himself. She was thought of as a beauty and as a talented actress with a very promising career ahead of her. Hollywood offers were coming at two a week for Simmons, according to one newspaper report. For a man in his late thirties, Jean Simmons was quite a catch and doubtless it fed Granger's vanity that this much younger woman was so devoted to him.

An Associated Press release of the time described Jean Simmons as putting on 'a piece of cotton thread as a temporary engagement ring as she said she was so excited over the engagement to Stewart Granger. Asked to pose with Granger for photographs, Jean said: "I wish you would make arrangements with Jimmy . . . he's the boss." ' The article explains that the engagement ring, which was a diamond in a yellow gold setting, had not been delivered by the jeweller, and so they had improvised for the moment. Simmons was either play-acting for the press in stating that Granger was the 'boss' or this was the reality at this stage in their relationship. That power equation in their relationship would certainly change within a few short years.

Granger, as an ex-pat in Hollywood, was homesick at that time, and missed both his children and Jean Simmons, after she had to return to England. He admits to 'star-gazing' at fancy Hollywood restaurants such as Romanoff's and Chasen's, as the likes of Gable, Tracy, Hepburn and many others paraded their stuff. However, this state of awe did not seem to last long as he got to know some of these 'legendary' stars. Clark Gable he described as monosyllabic and ill at ease on social occasions. He did later become firm friends with Spencer Tracy, Katharine Hepburn and, of course, Elizabeth Taylor through his friend Michael Wilding, who was to marry her a few years afterwards. But for the most part, familiarity with these stars bred something approaching contempt, and he had little admiring to say about many of his MGM co-stars, apart from the coterie to which he belonged. It appears that Granger did not find it easy to trust people or let people get close to him, so his close friendships were few and far between and often ended in disputes.

MGM clearly wanted to capitalise on Granger's success in *King*

Solomon's Mines and he was put to work in two movies, neither of which were to prove anything other than mediocre at best. The first was a film version of Rudyard Kipling's *Soldiers Three*, a jolly romp about three British soldiers serving on the north-west frontier of India. His principal co-stars were David Niven and Robert Newton. In his autobiography Granger complained about Niven's scene-stealing when he stroked his moustache, and as for Robert Newton, he was so drunk most of the time, they could hardly obtain a passable performance out of him. Perhaps Newton knew how awful the movie was and drank even more than usual to blot it out. It was directed by MGM hack director, Tay Garnett, and it was perhaps his decision to play it for laughs rather than as a roistering adventure tale. The result is a sad exercise in futile mugging that is embarrassing to watch fifty years on. It is one of those movies which seems to have been great fun for the cast and crew to have made but this sense of enjoyment is not shared by the audience. The cast act as though their antics on screen are much funnier than they really are, which results in cringe-making viewing. Granger was never at his best in comedy and, by his own admission, stoops to the most amateurish of pulling faces and other exaggerated comic gestures, which are a sure sign of an actor in a state of desperation. The film was greeted coolly by the critics and equally so by the public at large.

Thus, MGM had done Granger a favour by casting him as Allan Quatermain, but had botched his second assignment. *Soldiers Three* was decidedly not another hit for their new British star. Bosley Crowther in the *New York Times* commented that Kipling's original tale had been altered beyond recognition and 'reduced to sheer slapstick and bombast'. The three leading actors 'play the soldiers on the lowest level of nonsense' and the whole movie was 'silly, unimaginative and flavourless'.

The only interesting aspect of Granger's next assignment, *The Light Touch*, is that the writer-director of this completely forgettable film was Richard Brooks, who would later marry Jean Simmons when her marriage to Granger ended in divorce. This movie was definitely another strong reason why Brooks would not be very highly rated in Granger's estimation. It is one of those wispy gentleman-thief tales with Granger playing an elegant and amoral crook who sees the error of his ways in time-honoured fashion through the love of a good woman played by Pier Angeli, later famous for being the love object of James Dean and for having committed suicide at the young age of thirty-nine. Granger plays Sam Conride, a master thief who steals a religious masterpiece and then tries to sell it without sharing the proceeds with his partner, played by George Sanders. However, at the end of the movie, Conride/Granger returns the painting, an action, as *Variety* noted in its review of the movie, that was 'inconsistent with his larcenous nature'. However, the reviewer is kind to Granger, saying that he 'registers in the key spot'.

But the movie is devoid of wit and charm, essential ingredients if this kind of slender fare is to amuse at all. Granger flounders around with the rest of the cast and makes little impact. There was no challenge in this kind of role, but, worse, *The Light Touch* was a 'nothing' movie, indeed it was almost a 'B' movie and certainly it made no impact on the critics or the box-office.

The show business journalist Dick Richards recounted an incident that occurred during the shooting of some scenes for *The Light Touch* in Tunisia. On location, some rubber-necking Tunisians were causing problems for the technicians so Granger, according to Richards, suggested they set up a diversion. His suggestion was that he and a cameraman would go down the street and stage a fight between them in order to divert attention from the shoot. Yet again, Granger seemed anxious to prove his 'masculinity' even in a harmless diversionary ploy like this.

Granger had by this time borrowed money from MGM to buy a house in the very fashionable area of Bel Air, in Beverly Hills. He was acquiring the trappings of a Hollywood star, trappings which were clearly very important to him. It was the same pattern that had emerged when he first became a star in Britain. He needed, it seems, to surround himself with the conspicuous accoutrements of success. There had been the Elizabethan manor house and now there was this expensive Bel Air house, bought with money loaned to him against his future earnings by his employers. It can easily be seen that this made good sense from MGM's viewpoint. A star who was in hock to the studio was hardly likely to walk out on them or kick up too much of a fuss about the movies he was assigned to, not when he owed all that money on the expensive home he had just acquired. Yes, Granger had protested about *Soldiers Three*, but MGM executives would have assessed that their star had little real room to manoeuvre; Granger had to work to earn the money owed to him through his contract and some of that money had to be used to pay back what he had borrowed from them. In a sense, MGM operated a high-class slavery operation and the studio clearly encouraged their star employees to dig themselves deeper into a hole of financial dependence by offering these seemingly benevolent financial arrangements. Granger would from time to time rail against the chicanery of his studio bosses, but in his eagerness to acquire the material possessions which he considered a star of his magnitude should have, he became easy prey to a type of high-class bondage. He would be continually running on the spot, never quite making any headway to enable him to free himself from the chains that bound him. And this for a man of his temperament must have become increasingly frustrating.

Granger and Simmons now wanted to tie the marital knot, but there was the problem of the publicity that would surround what was their private affair if they went public about the details of the marriage. It was around this time that a particular bête noir of Granger's entered his life. This was no less that Howard Hughes, the multi-billionaire businessman and, at that time, the owner of RKO Studios, which made him a very big player on the Hollywood scene. Granger was introduced to Hughes by Cary Grant, who knew Hughes well and with whom Granger had become friends. In those early days of his friendship with Hughes, Granger admired his flying skills and his independent attitude to life. However, these warm feelings were not to last long as Hughes's lustful eyes turned towards the young woman whom Granger was to make his wife. Hughes had had this kind of unhealthy obsession with film stars before, notably with Jane Russell and Jane Greer.

It was Cary Grant who, in a sense, invited the viper into the nest by suggesting that Granger allow Hughes to organise the wedding so that they could escape the attentions of the press pack. Why exactly Granger allowed this to happen is difficult to explain. It was their wedding, after all, and Granger was a mature man of the world who could surely have thought up some way of avoiding the publicity hounds and having the kind of private wedding he and Jean both wanted. He also perceived himself as an independent man who gave not a tinker's cuss for any man's opinion, yet here he was, this headstrong, proud movie star in the first flush of international stardom, giving control over this very important event in his life to a megalomaniac whom he hardly knew. Why?

Perhaps he was awe-struck by Hughes's reputation as a sportsman, entrepreneur, adventurer, lover, movie mogul and rich man. Hughes was, by all accounts, rather shy and awkward, but he was one of the most powerful men in the United States and, incidentally, in Hollywood. Granger aspired to wealth and fame and power, and Hughes embodied all of these qualities. He very probably felt flattered by Hughes's concern about their wedding and that this powerful man should take time out of his busy whirl of business affairs and running RKO to bother with the details of a wedding between two British movie stars. Simply, Granger, new to the Hollywood scene and still rubber-necking at Hollywood stars, appeared to have been overwhelmed by Hughes. However, from the perspective of fifty years later, it seems a strange thing to have done.

Hughes arranged for one of his private planes to fly Granger and Simmons to Tucson in Arizona, where they were to be married in the home of one of Hughes's array of lawyers. A black Cadillac met the Grangers at the Tucson airport and they were whisked away to the Arizona Inn, where some of Hughes's henchmen awaited them. They were told they need not do anything, that everything had been arranged. No doubt the couple were impressed by this and felt valued, but it was to come at a heavy cost later.

They were married mainly among strangers with Michael Wilding as Granger's best man. They spent some time in Arizona, which they fell in love with, resolving to return there some day.

Shortly after they returned to Los Angeles, Cary Grant again phoned and said that Hughes wanted them to be his guests at the Grand Canyon, which they had not yet visited. The couple were to have a honeymoon at Hughes's expense. It was during this time that Hughes made clear he lusted after Jean Simmons. Granger overheard Hughes and Grant discussing her charms while he, unknown to them, was listening to their conversation in a lavatory cubicle. 'Well, what do you think of her?' Grant asked Hughes. 'I'd sure like to get my teeth into that,' Hughes purportedly replied, as though Simmons were a piece of especially succulent steak. 'I didn't realise until much later,' said Granger, 'what effect that innocent question of Cary's would have on our lives.' Whether Grant's question was that innocent is certainly open to question: given Hughes's reputation for chasing film stars, it could not have come as a surprise to Grant that Hughes wanted to add Simmons to his conquests and it was Grant who, after all, had been the intermediary.

In his autobiography Granger is bewildered by his own co-operation with Hughes's machinations, and well he might be. 'Jesus! Couldn't we have any say on our own marriage?' he commented nearly thirty years later. A wedding is, or should be, a private matter between two people. It is often necessary for a couple to fight family pressures when planning a wedding, but to have to accommodate the wishes of someone as wilful and dangerous as Howard Hughes is simply bizarre. From Granger's own account of the whole affair, it seems clear that he gave himself over to Hughes and surrendered control. He must have felt some kind of disempowerment because of this, which may partly explain his later, bitter tussles with Hughes. Impressed as he initially was with Hughes's charm and authority, Granger, being the kind of man he was, was bound to react negatively at some later date to this wholesale colonisation of something so important in both his and Simmons's lives.

Granger later mused that, at the time of his marriage to Simmons, he wondered whether Hollywood and the demands of their respective careers might tear them apart. The track record of the marriages of movie stars (when both parties are involved in making films often on location and abroad) is notoriously poor. Big-budget films involve months of production often in distant locations; spouses might well be acting and mixing with some of the most attractive stars in the film business; long separations are part and parcel of the movie business. Therefore, for the Grangers, it would require devotion to the cause of their marriage if it were to survive. The portents were not encouraging. Granger's first marriage had foundered partly for the reasons given above. If they were to make the marriage last, then one solution might be to find opportunities to work together. But even that was no guarantee of longevity of a marriage. In the 1960s, Richard Burton and Elizabeth Taylor made numerous movies together, but that only helped to prolong the marriage, not to save it. However, it would not be long before Granger sought opportunities to make films with his new young wife and he has to be given credit for wanting to make this marriage work.

One of the almost immediate strains that tested their relationship was the further interference of Howard Hughes in their private and professional lives. RKO was still a major studio in the fifties, although it would within a few years cease movie production. It was not as glamorous or large a studio as MGM, Warners, Fox or Paramount, but along with them, under Hughes's ownership, it still counted as one of Hollywood's Big Five, with Universal, Columbia and United Artists, kown as the Little Three, the other important production companies in the American film industry. RKO did not make expensive movies, but they had produced famous films such as *King Kong, Citizen Kane* and *The Outlaw,* which had starred Howard Hughes's 'discovery' Jane Russell. The studio also had a reputation for superior film noir, including such movies as *Out of the Past* and *Crossfire.*

Being a Hughes 'discovery' was a euphemism for being one of his numerous mistresses. He was a notorious woman-chaser although he was in many ways awkward with women. Becoming the target for his attentions would mean being showered with expensive gifts – diamonds, cars and apartments – but this bounty came at a steep price. He would have his ladies watched by private detectives and his many permanent employees to make sure that once they were in his 'stable', they did not stray and enjoy the favours of any stud in town. He was a persistent man, disliking being turned down in any sphere, and he usually obtained what he wanted, whether it was a woman or a President of the United States (Richard Nixon was clearly in Hughes's pocket). This persistence was manifested by his next move in his attempt to snare Jean Simmons.

In Britain Jean Simmons had been under contract to J. Arthur Rank, but the Grangers suddenly learned from a Hollywood journal that they had sold her contract to Howard Hughes. She was not party to this piece of business in any way; indeed, it was a fait accompli by the time she learnt of it. It seems astonishing that this could be done without her consent or participation, but the negotiating parties, the Rank Organisation and Howard Hughes, played hardball with their employees' lives and careers. Simmons had married Stewart Granger who was now resident in the States; the Rank Organisation must have realised that it would only be a matter of time before they lost one of their most important stars to Hollywood, so they cashed the remainder of her contract in while they could. On the one hand, this was good business because they were acknowledging the inevitable and making a financial gain from the situation. However, in human terms, it was surely indefensible. Simmons's total lack of involvement in the negotiations shows an uncaring, ruthless streak in the organisation, stemming largely from the coldly distant John Davis, whom Granger had disliked while he had been contract to Rank. This action borders on treating a young woman in their employ with contempt, as though she were not an interested party. Certainly, the Grangers claimed that the first time they learnt that she was now under contract to Howard Hughes was when it had been all signed and sealed, and there is no evidence available to contradict their account of the affair.

With due cause, the Grangers were furious. The fact that Hughes had gone to this trouble to get Simmons under contract to RKO had little to do with her worth as an actress or as a future Hollywood star, but everything to do with his lust for her. Hughes had frequently put actresses under contract to him and when they had failed to 'deliver the goods', that is, become one of his roster of mistresses, he had gone out of his way to ruin or curtail their movie careers. Jane Greer was an outstanding example of this pattern in Hughes's behaviour. She had become an RKO star in movies such as *Out of the Past* and *The Big Steal*, but her career was later put on hold by Hughes, who had, after all, that kind of power at his disposal and used it ruthlessly. Greer's career never really recovered from this interference. Thus, apart from their totally justifiable anger about the underhandedness and secrecy of the negotiations which led to Hughes 'owning' Simmons, they must have realised that this ogre was in some way obsessed with her and determined to have his way. They would have heard all the stories about Hughes's starlets and obsessions, and understood all too well that Jean Simmons had become his latest target. Granger, her new husband, must have felt insulted and so must have Jean Simmons. She had acted in movies directed by David Lean, Michael Powell and Laurence Olivier; and now she was being treated as though she were on a conveyor belt of Hollywood starlets who existed to serve their 'master', Hughes. For a talented, spirited and intelligent young woman with proven professional credentials, it must have been extremely galling to find herself under the control of such a man. It brought the Grangers in touch with a seamier side of Hollywood that they would rather have known nothing about.

Hughes's interference in Simmons's career soon began to manifest itself. He had claimed that he would make her one of the biggest stars in Hollywood if she agreed to sign a long-term contract with RKO (the Rank contract that Hughes had bought up had committed her to only three films). However, Hughes did not want other studios benefiting from his new employee's services. William Wyler was about to make *Roman Holiday*, and wanted Jean Simmons to play the princess who has a day out incognito in Rome and falls for reporter Gregory Peck. Hughes refused to allow her to play the role and Audrey Hepburn got the part. Hepburn had a tremendous personal success in the movie and it certainly launched her to major stardom. The movie, too, was a huge success, and there is no doubt that had Simmons been allowed to play the role, she would have had a similar success. Their anger with Hughes could only have been intensified by this loss.

Nevertheless, they accepted invitations from him, including a trip to Lake Tahoe accompanied by Liz Taylor and Michael Wilding. Hughes ostensibly wanted to show them his new flying boat, known as a PBY. His real motive was probably to further his courtship of Granger's wife. Granger suffered a perforated eardrum as a result of the dangerous flying stunts that Hughes put them through while showing his plane off to them. While Granger suffered from this affliction, Hughes wined and dined his wife in Tahoe hot spots.

Hughes was putting more and more pressure on Simmons to sign an exclusive seven-year contract and he resorted to threats to gain her consent. Unless she agreed, he said, he would put her 'in three of the lousiest movies you've ever seen'. Granger later described how Hughes would call them up all the time 'in that high-pitched strangled voice' and he became convinced that not only was he after his wife, but he wanted to smash their marriage. To start with, Granger had looked upon Hughes as a 'fascinating enigma', but now he had become a monster.

Granger was definitely furious about Hughes's control over, and his lust for, his new wife. In all Granger's dealings with Hughes from now on – and he was to continue to be an important factor in both their lives for some years yet – there was an element of highly charged male competitiveness. Hughes's machinations were a challenge to the masculinity Granger valued so highly. Between the men, it was a power struggle and in taking on Hughes, Granger would be locking horns with one of the most powerful men in the United States. However, he had never shirked from a challenge like that; indeed, it might be said that he had gone out of his way to seek these confrontations, judging by the difficulties he had had with film executives, directors and other men in positions of authority over him. Hughes had laid down the challenge and the swashbuckling Granger was not the man to refuse such a test of his manliness. His pride was at stake and, of course, so was the well-being and career of his beloved young wife.

Meanwhile, back at the MGM ranch, Granger had now two strikes against him (*Soldiers Three* and *The Light Touch*) and he needed a success to restore his standing in the film world. The old Hollywood adage about only being as good as your last film haunted most stars and after these two flops Granger must have been desperate to make up for lost ground as well as frustrated that MGM had shunted him into two such lack-lustre movies. Despite the fact these two movies had not been successful, a Kinematograph Weekly poll at the end of 1951 made Granger the most popular film star, and that included Hollywood stars as well, so his departure for Hollywood had not at all harmed his standing with the British film-going audience.

His foresight in insisting that a screen version of *Scaramouche* was included in his contract was now about to pay off. Anxious as he must have been about his wife's career and the struggle with Hughes, he must have needed to focus too on his own Hollywood career. He had had one huge success with *King Solomon's Mines*, but he had now to consolidate that success and show he could cut the mustard in another major success. Granger fancied himself as a swashbuckler both on screen and in life. His life, it appeared, had become a constant gamble and challenge. He took risks and wanted to continue taking them. *Scaramouche* would be a real challenge not only in terms of his Hollywood stardom, but also physically. It was exactly the kind of role in which Granger could expect to show off his 'manly' qualities and prove conclusively he was not one of those weak-kneed limey actors. It would turn out to be an adventure in more ways than one and provide one of the peaks, if not *the* peak, of his movie career.

Chapter 5

THE MASK OF SCARAMOUCHE

WHAT IS A swashbuckler? As a genre, swashbucklers are period adventure movies, the action of which usually takes place in historical eras that mass audiences would recognise: the French Revolution, Early Tudor England, the Middle Ages, the Spanish Armada and Elizabethan England. Staple elements include daring, chivalrous heroes, high-born ladies in peril, courtly intrigue, dastardly villains, sword fights and other duels, the storming of castles, dungeons, ships and all kinds of fortresses, battles at sea and on land, jousting and archery tournaments, highwaymen and gentlemen thieves, and ladies of dubious virtue. The production values in the more expensive of these movies include colour photography, elaborate costumes and sets and exotic locations. The pace of the film has to be fast and action is the driving force. Attention has to be paid to the details of the plot, but the brain cells of the audience are not to be overtaxed. Recently, *The Mask of Zorro* with Antonio Banderas and *Pirates of the Caribbean* with Johnny Depp have revived the genre.

Among the most famous of the actors who had made their name in swashbuckling roles were Douglas Fairbanks Senior and Junior, Rudolph Valentino, Errol Flynn, Tyrone Power, and Louis Hayward. Others such as John Barrymore, Ramon Novarro, Ronald Colman, Cornel Wilde, Gene Kelly, Burt Lancaster and Tony Curtis had also made their mark in the genre. All these stars could play heroic and had an athletic grace that suited the physical pyrotechnics of these roles. Thus, Stewart Granger was challenging some of the legends of the screen in taking on the role of Scaramouche, first played by Ramon Novarro in a 1923 MGM version of Rafael Sabatini's historical novel.

Granger had been worried that MGM would cast Gene Kelly in a musical version of the story. Somehow he had got it into his head that MGM's great 1948 success *The Three Musketeers* starring Gene Kelly had been a musical, which, it has to be said, does not say much about Granger's knowledge of even the recent history of the studio he worked for. In fact, in his autobiography, he makes some slighting remarks about Kelly's height, something he was prone to do about other men. He also tells of an occasion of a royal film premiere he attended in London where he was photographed with Alan Ladd, who was very self-conscious about being quite small. Ladd was seemingly very grateful to Granger when he (Granger) crouched for the photograph so that he did not tower over the smaller actor. Granger communicated an intense competitiveness with other men, especially over rather superficial matters such as height and physical strength.

George Sidney, the eventual director of *Scaramouche*, made it clear in a BBC radio feature in 1993 (written and produced by Tony Sloman) that he had in fact been seriously considering making *Scaramouche* as a musical, which would certainly have put paid to Granger's hopes of playing the lead role. However, in the same interview, Sidney also states that he had first realised Granger was the actor they needed for the role when he ran *Caesar and Cleopatra* and was impressed by Granger's playing of Apollodorus. So much for Granger's worries that Shaw had intended the character to be 'queer'! His playing of that part had helped land him the role of his career.

Although Granger had made numerous period movies in Britain, none of them could properly be called a swashbuckler. *Scaramouche* was the genuine article, however, and MGM were to mount an expensive production in their aim to have another commercial hit. For Granger, it must have seemed that this was make-or-break time if he were to maintain his drive towards international stardom and consolidate his standing with the MGM executives, with whom he was not universally popular because of his perceived truculence. Two mediocre movies on the trot had not done him any favours and he needed a success. He had, to a certain extent, initiated the project, although it seems likely that MGM had been already seriously contemplating making a new version of *Scaramouche*, if rumours about a Gene Kelly version were circulating, and Sidney confirmed this in the BBC interview. In terms of his own personality and how he wanted to project himself on screen and in life in general, his choice of the Scaramouche project tells us much about Granger.

Scaramouche is the story of a foundling, André Moreau, who discovers, after numerous adventures, that he is the bastard son of a French noble, the Marquis de Maynes, who was unable to acknowledge him as his son at the time of his birth and asked two members of the minor aristocracy to bring the boy up. At the beginning of the movie, Granger/Moreau is a spendthrift, a compulsive womaniser and useless at swordsmanship. By the end of the film, he has become a master swordsman, has left the 'bad girls' of his past behind and marries an aristocratic beauty. Indeed, the story is an aspiring bourgeois' wet dream. The hero finds out he is not of the common herd and indeed belongs to the highest echelons of society, a status he further reinforces by marrying 'well'. Along the way, he has had to bide his time play-acting as Scaramouche, a performer in the *commedia dell'arte* Parisian theatre, a profession into which he literally stumbles and in which he has his triumphs but which he will inevitably leave once his real self is revealed to the world.

It is a mistake to identify actors too closely with the roles they play, but perhaps it not reading too much into things to remark on the relevance of this role to Granger's own life. Granger was born into an upper-middle-class family, where money had not been in plentiful supply, but there had been enough to supply the conventional education (nanny and private schools) associated with this background. Granger, like the character he plays in *Scaramouche*, is confused about who his real father is: his first allegiance was to the 'uncle' figure in the family until the secret of his mother's real relationship with him is revealed. Like Moreau, Granger had 'stumbled into' the acting profession, and like the film hero, by donning the actor's mask, had elevated himself to fame and wealth. He, however, spent his new-found money like the nouveau riche he was on fancy period houses, land, servants, motor cars and schemes for breeding pheasants. When that had ended in financial trouble, he had chanced his luck in the States, where he had just bought expensive real estate, and he was to make future business ventures that smacked of adventurism. Of course, Granger in his rational mode did not imagine he was the son of anyone other than his father, a decent, hard-working army major, but in his fantasy life, he may have had a different view of himself. The fact of his mother's long-standing affair with the man he thought was his uncle could only have encouraged the young Granger's fantasies of escape into a more glamorous world where, indeed, he was not the minor public schoolboy, but a true aristocrat, if not by birth, but by natural inherent worth. A convincing case can be made that *Scaramouche* meant more to Granger than just a movie vehicle for him to exploit his particular talents. It met some other needs in him as well.

Of all the masculine prototypes that Hollywood serves up in its genre movies, the swashbuckler hero is perhaps the most flamboyant and 'free'. The western hero is generally weighed down with a sense of duty to right wrongs and re-establish law and order (think of Gary Cooper in *High Noon*, Henry Fonda in *My Darling Clementine*, even Alan Ladd in *Shane*). The war hero of genre war movies is equally driven to do his duty and serve his country (John Wayne, for example). The gangster anti-heroes are troubled human beings bent on a path of self-destruction. Even the heroes in Hollywood musicals are driven towards success and fame (Kelly in *Singin' in the Rain*, Astaire in *The Band Wagon*). But the swashbuckler generally has a much jollier time of it, whatever wrongs are inflicted on him. He is usually an outsider of some kind (a pirate, an unacknowledged son of a nobleman, a maverick soldier or sailor), who has to come back into the fold of conventional order but symbolises an eternal free spirit, a boyish sense of adventure, a refusal to observe the boundaries of traditional life. The heroine invariably starts out disapproving of his counter-culture attitudes but comes to value his courage and integrity both in her service and the service of legitimate authority. Robin Hood, Captain Blood, Zorro, the Count of Monte Cristo, the Man in the Iron Mask all start as outsiders and are brought into the fold, although they appear to keep their independence while reaping the rewards of a grateful state and heroine.

The opening credits to *Scaramouche* start with a quote from the author of the original novel on which the movie is based, Rafael Sabatini: 'He was born with a gift of laughter and a sense that the world is mad' – as useful a definition of a swashbuckling hero as there is. Granger was a man who in real life seemed to have a gift of laughter, but too often was in fact unhappy and dissatisfied with himself. Some part of him, too, probably did believe the world was mad, and his impulsive acts throughout his life were his way of trying to create order out of the craziness.

Errol Flynn was perhaps the most successful swashbuckler star in screen history. For many men, he embodied the free masculine spirit and the quest for adventure, thrills, wealth, women and pleasure in all its forms. Flynn was the hero who never grew up, who seemed to defy augury and the passing years, until time and his self-destructive ways finally caught up with him and he died at the age of fifty-nine. The interaction between Flynn's own personality and the swashbuckling roles he played, what he brought to these roles and what these roles did to him, is the subject of another book. But can it be denied that actors can be affected by the role models they themselves embody? Was Flynn 'destroyed' in part by the driving need to live up to his swashbuckling image on and off the screen? With Flynn, the conclusion cannot be avoided that the public perceived him in a certain way because of these roles; perhaps Flynn himself began to think of himself in the same way and felt a compulsion to live up to the legend.

Stewart Granger never indulged in the kind of unceasing self-destructive antics of Errol Flynn, but he had his own way of making difficulties for himself and that had partly to do with the shaping factors of his early life and how he thereafter wanted to be perceived by the world and, indeed, himself. It was not an accident of casting that had him playing Scaramouche, but something he actively sought. It could be argued that it was just an example of an actor recognising his own strengths and going after a juicy role to exhibit them. That is part of the story, but there is something deeper there, too. Throughout his life, he was looking for freedom, but he also wanted to enjoy fame and wealth and success, while living the life of a 'manly man' indulging in masculine pursuits and gambles of one kind or another. The profession he had stumbled into offered a kind of bohemian life, but he appeared to aspire to something more respectable – the status and life-style of the upper classes. This drive would lead him into difficulties as his need for money to indulge in these status symbols inevitably lessened the freedom he so treasured and he became more of a slave to the power brokers he despised. There would always be a tension between Granger's instincts towards freedom and his desire to move upwards in society. It was a tension that he was never able to resolve.

MGM cast Mel Ferrer as the villainous half-brother of Scaramouche (very insightful casting because Ferrer on screen made it easy to dislike any character he played), Janet Leigh as the aristocratic beauty, Aline de Gavrillac, whom Granger rides off with at the end of the movie, and Eleanor Parker as the 'bad girl' actress, Lenore, with whom he is dallying when the action of the movie opens. The sexual politics of *Scaramouche*, from today's perspective, do not withstand much scrutiny. The sexy bad girl has to be rejected finally in favour of the respectable 'good girl' who, handily, happens to be a rich aristocrat. Granger's interaction with Parker (the 'bad girl') on screen is teasing, double-dealing and explosive; he rarely addresses her as an equal or without manipulating her in some way. His behaviour with the

Janet Leigh character is respectful, chivalrous and almost paternal: she is destined to be his wife and so she is a virgin, it is implied, unlike the promiscuous Lenore. This is the familiar good girl versus bad girl pattern of genre movies; it is especially common in western movies where the hero is often torn between the virtuous and respectable heroine and the 'immoral' saloon girl, who loves him but knows she will lose out in the final reel.

As usual, Granger was determined to perform as many of his own stunts in the movie as possible and he was also determined to improve his swordsmanship so that a double (Jean Heremans) need not fill in for him too often. Heremans, who was a master swordsman and employed by MGM to teach Granger and Ferrer the moves that would make their duels convincing, would stand in for Ferrer during much of the long duel scene that would be the climax of the movie. That might have been all right for the 'namby-pamby' Ferrer, but it wasn't going to be the case with Stewart Granger. He was going to show these Yanks he could cut the mustard when it came to duel sequences and dangerous balancing acts. This determination to prove his dexterity was a set pattern now in his film career. It could be legitimately asked: to whom was he trying to prove his courage? His late father, perhaps, or indeed, himself?

Granger had to memorise eighty-seven separate sword moves, and was involved in twenty-eight stunts and situations that demanded athleticism. Heremans himself had a narrow escape when he was fencing with Granger, as Granger's sword broke and part of the blade embedded itself in Hereman's eyelid. If it had been the eyeball, then the consequences would have been horrendous. Granger's insistence on doing so much of the sword fights himself resulted on another occasion in which Heremans, while parrying a lunge from Granger, sliced Granger's eyelid. Blood poured out and there was a fear that his eye might have suffered some lasting damage. It looked worse than it was, however, and Granger was able to resume shooting the next day, although it had been a narrow escape, and one which must have alarmed the MGM executives when they heard about it: not only would the movie have been seriously delayed if Granger's injury had been really serious, but they would have been faced with a probable law suit. Granger being Granger angrily enquired about insurance. He was told, to his amazement, there was no insurance as no other stars had ever asked for it. Granger forced Eddie Mannix, the tough MGM executive who handled such matters, to arrange it. It does seem astonishing that MGM, the doyen of Hollywood studios, did not bother, or incur the expense, of insuring their highly paid stars against injury while shooting potentially dangerous stunts. This oversight on the part of his employers only fuelled Granger's conviction that they were a callous, profit-chasing bunch of bastards, while, from MGM's viewpoint, Granger's insistence could only have reinforced his reputation as an awkward customer.

Granger was intent on taking risks and doing his own stunts, but he also had an instinct for self-preservation and a distrust of other people's assurances that all had been done to avoid accidents. In one scene where the hero and villain square up to each other in a kind of rehearsal for the final climactic duel scene, Ferrer at one point cuts the ropes of a gigantic chandelier, which then drops towards Granger and narrowly misses hitting him. The stunt was set up by the director George Sidney and he asked Granger to shoot the scene without a rehearsal. The chandelier was on metal ropes that would stop its fall a few feet above Granger; its further descent would be filmed separately. Granger was sceptical about the lack of rehearsal because, after all, if the stunt went wrong, he was directly in the firing line. Much to the irritation of Sidney because of the delay in time and also the expense involved, Granger insisted that the fall of the chandelier be rehearsed without his lying underneath it. When it was tried, the chandelier fell straight down to within two inches of the floor where Granger would have been lying. It would probably have killed the star of the movie.

Granger, understandably, was furious, and Sidney was aghast at the narrow escape from disaster, being violently sick on the spot. Granger had, for once, not taken an unwarranted risk and thereby had probably saved his own life. However, this lax and unprofessional approach to such a dangerous stunt only fed his paranoia about how MGM treated its stars and, in the final analysis, how unimportant they were if their well-being and safety conflicted with the need to 'keep them rolling' and minimise expenditure. His anger was increased when he discovered that the insurance cover that he had fought so hard to obtain was not yet in place at the time of this debacle. He had had the same complaints about how the stars of *King Solomon's Mines* had been treated on location in Kenya and now he had a further serious example of the studio's lack of care. Granger, however, was a grumbler, he complained about everything and he had a reputation for it. This meant when he had a legitimate excuse to complain, it carried less impact because he did it so frequently.

However, when, during the duel scene, Granger had to fence while balancing on the ledge of a theatre box twenty feet above the floor, he had only himself to blame when he incurred an injury. This was exactly the kind of scene where a stand-in could have taken Granger's place without the audience being too aware of it. However, Granger would have none of that; he had to balance himself precariously on the edge of the balcony while fencing with Heremans/Ferrer. MGM did take some care over this stunt and fitted Granger with a corset with a wire attached to the ceiling so that if he did fall, he would dangle in mid-air and not plunge to the floor. When rehearsing the scene, Granger found he could not move freely enough so he insisted on removing it. Almost inevitably, he fell off the ledge, plunged to the floor and hurt his shoulder so badly that he had problems with it for the rest of his life.

In some ways, Granger's courage and determination are wholly admirable. He wanted to make the scene as realistic and convincing as possible and the way to accomplish that was for the star to be seen up there on the screen performing this dangerous feat. However, from a personal point of view, it was a foolhardy and risky move that resulted in a lifelong injury. What was driving this man to do this kind of thing? It is almost as if, deprived of a 'good war', he had to show, even if only in the make-believe world of the movies, that he would not shirk danger and would take risks.

Another part of the duel scene had Granger fencing his opponent across the back of the theatre tip-up seats, which had been bought from a cinema. He had to balance on the narrow top of the seats while continuing to thrust and parry and appearing to be engaged in a life-and-death struggle. While they were shooting the scene for real, he lost his balance. His leg got caught up in the gap between the back of the seat and the cushion with the inevitable result that the seat was torn from its moorings. Granger fell to the floor, badly twisting his knee, and took full advantage of the situation by pretending that something much more serious had happened. When the assistant director rushed up, he saw that Granger appeared not to be breathing and screamed to George Sidney that 'the poor bastard' was dead. According to Granger, Sidney's first response was, 'What the hell are we going to do? The picture's only half-finished!' whereupon Granger 'came to', called his director 'a mercenary prick' and ordered him to call a doctor. Sidney's supposed response to this accident is almost certainly apocryphal, part of Hollywood mythology that reveals the hard-nosed nature of the film business and an amusing anecdote for Granger to tell in later life about his adventures in Hollywood. However, the damage to Granger's knee was indeed a serious injury; but although he had to hobble around for days, he did not allow that to hold up shooting for long. More importantly for him, the knee never really recovered from this injury; he had to have an operation on it some years afterwards, and it too gave him problems for the rest of his life.

One accident on a movie such as *Scaramouche* is understandable, but this series of near disasters involving Granger does seem excessive. Can it all just be put down to MGM's cavalier attitude to the safety of its stars? That does not seem very likely because an incapacitating injury to the star of a movie can lead to delays and budget overspend. It was just not in the studio's interest to put their stars into dangerous situations, and any director, such as George Sidney, who allowed his leading man to suffer serious injury that delayed production would surely have been in serious trouble. No, the evidence points to Granger's own over-eagerness to take the risks himself. He was displaying his courage and physical prowess for all to see: the cast, the crew, the director, and finally the screen audience. Once again, it has to be surmised that he had an overwhelming need to prove that he had guts, and that physical danger did not worry him. However, all the risks involved in shooting the long final duel scene paid off handsomely in screen terms. The much-maligned George Sidney made the decision not to underscore the duel with the kind of dramatic music that composers Erich Korngold and Max Steiner had created for similar Errol Flynn sword fights. The absence of music emphasises the sound of the cold steel as the duellists make their way round the theatre set to the climax on the stage itself. In terms of screen fencing duels, it is the tops and Granger looks tremendous executing it.

George Sidney in the 1993 BBC radio interview mentions that during the shooting of *Scaramouche* when Granger was in one of his 'grumbling moods', Spencer Tracy visited the set. Granger said to Tracy that all the movies he had made and his performances in them were not worth just one of the great screen performances Tracy had given, whereupon Tracy replied that he would give all his roles up for the chance to play Scaramouche as Granger could. We all tend to despise what comes easily to us: playing Scaramouche was a role Granger was born to play, but because it was no real challenge to him, he tended to discount his achievement. The immensely more talented but rather portly Spencer Tracy envied Granger for the ease with which he played this athletic swashbuckling role. The grass is always greener.

There is no doubt that *Scaramouche* marks a peak in Granger's screen career. Indeed, in the opinion of many critics and fans, it was *the* peak, and from that point on there was a gradual decline in his fortunes. It is certainly one of the few roles he will be remembered for as long as Hollywood movies from this era continue to be shown. The movie itself has lasted well and is almost as fresh today as it was in 1952. It has pace, verve, a richness of texture and looks wonderful. It is MGM almost at its very best in terms of opulence and sheer entertainment. Granger's talents as a performer are also displayed at their very best. He is even rather touching in some scenes, for example, when the villain played by Mel Ferrer kills his best friend (Richard Anderson). Granger wasn't able to act with any great depth or understanding, but he could carry off a heroic role like this and also play the clown in the theatrical scenes. Indeed, to MGM's credit, the representation of the theatre performances with Scaramouche in his mask are excellently mounted. They clearly employed theatre and design experts to advise the director so that the theatrical period is reproduced with convincing authenticity. The costumes and other sets are sumptuous and the colour photography by Charles Rosher is impressive. Ronald Millar provided a literate script based on Sabatini's novel. All in all, *Scaramouche* is an example of Hollywood entertainment at its near best and the movie must rank highly in any swashbuckler order of merit.

Granger got the hit he so badly wanted, because when *Scaramouche* was released in 1952, it was a huge success with many of the critics and most of the public. Granger, on the whole, received good reviews. Bosley Crowther opined: 'Granger delivers along the line that he was born with the gift of laughter and a sense that the world was mad. He's got the teeth for laughing and the manner for confronting a mad world.' Crowther also praised the movie's 'extraordinary richness and high flippancy'. This 'flippancy' disturbed other reviewers, however, including *Variety*'s who complained that the movie 'never seems quite certain whether it is a costume adventure or a satire on costume adventure dramas'. Interestingly, it also notes that the French Revolution had been almost eliminated from the story 'because of the inevitable Red analogy were the hero to spout the 1789 theme of Liberty etc.' *Variety* damned Granger with faint praise by commenting 'Granger is handsome enough but seems quite unable to keep from letting his smirk show through at some of the ludicrous lines and situations he's forced into.' The *Monthly Film Bulletin* also commented on the dialogue that 'alternates between primitive cliché and absurdities that one feels must be intentional'. It is true that some of the lines Granger and others have to deliver topple into melodrama, but these work for the movie, otherwise the overall tone would veer too much towards farce. *The Saturday*

Review described Granger as 'more buckle than swash'.

Granger's stock was now very high with MGM, although his various grouses and generally 'bolshie' attitudes had not endeared him to everyone in the studio or the film community in general. His judgement about the project had been proved right and he had created a movie vehicle for himself that reinforced his star status and box-office appeal.

One example of how Granger sometimes went out of his way to lock horns with important people in Hollywood is illustrated by his account of how he tore a strip off the notorious Hollywood gossip columnist, Hedda Hopper. Granger's attitude to scurrilous journalists like Hopper and Louella Parsons was entirely proper: he wanted no truck with them and did not pander to them. Both those women made their living by peddling vicious gossip and they wielded an unhealthy power in Hollywood where they could make or break someone's career by revealing details of private lives that might not sit well either with the studio bosses or the general public. This was in the early 1950s when the McCarthyite investigations into communist influence in the Hollywood film industry were in full swing and careers were in jeopardy because of past affiliations with 'un-American' activities. No one would be able to accuse Granger of any of that, but the kind of paranoid climate that was created by such persecutions aided muck-rakers like Parsons and Hopper to ply their lowly trade.

The occasion that sparked Granger's rage at Hopper involved his old and good friend Michael Wilding, who was forging a Hollywood career of sorts, and had married Elizabeth Taylor, one of the beauties of the time and a very famous movie star indeed. Hopper summoned the pair and, in front of Wilding himself, upbraided Taylor for marrying this English actor whom everybody knew was a homosexual. The insensitive arrogance of Hopper, if this incident did happen as Granger told it, is quite staggering. Here was this talentless tabloid hack laying down the moral law for Taylor and Wilding. How Wilding could have sat there and allowed that to be said in front of him defies belief.

If Wilding did not react to Hopper's poison with enough aggression, his best mate Stewart Granger certainly made up for it. When Wilding and Taylor gave their account of the meeting and what Hopper had said about Wilding, Granger telephoned the columnist directly and in no uncertain terms (obscene epithets and all) told Hopper exactly what he thought of her. This was very typical of Granger: he was loyal to only a few people and Wilding was one of those. Even though attacking Hopper in this very personal way might lead to future trouble from that quarter for himself, he leapt in to defend his pal, hang the consequences. That sounds wholly admirable, uncalculating and selfless. However, Granger's comment in his autobiography – 'How dare she call my friend a faggot!' – somewhat lessens our admiration, perhaps. It was not so much that Hopper had advised Taylor against marrying this English fop, but that she had called him a homosexual, when everybody who knew Wilding considered him a 'cocksman'. What Granger fails to mention in his account of this sordid little contretemps is that Hopper had linked him directly with Wilding and implied to Taylor that Granger and Wilding's relationship had been 'too close'. Thus, Granger's conduct is revealing in several ways: it showed his impulsiveness, his loyalty, his determination to defend his friends' reputations and to ward off obtrusive journalists. At the same time, it also revealed the less admirable rampant homophobia that is evident in Granger's ragbag of attitudes to society in general. A coda to this incident is that Hopper repeated her charges against Wilding in her 1963 book *The Whole Truth and Nothing But*, whereupon Wilding sued her and her publishers and won damages of $100,000.

Granger and Simmons had now settled into their Hollywood home. Kenneth Tynan, the famous theatre critic, describes the Granger domicile in an article called 'Days in the Dream Factory' written for *Punch*. According to Tynan, the area itself manifested 'a head-on collision of architectural styles, baroque encroaching on Frank Lloyd Wright, which is muted by profuse vegetation: palm cypress, jacaranda, bougainvillea, flaming eucalyptus, plumbago'. Among 'the shrouded mansions of Summit Drive' is 'the empty Chaplin palace and deserted Pickfair' and the 'bizarre big-game museum occupied by Stewart Granger, wife and assorted buffalo skulls'. Not far from the Grangers' house was the 'multi-terraced villa once owned by Buster Keaton, now transformed by James Mason into a cat sanctuary. Am told "mot" of Fred Allen's: "When Mason wants the butler, he just steps on an adjacent cat." '

Tynan paints a bizarre picture of the Hollywood lifestyle and these highly paid ex-pats living it up amidst this excess. He describes it as festooned with hunting trophies and animal-skin rugs, as well as paintings of Jean Simmons. Perhaps Granger also perceived Simmons as a trophy. They had the regulation Hollywood swimming pool and at weekends they lived the good life, Hollywood-style, laying on barbecues for their friends the James Masons, Liz Taylor and Michael Wilding, Deborah Kerr and her then-husband Sam Zimbalist, Spencer Tracy, Richard and Sybil Burton. It must have seemed an idyllic existence to envious outsiders, but life is never that simple. Beneath the surface, there were worries and tensions. Success in Hollywood brings with it the anxiety of how long it is all going to last.

If Granger had thought that the success of *Scaramouche* would improve the quality of movies MGM offered him, then his next assignment quickly knocked that notion on the head. MGM cast him as a French-Canadian trapper, Jules Vincent, in *The Wild North*, an adventure story set in Alaska. The director assigned to this routine programmer was Andrew Marton, whom Granger had praised when he took over from Compton Bennett on *King Solomon's Mines*. The story concerns a Canadian Mountie played by Wendell Corey who in 'getting his man' (Granger, who has been falsely accused of murder) is injured and needs the help of the character played by Granger to survive the frozen wastes. The Mountie ends up, rather implausibly, suffering from 'snow madness', which only drastic methods will cure. The dilemma for the Granger character is whether to seize his chance of freedom or help the policeman regain his sanity. There are no prizes for guessing which choice the hero makes.

There is also the usual roster of arctic clichés including avalanches and wolf attacks. Indeed, Granger was bitten by a wolf on one occasion when a stunt went wrong. Once more he was insisting on doing as many of his own stunts as possible and, not for the last time, he found himself injured as a result. It has to be asked whether he had anyone else to blame for this because he was volunteering to put himself in some danger. He was no Leslie Howard or David Niven.

The Wild North is another routine action movie, indistinguishable from others of its type. Basically, it is a clichéd western, but a western set in Alaska, although much of it was actually shot in Sun Valley, Idaho. Granger handicaps himself by adopting a terribly phoney French accent, a ploy which he later admitted was a bad error of judgement on his part ('that bloody frog accent', as he characteristically called it later). The movie is the type of adventure story that MGM clearly believed offered the cinema audience something that television could not: it was shot partly on location and the actors clearly were struggling with real ice and snow, not some studio-bound imitation. Television was still studio-bound; the days of the television movie were still distant. Thus, the film studios had to offer something the box in the sitting room could not, and 'exotic' locations like Alaska were part of that strategy. The difficulty was that they did not pay enough attention to the quality of the scripts they commissioned so that the locations could not make up for the poverty of the storylines and characters. *The Wild North*, like Granger's two previous movies before *Scaramouche*, never rises above cliché and the conventional elements of a Hollywood adventure tale. It was another 'so-so' movie under Granger's belt and he had to live with the reality that his cod French accent did him no favours at all on screen. However, *Variety* considered that Granger 'sharpens the masculine flavour of the screen story'. Bosley Crowther praised the 'remarkable colour photography' as well as noting the phoney studio snow. 'At times Mr Granger is solid as the simple backwoodsman,' Crowther wrote, 'at others he is foolishly comic and absurd.' Playing the fool was still something Granger could not master on screen.

If Granger needed reminding that in Hollywood you were only as good as your last picture, he need only have read the press. The well-known show business writer Donald Zec wrote an article in 1952 in which he commented that the British 'must do better than Jean Simmons and Stewart Granger, who have so far failed to capture, or captivate, Hollywood'. Despite his success in *Scaramouche*, Granger was being warned not to get too complacent about continual Hollywood success.

However, the temporary setback to his career that was *The Wild North* was quickly followed by another success in a swashbuckler remake. This time it was a new MGM version of *The Prisoner of Zenda* based on Anthony Hope's famous novel and very much a retread of a 1937 MGM version which had starred Ronald Colman. There had also been two silent versions of this movie, so it was not much of a gamble for the studio to bow to their star's wishes and finance a new production of this familiar tale of an Englishman on holiday in Ruritania who looks exactly like the country's drunken king, against whom there is a dastardly plot to replace him with a much less appealing character. Colman had had quite a success with this dual role and Granger clearly felt he could consolidate his MGM standing by replicating that success. He had to persuade MGM to pay David Selznick half a million dollars for the film rights of the book, but on the back of the huge success of *Scaramouche*, which the star had also suggested to the studio, they were willing to pay what was a huge amount of money in those days.

Granger seemed to make it a habit to suggest projects to his employers, which they may, or may not, have welcomed. He had clearly studied the MGM inventory and knew which movies had been successes in the past for the studio and for the stars who had had top billing. Granger must also have known that in the MGM 'family', as that old phoney Louis B. Mayer was wont to call the studio, competition among the leading stars was rampant. In a shrinking movie market, there were only so many important roles in top-budget movies to go round and he had to be in there pitching to land some of them. That meant he had to 'audition' for parts, or, at least, meet the director, read lines and try on costumes.

For example, another top MGM production of this period was *Quo Vadis*, the Roman epic, which proved a tremendous success for the studio. For a while, it appeared that he was favourite to play the Roman centurion who falls in love with a Christian slave girl, renounces Rome and becomes a follower of this new faith. But it was not to be, despite the fact that Hollywood epics were festooned with British actors who, it was believed, could speak like Romans or Greeks without too many jarring tones. Richard Burton would land the lead in the first Cinemascope movie *The Robe*, the little-known Edmund Purdom would star in *The Egyptian* and even Laurence Olivier would co-star in *Spartacus*. But Granger missed out to Robert Taylor in *Quo Vadis*, which must have been another disappointment and increased his irritation with the studio bosses.

It had been decided by MGM that their remake of *The Prisoner of Zenda* would be a virtual shot-by-shot copy of the 1937 version. The director was to be Richard Thorpe, who was known in the business as 'One-Take Thorpe' because he was usually satisfied with one take of a scene and did not bother with repeated takes to perfect shots or performances. This propensity no doubt endeared him to his MGM bosses, conscious as they always were about the dangers of indulgent directors over-running shooting schedules and going over budget. Thorpe seemed also to have gained a rare seal of approval from Granger, because he was not an actor who usually had warm words to say for directors. It was not that Granger considered Thorpe a particularly sensitive director or that he had much artistic input, but the man gave the actors their heads and just got on with the professional job of putting scenes onto celluloid.

As MGM had decided on a virtual copy of the Ronald Colman version, the director had little to do other than to point the cameras at the action, keep them rolling and make sure the finished version was as close to the earlier version as possible. It seems an extraordinary way to make a movie, but this was not art, after all, it was a Hollywood movie. Granger seemed to give himself over to this copycat syndrome and whether to please his bosses at MGM, or because he felt some kind of inferiority to Ronald Colman, he set out, by his own admission, to reproduce Colman's earlier performance as closely as possible. It seems a very limited objective for any actor to copy the gestures and tones of an actor from a previous generation. Granger makes a revealing comment in *Sparks Fly Upward*: 'I could never compete with Ronnie Colman as an actor, but at least I could fight better.'

Is this merely a self-deprecating false modesty on Granger's part or did he really feel he was inferior to Colman in the acting stakes? If he really believed that, he is perhaps voicing the self-doubts of someone who had indeed stumbled into acting and never really believed he was any good at it. If he had been comparing himself to Laurence Olivier or even Richard Burton, then it would have been understandable, but Ronald Colman? Colman had been a big star in the 1920s, 1930s and early 1940s. He was, par excellence, Hollywood's idea of what an English actor should be: well-spoken, with matinée idol looks, a certain gravitas and a gentlemanly air. In fact, he was usually wooden, inhibited, self-regarding and pompous on screen. Granger may not have been a great actor himself, but to say he could never compete with someone like Colman is just nonsense. The other interesting aspect of this comment is that Granger, while giving Colman the upper hand in the acting stakes, claims what is important to him: his superiority at 'fighting', by which he meant the duelling and action sequences. The implication is that he was more masculine, a better action hero than Colman.

Remakes always suffer at the hands of critics who have fond memories of an earlier version, even though the later movie may be better. An outstanding example is *The Postman Always Rings Twice*. Most critics favour the 1946 Lana Turner and John Garfield version, despite the total miscasting of Turner in the femme fatale role and her very limited acting talents. However, any objective analysis would surely judge that Bob Rafelson's 1986 version starring Jack Nicholson and Jessica Lange is superior in almost every way, except for Garfield. However, Nicholson the drifter who gets caught up in a murderous plot is arguably equally as convincing in the role.

Some of this snobbish attitude rubbed off onto the 1952 *Prisoner of*

Zenda. You could argue about their relative merits, but only a blinkered critic could sustain an argument that the Colman version is vastly superior to the Granger movie. This new version is in Technicolor, and the lavish costumes and settings benefit from that. Additionally, apart from Granger himself, the 1952 version boats a fine villainous performance from James Mason. Granger had played second fiddle so often in the British film industry to James Mason that it must have given him some satisfaction to be the star of this movie and well above Mason in the credits. The cast also included Jane Greer in a supporting role; perhaps Granger had opportunities to discuss Howard Hughes with her. The actress had been under contract to Hughes, and had suffered when his unwelcome attentions had been rejected.

As for Granger himself, he really need not have worried about his performance in the dual role of Rudolf Rassendyll, the English pretender, and Rudolf, the real king. Most people who saw the movie at the time of its release would not have made the connection between the performances of Granger and Colman. Of the two many would have preferred Granger, because Colman was an insufferably smug actor, depending on his appeal on that corny, over-ripe voice of his and his cosy matinée idol looks. He had a heavy quality on screen so that when he was meant to be light-hearted and breezy, it always came over as forced and unnatural, whereas that was what Granger did best, however troubled he was in real life. *Picturegoer* in a feature article on the movie on 7 February 1953, agreed: 'Granger is more comfortably "right" than Colman: his romance is more energetic, less idealistic. And he has lost some of the arrogance of his *Scaramouche* portrayal.' At any rate, *The Prisoner of Zenda* was another hit for MGM and Granger. *Variety* praised Granger for giving the roles 'the proper amount of dashing heroics'. The *Monthly Film Bulletin* complained the 'film lacked inner conviction'. Nevertheless, the star had now repaid MGM's faith in him by starring in three resounding successes: *King Solomon's Mines*, *Scaramouche* and *The Prisoner of Zenda*.

Granger did not escape injury from this latest swashbuckling adventure.

Jean Heremans was again the fencing expert employed by MGM to stand in for James Mason, in particular in the duel scene. During the shooting of the scene, Heremans managed to cut Granger's mouth with his sword. Granger's gums were sliced open and blood flowed freely. Obviously, it caused no lasting injury, but it was another example of the injuries that beset this accident-prone star who was so intent on taking risks. MGM must have wondered whether one day they would be faced with a gigantic lawsuit from their unruly star for injuries incurred in the line of duty.

No one could deny, not even Granger's enemies – and he had made a few – that he had well and truly arrived in Hollywood and had made a successful transition from the domestic British film industry to become an 'A'-list international star. As testimony to this, Granger received a comparatively rare accolade for a Hollywood star by appearing on the cover of *Life* magazine. Garbo, Gable, Vivien Leigh, Tyrone Power and, later, Marilyn Monroe were among the stars who had been deemed important enough to feature on *Life* covers. Now Granger had been added to that list: 'Stewart Granger, Swashbuckler', the front cover proclaimed. It was a yardstick of how far Granger's career had progressed in a period of two to three years.

Meanwhile, back on the home front, Jean Simmons was having more and more trouble with Howard Hughes, who had now propositioned her directly and had been refused. He was not used to being turned down in any sphere and he took it badly. Apart from this aspect of their relationship, Simmons was unhappy with the movies that Hughes designated for her at RKO. Her first movie for the studio was *Angel Face*, which co-starred Robert Mitchum. In it she plays a neurotic, destructive and spoilt rich girl, who finally kills herself and her lover, Mitchum, when he tells her he is leaving. Then there was *She Couldn't Say No* (in Britain *Beautiful But Dangerous*), a light-hearted comedy, again with Mitchum. Victor Mature was her co-star in *Affair With a Stranger*, another light comedy. *Angel Face* is not that bad a movie, although the other two were lightweight fodder. Simmons had worked with Lean, Powell and Olivier. It must have seemed to her that her career had taken a backward step, but her protests fell on the deaf ears of Hughes. The stalling in her career made a stark contrast with her husband's standing in Hollywood. He was appearing in big budget movies and was a major star. She was appearing in cheap RKO-Radio quickies with little prospect of anything changing. Power relations are a factor in all marriages and the Granger–Simmons would have been no exception. At this juncture, Simmons was in a distinctly disempowering bind, whilst Granger was on an upsurge.

Granger backed his wife in standing up to Hughes. The two were undoubtedly rival males competing for 'ownership' of this young beauty, but Granger was also a loving husband who wanted the best for his young wife. Simmons made it clear that she no longer wanted to be under contract to Hughes and that she wanted her freedom. Hughes was not a man who was accustomed to, or took kindly to, being challenged in this way, especially by young women whom he lusted after. When Simmons (with Granger at her side) finally told Hughes she would never sign a long-term contract with him, Hughes warned the other Hollywood studios not to employ her because he had a 'moral contract' with her. The idea of Howard Hughes, the arch-corruptor of politicians and women, having a 'moral' contract with anyone is laughable. However, a warning of future litigation from Hughes, one of the richest and most influential people in America, with ugly tentacles reaching into the lower depths of American politics, the underworld, the gambling industry and, of course, Hollywood itself, was bound to be taken seriously. The other studios would not want to lock legal horns with Hughes and his battery of highly paid lawyers. Jean Simmons might be a tempting property for the major studios, but not enough to make it worth entering into expensive and prolonged legal tangles with Howard Hughes, who was, after all, one of their own, while Granger and Simmons, in their eyes, were just two actors. There were plenty more where they came from, but there was only one Howard Hughes and he could do them all some lasting damage.

Nevertheless, Granger and Simmons decided to take Hughes to court, claiming that he was placing an unlawful restraint on Simmons's freedom to work in Hollywood. They were backed in this decision by Granger's new agent, Bill Allenberg of the William Morris Agency, even though the agency itself, the biggest handler of star names in Hollywood, warned against it. Allenberg would remain a lifelong friend of Granger's, one of the few men in the industry for whom he had lasting respect and affection. Joe Schenck of Loew's Inc, the New York-based conglomerate that actually owned MGM, also advised strongly against taking on Hughes, and Benny Thau, one of MGM's top executives, also warned them against it: 'You can't beat this man. Howard Hughes takes on governments, for God's sake. He's beaten Washington. He's tough and he's powerful.'

Granger had never backed off from bullies and now he saw his wife being intimidated by, in effect, the biggest bully in the playground. Perhaps the fact that they were British and new to the American and Hollywood scene emboldened them in this legal adventure. An additional factor might have been Granger's own experiences with Rank executives in Britain. This time he was not going to back down. He had hoisted their colours and declared war on one of the most powerful men in the world. He had faith in the American legal system and so, despite most of the advice they were receiving, the Grangers proceeded to legal action.

Granger in a Gainsborough heart-throb publicity photo, which was no doubt sent out by the thousand to adoring fans. Notice the Latin look. *Moviedrome*

Granger on stage at the Birmingham Rep in the play *The Devil's Disciple* by Bernard Shaw, whom he met while playing later in Shaw's *The Apple Cart*. Notice the mugging style of his acting. *Getty Images*

Granger plays second fiddle to Rosamund John in *The Lamp Still Burns*, a wartime morale booster. *The Man in Grey* had made him a star by then, but he still had to fulfill his commitment to this modest production. *Moviedrome*

Granger with his first wife, Elspeth March, and their two children, Lindsay (left) and James (right). *Popperfoto*

Granger down on his manor feeding his horses: he was an able rider, which would stand him in good stead in Hollywood. *Getty Images*

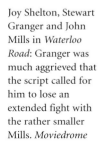

Joy Shelton, Stewart Granger and John Mills in *Waterloo Road*: Granger was much aggrieved that the script called for him to lose an extended fight with the rather smaller Mills. *Moviedrome*

A cinema lobby card of *Saraband for Dead Lovers*, one of the few films Granger was proud of. *Moviedrome*

Granger with Flora Robson in *Saraband for Dead Lovers*: a film that looked exquisite and had Granger dressed once more in lavish period dress. *Moviedrome*

Granger sparring with Freddie Mills, at one time light-heavyweight champion of the world, who would die in mysterious circumstances not many years after this late 1940s photo was taken. *Popperfoto*

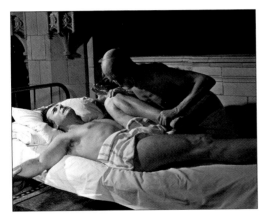

Granger suffers for his art: a trainer makes sure the heart-throb stays supple. *Popperfoto*

Granger can't help mugging for the camera even when he is in a steam bath. *Popperfoto*

Granger proves himself useful to his ex-lover Deborah Kerr whilst relaxing between takes during the shooting of *King Solomon's Mines*. *Getty Images*

From left to right: Richard Carlson, Hugo Haas, Granger and Deborah Kerr in a scene from Granger's first Hollywood film, *King Solomon's Mines*. Note the leopard-skin band round Granger's hat: it became fashionable for African hunters. *Moviedrome*

A poster for MGM's *King Solomon's Mines.* It was an arduous shoot and Granger complained about the studio's cavalier ways with its stars, which did not endear him to his new employers. *Moviedrome*

Granger discusses matters with director Richard Brooks while on location for *The Last Hunt*. Granger detested Brooks and later even more so when Brooks married Jean Simmons after their divorce. *Getty Images*

Granger swings in mid-air while duelling with Mel Ferrer in *Scaramouche*. He would fall while making the scene and damage his shoulder. *Moviedrome*

Two Grangers for the price of one in The *Prisoner of Zenda*. The studio set out to replicate exactly the earlier Ronald Colman version. Granger opined that he could not act as well as Colman but was a more convincing fighter. *Moviedrome*

A movie poster for what many people believe to be Granger's greatest triumph. It was Granger who suggested to MGM that they remake *Scaramouche*. *Moviedrome*

Granger and Jean Simmons relax for the cameras in their Bel Air home. Kenneth Tynan, the famous theatre critic and wit, commented on the bizarre trappings of their home: leopard-skin rugs, lions' heads and animal trophies of various kinds. *Getty Images*

Granger, Jean Simmons and Frank Sinatra: when Simmons was making *Guys and Dolls* with Sinatra, Brando and director Mankiewicz, Granger worried about her being surrounded by those notorious womanisers. *Empics*

Granger and Simmons on their New Mexico ranch. Granger fell in love with the American West and fancied himself as a cowboy and a rancher.

Granger woos Grace Kelly in *Green Fire*. This film was not a great success either critically or commercially. Granger's days as a top Hollywood star were numbered. *Moviedrome*

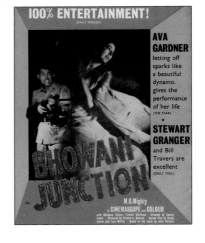

Granger starred with Ava Gardner in *Bhowani Junction*. According to Granger, Gardner made repeated attempts to seduce him, which he resisted in order to remain faithful to Jean Simmons. *Moviedrome*

Granger, John Wayne and Tommy Sands in *North to Alaska*. Playing Wayne's sidekick, Granger lost the girl and a fight with Wayne as well. *Kobal Collection*

Granger (Lot), in his fifties by now, carries Pier Angeli (Lot's wife) in the biblical epic shot in Italy, *Sodom and Gomorrah*. By this stage in his career, most of his films were made in Europe and many of them did not obtain a British or American release. *Moviedrome*

The Last Safari was a rather tired attempt to rekindle past glories by giving Granger a role once more as an African hunter, but the success of *King Solomon's Mines* eluded this minor production. *Moviedrome*

Granger arrives at Heathrow with his third wife Caroline Lecerf, a former Belgian beauty queen. 'I suppose she keeps me young,' said Granger, but the marriage ended in divorce in 1969. *Rex Features*

Unlikely casting! Granger played Sherlock Holmes in a 1972 made-for-television movie. Holmes fans reeled with shock.

Granger returned to the big screen in the 1978 mercenary adventure *The Wild Geese*. Granger plays a Tiny Rowland-type tycoon and is shot dead near the end of the movie by pal Richard Burton, who had recommended Granger for the part. *Kobal Collection*

Granger on television in 1981, plugging his autobiography *Sparks Fly Upward*. *Rex Features*

Granger with his daughter Samantha, the child of his marriage with Caroline Lecerf. *Corbis*

An elderly and frail Granger in his Malibu home shortly before his death. He had kept many of his African hunting trophies to the last. *Rex Features*

Chapter 6

TAKING ON THE BULLIES

GRANGER HAD CLAIMED to have been persecuted at his prep and public schools, an experience which often leaves lasting scars. He had learnt to 'look after himself' at Epsom College where he had honed his boxing skills as well as other sporting expertise. R. Bryce Taylor, another contemporary of Granger's at Epsom College, remembers him as being very good at fencing, and also remarks that he was a very popular fellow. Granger's own account of his schooldays, however, hints at the opposite. As a good-looking young man with a talent for speaking poetry and projecting himself, he would undoubtedly have been the target for the envious, and in some ways it is clear he always thought of himself as under attack throughout his life.

It is a harsh fact that many people are indeed very envious of the intelligent, the good-looking or even the successful. It explains the love–hate syndrome shown towards over-publicised celebrities in our contemporary culture; there is inevitably a great deal of Schadenfreude when any so-called celebrity is somehow caught out or when their success brings unhappiness or disaster. Granger often referred to the envious people in the movie world and although some of his attitudes might be attributed to an inherent paranoia, there can be no doubt that Hollywood fame is a double-edged sword: it comes with the territory.

Thus, when the news broke that Granger and Jean Simmons were about to take on the mighty Howard Hughes in the courts, those who wished Granger some ill would have been rubbing their hands with glee. At last, it looked as though this arrogant limey had overstepped the mark and would get his come-uppance. And it wasn't as though he hadn't had good advice from people in the Hollywood know: they had told Granger not to be so foolish and he hadn't listened. However, Granger was very angry with Hughes: not only had the man lusted after his wife, but he had also moved to block Simmons's career in Hollywood so that in essence she could not work there. For a man of real spirit like Granger, both these injuries required satisfaction, and as duels *à la* Scaramouche were no longer allowed by law, then a legal duel it had to be. But a duel it certainly was, a struggle between two alpha males, and the prize was the possession, in more than one sense, of the young beauty, Jean Simmons.

It is likely that Granger was the prime mover in all of this, although naturally Jean Simmons must have been very angry about the restrictions placed on her by her would-be lover, Hughes. However, in a newspaper interview much later in his life, Granger expressed some criticism of his ex-wife: 'Jean was a flirt. When women are beautiful and powerful, they're real ball-breakers.' Clearly, he felt threatened by women of influence and power, and this may be a pointer to why his marriage to Simmons eventually ended. When they first met and became lovers, the power equation in their relationship swung dramatically towards Granger: he was much older, had become an established and famous film star while she was barely out of her teens and only starting on her chosen profession. As time passed and she matured as a woman and as an actress, achieving major star status, Simmons would have been less dependent on her husband's advice and support; the power equation would have lurched her way. Judging by Granger's public pronouncements about gender politics, this would not have been a very comfortable situation for him. If Granger was the prime mover in the decision to take Hughes to court over his wife's career prospects, he was attempting not only to see off a rival male but also to control his wife's professional life.

In a feature article published in the *Daily Mail* shortly after Granger died in 1993, Robin McGibbon wrote of a time in 1978 when he listened to Granger expressing his feelings about the whole Hughes contretemps. 'Granger found the powerful presence of Hughes difficult to live with,' wrote McGibbon. It is clear that Hughes symbolised something very important for Granger and that he had a damaging effect on his psychological state and his marriage. According to McGibbon's account, Granger felt that the joy had gone out of his life and his marriage, and is quoted as saying 'within two years the initial excitement and hopes had faded'. If this is an accurate judgement, then it did not augur well for the remaining eight years that they were together. Granger had grown irritable and was drinking too much, added to his forty-cigarettes-a-day addiction, which did not presage well for his health in later years. Granger felt 'damaging blows were being dealt to his marriage' and that Hughes had 'ripped into the fabric of his life'.

It would be foolish to underestimate the damage that a bullying billionaire ogre like Hughes, with all his power ploys and influential connections, could do to anyone who stood up against his will, but it is a fair question to ask why it affected Granger quite so much. Was it some kind of displacement anxiety? Did the Hughes problem become the focus of his life at this time as a diversion from his real emotional and professional problems: his early traumatic experience in his first family, his doubts about his career and his abilities, his excessive need to express his masculinity on all occasions and even his feelings about his marriage to Jean Simmons? In McGibbon's article, Granger describes Hughes as a 'giant of a man, a genius whose problem was the scale of his obsessions'. He was in awe of this man who 'seemed to own everything'. Granger also wanted to own things, to wheel-and-deal and be a highly successful businessman, but his past business ventures had failed and others would fail in the future. Perhaps Granger was also envious. By taking on Hughes in the courts, he was surely backing his judgement against this 'genius' and it was one businessman against another, with a beautiful young woman as the prize.

In order to boost Simmons's career and perhaps – in part at least – to control it, Granger had agreed to play Sir Thomas Seymour in *Young Bess*, with Simmons playing the young Queen Elizabeth I. It was to be made at Elstree Studios in England. Granger has a major role in the movie, but the picture is mainly a vehicle for Simmons, with Charles Laughton playing her father Henry VIII, whom he had also played in the Alexander Korda 1933 production *The Private Life of Henry VIII*. Laughton would seriously annoy Granger during the making of his next movie, but he does not seem to have had any problems with him during the shooting of *Young Bess*.

Granger had the director of *Scaramouche*, George Sidney, guiding his wife and himself though the clichés of this routine Hollywood historical drama, but, in truth, it is anonymously directed. Simmons as the young Elizabeth is in love with Seymour, the Lord High Admiral, but he marries Catherine Parr, Henry's widow (Deborah Kerr). Seymour has a love affair with Bess, even though he still loves his wife. After his wife conveniently dies, Seymour/Granger is accused of treason by plotting to marry the royal princess as a ploy to steal the affections of the people from the young king Edward VI and thereby to ascend the throne himself. Bess/Simmons tries to save him when Seymour's brother Ned persuades the High Council to issue an order for his execution. Granger as Seymour goes nobly to his death, pronouncing his enduring love for the princess. The story is told in flashback and at the end of the movie Young Bess has grown up to be the steely Elizabeth I.

The treatment is nothing if not hackneyed and there are no surprises in this pageant, only tired predictability. There is an inbuilt reverence for the idea of the British monarchy, despite the depiction of the sordid power struggles that encircled the royal throne. However, Charles Rosher again was the cinematographer so the movie never looks less than sumptuous, and the musical score was by Miklos Rosza, one of the top Hollywood composers, so this was not a cheaply produced quickie. In playing Elizabeth, Simmons was following in the footsteps of Bette Davis and Flora Robson, among others. It was a prestigious role, although not one that challenged her acting talents, and the movie itself was tepidly received by critics and public alike. There are some excruciating scenes between the boy playing Edward VI and Bess/Simmons, as well as genuinely comic lines such as when Granger has to say, 'I wish that Italian fellow – what was his name? – Michelangelo, was still alive. Now he really knew how to paint women.' Bosley Crowther in the *New York Times*, however, noted that Granger was 'tall, handsome and strikingly noble in the uniforms of the day'.

It can be argued that Granger made something of a sacrifice in accepting the lesser role in this movie. His wife's name appeared before his name in the credits and she had the title role. Laughton was able to make a scenery-chewing meal of his reprise of his Henry VIII act, whilst Granger had little to do as Seymour other than look suitably handsome and be his usual slightly arrogant self. However, it was not that much of a sacrifice, because *Young Bess* was a top-budget MGM movie, and it enabled him to work with his wife and influence the development of her Hollywood career. Granger is, in fact, quite effective in the role of Seymour, especially as the uncle to the young king and when he plays 'sincere'. There is no real pain or deep emotion in the movie, however – all is surface and outward show – so that there is a deadness to the whole proceedings that the actors cannot break through. It is not accidental that MGM released this movie in 1953, the year that Elizabeth II was crowned the new young Queen of England. The studio clearly wanted to cash in on the wave of royal enthusiasm and interest in the new young queen by making yet another movie about her distant predecessor. There was much journalistic twaddle written about the ushering in of a 'new Elizabethan age' and the movie suffers from a surfeit of this kind of sycophantic over-reverence towards the tradition of British monarchy.

Interestingly, the movie inaugurated the giant panoramic screen at the Empire in London's Leicester Square.

The story of the movie, however, does reflect in an odd way some of the issues between Granger and Simmons in real life. When the movie opens, Young Bess is very young, in her early teens, but she already has a crush on Thomas Seymour, who is much older than her. Their first scene together has Granger/Seymour coming to Hatfield House in order to persuade the very reluctant Bess to join the royal court. He manipulates her with his charm and flirtation. However, he also treats her like a child and seems blind to her real feelings for him. When his brother, Ned Seymour, accuses him of encouraging the young Bess, he scornfully dismisses this by saying, 'If I want to start a love affair, I won't be looking in the nursery.' As she matures into her late teens, however, he realises he has fallen in love with her. He is jealous, especially as she indulges in some manipulation of his emotions herself. Once they declare their love for one another, he becomes her protector and guide through life. There are definite parallels between the story they enacted on screen and their own lives. Granger had met Simmons when she was a very young girl and had started a relationship with her when she was eighteen. Like the character she plays in the movie, Simmons was maturing into a powerful woman in her own right and there were definite issues about possessiveness and power within their marriage.

Granger had never been adept at nurturing friendly relations with the media, especially with the hacks who peddled cheap tittle-tattle about the home life of the stars. He had therefore been acquiring a reputation among the Hollywood press corps of being 'uncooperative' and this reputation was enshrined when they dubbed him 'the most unpopular British actor in Hollywood: arrogant, overbearing, superior'. The question is whether this accolade rebounds to Granger's credit or discredit. As we have seen from his run-in with Hedda Hopper, he was willing to take on the hacks and give them the benefit of his salty language skills. By his own admission, Granger was a lifelong 'swearer' and he did not inhibit himself in his choice of language when he spoke to the show business journalists he so despised.

This can be interpreted as the expression of an independent spirit who would not cut his cloth according to the dictates of a Hollywood press corps with the professional and ethical standards of the average tabloid journalist. Or, as the hacks saw it, the behaviour of a conceited and disdainful limey movie star who used his star status to act rudely to those whose job it was to report on the Hollywood scene.

It is easy to sympathise with Granger if he was anxious to avoid the grosser intrusions in his and his wife's private lives, and we can share his contempt for the level of most of the show business journalism that found its way into the pages of newspapers and film fan magazines. However, our hero did appear to have an undisputed talent for treading on toes and raising hackles. He almost certainly projected a kind of breezy arrogance (some of that manner comes over in many of his film roles) and the fact that he was a Brit in Hollywood probably did not help matters with the hacks, many of whom would certainly have had attitudes about the 'superior' British. James Mason, a fellow Brit, had been the target of attacks and smears when he first came to Hollywood, especially about the 'lax' manner in which he and his wife at that time, Pamela Kellino, were bringing up their daughter, Portland. Nevertheless, it was not only the hacks of the show business publications who found Granger arrogant. He had also made himself unpopular with fellow workers in the industry and with studio executives. Some co-workers dubbed him 'Stupid Granger' because of his apparent insensitivity and irascible ways.

As an example of the kind of show business 'journalism' that so infuriated Granger, we can look at a 1957 feature in the British movie magazine *Picturegoer*. The article by Donovan Pedelty is headlined 'The Marriage They Said Wouldn't Last'. According to Pedelty, Hollywood had started calling Simmons and Granger 'Beauty and the Beast'. Granger 'gave an impression of lusty grossness that seemed ill-assorted with her appearance of gracious delicacy'. In addition his 'off-set speech' was liberally 'peppered with the present tense of an active verb much heard in the Army, Navy and the Air Force'. The article goes on to state that Granger had chosen their Bel Air home and all the decor and furnishings; he even did all the cooking. Jean Simmons is portrayed as an unworldly idiot whose 'eyes glaze over when he tries to explain matters to me'. Granger, according to Pedelty, was 'a man who has to prove things – his own competence and virility among them'. It perhaps does have some significance that even then, when notions of what constituted conventional models of masculinity were much more restricted than they are nowadays, Granger was seen as somewhat over-emphatic in the expression of his maleness. However, such show business yarns have to take an angle towards their subjects and that was Pedelty's in this feature, so it needs to be interpreted in that light. Overall, the article gives an image of an overbearing, possessive and jealous man who controlled his wife's life and career in almost all its aspects. Although it appears that the Grangers gave Pedelty access to their Hollywood home and granted him an interview, the article cannot have pleased them.

Another illustration of how Granger was viewed by the press comes from a *Picturegoer* feature titled 'Stewart Granger's Charm School' from January 1953, when the actor was in England to promote *All the Brothers Were Valiant*. The feature writer, David Marlowe, describes Granger as the former 'pressman's grouch' and confesses he had been of 'the not-so-few who loathed the Granger legend'. Now, it appears, Granger was a changed man: he talked freely about his money troubles, about the troubles he was having at the studio because of his prematurely greying hair and his frustration that he could not return to Britain yet to make films because the tax man would pounce on him. Granger was asked whether it was true he was bad-tempered and that he resented all criticism. Granger admitted he was 'nervous, worried and ill-at-ease on the set' because so much was riding on every film. Marlowe concluded, 'There's been a certain amount of maligning of Granger in the past. He may have deserved some of it. He may not have deserved all of it. Anyway, let's give the man a break.' Thus, it appears that on this occasion at least, Granger had tried a charm offensive and had been successful with at least one of the journalists present. It is likely that the presence of MGM minders had something to do with his 'reformed' behaviour.

The press also liked to portray Granger as being extremely possessive and obsessed with his beautiful, young film star wife. In an *Evening Standard* article of November 1953, the reporter noted: 'On the mantelpiece of Granger's flat was an outsize photograph of Jean Simmons. Her name came into our conversation thirty-seven times in a half-hour.' When the reporter tentatively mentions a Hollywood rumour that there was a rift between Simmons and himself, Granger 'replied with a rumbling laugh and an expressive Chaucerian word'. Granger is then asked whether he talked to his present Hollywood bosses in the same way he used to address the J. Arthur Rank executives: 'I am told I am tactless. Maybe that means I refuse to say yes, Mr So-and-so and no, Mr So-and-so.' Granger pleads guilty to the charge of arrogance, however: 'I am an arrogant fellow. I have always been arrogant. But I deny that I have ever been deliberately offensive without cause.'

Hollywood columnist Roderick Mann gives us some idea of what it was like for Granger to be in Hollywood and how Hollywood perceived him. Referring to both Granger and James Mason, he noted that 'they were both rather alike, English loners in Hollywood desperate to do better work, but somehow unable to fit in totally with the local community or to form their own. They didn't seem even to get terribly close to each other and whenever you saw them on screen or at parties, they always vaguely looked like they wished they had gone somewhere else.' Mann is almost certainly right in stating that Granger never became part of the Hollywood scene, but then 'fitting in' in any environment seemed to be difficult for him. It is interesting that Mann describes him (and Mason) as a loner, because it is clear Granger saw himself like that and he must have somehow emanated that quality to observers of the Hollywood industry.

An illustration of Granger's propensity to upset people in the film industry revolves round George Cukor, the famous director of *The Philadelphia Story* and *A Star Is Born*. Granger was being considered for the lead role in the latter movie, a part that James Mason eventually played with resounding success. Cukor was one of Hollywood's 'closet queens', a homosexual at a time when a whiff of scandal in that area could ruin someone's career. Now it would have been a well-known fact among the Hollywood community that Cukor was gay, but he was such a successful director that his employers chose to overlook his predilections and protect him from the intrusions of the press. One rumour had it that Cukor had lost the job of directing Hollywood's biggest-ever movie, *Gone With the Wind*, because he, Cukor, had known Clark Gable when MGM's top star had been making his way in the industry and had used his good looks to ingratiate himself with some of Hollywood's top homosexuals. The story was that Gable could not stand the fact that Cukor knew about his shady past and refused to sanction Cukor as director, and as Gable had already been announced as the screen's Rhett Butler, Selznick, the producer, had had no option but look elsewhere for his director.

Whatever the truth of those rumours, Cukor was hardly likely to be the type of man to whom Granger would warm. He undoubtedly nurtured strong homophobic attitudes and this must have come across when he met Cukor for preliminary readings and discussions about Granger taking on the role of the alcoholic movie star in *A Star Is Born*, who finally sacrifices himself for the sake of his wife's career. Granger's account of the encounter ascribes to Cukor a strong tendency to tell him how to read lines and act in general, which he did not appreciate. He refused, in essence, to accept Cukor's direction and Cukor dropped him from the project. It is likely that Granger resented taking direction from this Hollywood 'cissie' and alienated Cukor so much that he no longer considered him suitable for the project. What Granger would have made of the role is hard to contemplate, but it is a fact that Mason won rave reviews in the part and an Academy Award nomination. It is doubtful if Granger could have equalled Mason's performance, but it would have been a new challenge for him, just as playing Stanley Kowalski in *A Streetcar Named Desire* on the London stage or the James Mason part in *Odd Man Out* would have been. These opportunities were passed up, one because Granger probably believed it was beyond him and the other because he fell out with the director. Such prime opportunities do not come often to an actor and Granger spurned them to his cost.

Granger's homophobia almost certainly had something to do with the problems he encountered when he co-starred with Charles Laughton in his next movie, the quite dreadful *Salome*. From time to time, the top Hollywood studios would loan one another their top stars if a particular studio had a specific casting need that only another studio's contracted star would satisfy. MGM in this case loaned Granger out to Harry Cohn's studio, Columbia, to play Claudius, a Roman soldier and a secret Christian, who somehow becomes embroiled with Salome, Herod's stepdaughter. She, to spite him, dances the dance of the seven veils for the head of John the Baptist.

Salome is one of Hollywood's disagreeable mixes of religiosity and sex, and, despite the talents of director William Dieterle and a cast that included Judith Anderson, Rita Hayworth, Cedric Hardwicke and Alan Badel, it sank like a stone. The whole farrago leads up to Hayworth's dance striptease, which, even for those days, turned out to be very tame stuff. The 1950s was Hollywood's peak decade for spurious religious epics such as *The Robe, The Egyptian, The Silver Chalice, The Prodigal, Demetrius and the Gladiators* and *Ben Hur. Salome* ranks among the worst of them. Granger suffers like the rest of the cast with the impossible dialogue and insufferable piety, which is all the more indigestible because the whole marketing of the movie was based on the prospect of Rita Hayworth taking her clothes off at the end.

In his account of the making of *Salome*, Granger claims he became so incensed with Laughton's attempts to undermine him on set, that he took the elderly and obese actor aside one day and threatened to 'kick him in the balls' if he did not desist from these games. It is very likely that Laughton emanated a kind of disdain for this handsome star who had very seldom attempted any really serious acting in his career and whom Laughton would have considered a mere movie star rather than an actor. In a letter written to Elsa Lanchester, Laughton's wife, by William Dieterle, the director of *Salome*, Dieterle mentions that 'when it came to dialogue, the gap between Laughton and the rest of the actors was unbridgeable'. Laughton, according to Dieterle, was anxious to make something out of his role and the film, so he rehearsed with his fellow actors in the hopes of improving his scenes. However, Dieterle also quotes Laughton as saying, 'A fencing master cannot fence with amateurs.' That kind of lordly attitude would have been exactly the kind of behaviour to stoke Granger's anger.

There might even have been some sexual tension at work here (Laughton, for all his lofty airs, may have been attracted to Granger), but Granger's account of his conduct does him little credit. To threaten in this way a man of Laughton's age and obvious physical infirmity was not the action of a hero figure, but it is once more not only a manifestation of Granger's whole-hearted homophobia, but also an unattractive bullying trait that ill-became a man of his physical prowess. It is also likely that Granger did feel a certain sense of inferiority in the acting stakes to Laughton who, despite his propensity to ham it up, had a reputation as a 'serious' actor, a status to which Granger could not lay claim, and could steal scenes. Added to that would have been Granger's knowledge that this movie, for which he had been loaned out, was going to be a substantial turkey and likely to be rained on from a great height by the critics. Granger called the movie 'truly terrible', the German-born Dieterle a 'Nazi' and Laughton 'extremely difficult and unpleasant'.

It was while he was making this 'truly terrible' film that the Grangers' case against Hughes reached the court in Los Angeles. In a *Picturegoer* article, Jean Simmons is quoted as being very proud of her husband putting 'his own career on the block to save mine'. Granger must have known that there was a possibility it would harm his career, whether they won or lost the case. The question is what was the more important motive in this ostensibly brave action: his wish to free his wife from the control of an unscrupulous mogul or his need to defeat one of the most powerful men in the industry, thereby proving his virility to himself, Jean Simmons and the world at large?

Hughes was claiming that an oral contract bound Simmons to RKO after the initial six months of the Rank contract he had bought up expired. Hughes also claimed that Granger had demanded that RKO pay Simmons $500,000, that the studio should buy their Beverly Hills home and an option on a story Granger had been working on for $10,000. Hughes was an old hand at legal wrangles and he employed top lawyers to argue his corner, lawyers who knew every legal trick in a fairly dirty book. For example, before the case came to court, Hughes sent by courier a cheque for $187,000, which the Grangers were meant to sign for. Granger realised that if they signed the receipt, Hughes would use this against them and the case would be settled in his favour. He was wise enough in the ways of the world to refuse to do this so the case came to court.

As Howard Hughes and two movie stars were involved, the case was bound to attract massive publicity. If nothing else was achieved, the name of Jean Simmons would be known by the end of the case by far more people than had hitherto been aware of her. Here was a handsome British swashbuckler and the 'legendary' Hughes publicly quarrelling over control of this beautiful young woman. It was the stuff of melodramatic soap opera.

In *Sparks Fly Upward* Granger makes much of a supposed plan to bump Howard Hughes off, so exasperated had he become with him at the time of his attempted stranglehold on Simmons's career. According to Granger, he suggested to Simmons that she pretend that he (Granger) had gone away for a few days. She should invite Hughes round to their Bel Air home, which was perched on the Hollywood hills. The terrace of their house jutted out over a steep 100ft drop onto the rocks below. Simmons would entice Hughes onto the terrace and position him against the railing. She would scream loudly, Granger would rush in and throw Hughes onto the rocks below. They would then phone the Los Angles police and allege that Hughes had attacked her sexually. Granger and his wife would then claim he had acted in defence of her honour and that it was justifiable homicide. 'I hit him on the jaw and he went over the rail,' Granger was to claim.

Well, it made a good story for his autobiography and an anecdote for the chat shows he appeared on in 1981 when his autobiography was published. It is probably true that Granger was so frustrated that, during one alcohol-fuelled evening, he raised the possibility with Simmons of doing something like that, but it is extremely unlikely that it was anything more than a passing fancy, a plan thought up as the result of too much indulgence in alcohol and forgotten about the next morning. Indeed, in McGibbon's article, he states that the next morning he realised what madness his plan had been. It is revealing, however, that he did entertain such a fantasy. There was a deep well of aggression within Granger that came out in fantasies like this and in his contretemps with many antagonists throughout his life.

The legal battle inevitably turned very nasty indeed. Hughes's lawyers tried to dig up any dirt they could about the Grangers' private and professional lives. They tried to find out whether he had ever been a homo-sexual (this must have especially offended the homophobic Granger), or taken drugs or committed adultery while married to Simmons. Drawing a blank on all three counts, they then claimed that Granger had suggested an illegal tax-evasion strategy in connection with Simmons's RKO contract. Granger countered by requesting all RKO records to investigate possible tax evasion and irregular financial dealings on Hughes's part while he ran RKO. The vans rolled up to the RKO headquarters and court officials loaded the records onto them. Federal tax officials started investigating and Mr Bernard Laven, US Assistant Attorney, was quoted by the press as saying he would make a full report.

The Grangers' case against Hughes alleged that RKO had stopped Simmons from working for other studios and that their contract was broken by Mr Hughes refusing to buy property from Mr Granger. That property was the house that they lived in in Beverly Hills. Hughes's lawyers countered by claiming breach of contract and that the couple had agreed to a three-year contract under which Simmons would have been paid £71,000 a year.

Two conditions applied to the contract: that RKO-Radio Pictures would buy the house from Granger for £35,700 and that they would also buy the film story from him for £8,640. The lawyers then raised the issue of tax evasion, stating that the couple demanded that the house price be recorded as £53,570 and the price paid for the story £26,780. They had also asked that Simmons's salary for the three-year-period of the contract be recorded as £178,500 instead of £214,800. The recorded price of the house and the story were to be reported as capital gains. In simple terms, Hughes's lawyers were accusing the Grangers of serious tax evasion. If there had been any substance in these charges, then it must have been a source of serious worry to both of them.

When Granger went into the witness box, he did not use euphemistic language to describe why he felt such enmity towards Hughes. 'I objected to the studio's boss wanting to screw my wife,' he said. There could not be a clearer expression of the prime motivation for Granger taking on Hughes than this. While the lawyers argued the fine points of Simmons's contract with Hughes and RKO, and the rights and wrongs of Hughes's moral claim over Simmons's services, Granger went to the heart of the matter. Hughes was attempting to tread on his sexual preserve and he was having none of it.

It is not clear whether it was the court granting Granger's request to be able to examine RKO records that forced Hughes's hand but Hughes suddenly decided to settle the case, after all-night negotiations between the opposing lawyers. The Grangers accepted damages of $250,000 plus their legal expenses ($35,000) but nothing more. Simmons was to complete the three films she was contracted to make under the terms of the J. Arthur Rank contract that Hughes had bought and she agreed to make three other movies for RKO, but on loan-out to other studios at $200,000 per picture. She also agreed to make a movie for 20th Century Fox, in return for which RKO would obtain the free services of Victor Mature for one movie.

The important outcome was that Hughes would not have the right to control Simmons's career or prevent her from working for other Hollywood studios. Judge Tolin, the presiding judge in the hearing, expressed the opinion that 'it was unfortunate that fraud had been brought into the case by suggestion' because it hadn't been substantiated by evidence. There was simply no proof of 'unclean hands' on the part of Granger and Simmons or any attempt to illegally evade taxes. Thus the couple had been vindicated in their action and Simmons's career was no longer under Hughes's direct control.

Granger had seen off the big bully and he could now plan the next moves in his wife's career. 'We had made waves and challenged the Establishment,' wrote Granger, 'but it almost ruined our marriage.' In the McGibbon article, he was quoted as saying, 'When we did come through it all, we were changed and there was no changing back. We could try and we did. But we couldn't get back that first, bright thing.' That was an admission that the strain of taking this legal action had affected their marriage irrevocably. Granger in the McGibbon article puts forward the theory that Hughes did not so much love women as hate men: 'Maybe it was the result of his first marriage when he caught his wife in adultery and burned the house down.' Granger confesses that for six months afterwards he kept telling himself that he had won but he also had nightmares and his marriage to Simmons continued to deteriorate. 'Yes, I won,' he is quoted as saying, 'but I don't know. Right up to this day, I don't know.' Granger changed his story about the wrangle with Howard Hughes according to who he was talking to. On other occasions he said that defeating Howard Hughes in the courts was the proudest achievement of his life.

It is clear that Granger was not the type of man who could enter into this kind of legal affray and not worry about it. He was not a carefree adventurer: he suffered from stomach ailments and other minor physical ailments for most of his adult life. His over-indulgence in alcohol and his chronic addiction to cigarettes would cost him dear. These fierce struggles he insisted on having, because of his innate embattled nature, also had their cost in the state of his health, not only physical but mental. That breezy screen manner disguised a troubled man. When Scaramouche took off his mask, what was revealed was not a happy, smiling face, but the features of a man who was too often the victim of his own impetuousness and inner demons. The price of taking on Hughes had been high in terms of the anxiety it caused both himself and his wife and the lasting damage it did to their marriage.

Some of those Granger inner demons found an expression in the way he dealt with the press and working colleagues. In a *Sunday Express* article of January 1953, it is reported that his critics had called him 'one of Britain's worst unofficial ambassadors' and 'the most unpopular Englishman in Hollywood'. Granger is asked whether he had had delusions of grandeur when he bought his first house in Hollywood. He replied that he bought it because he thought it would make Jean Simmons happy, but that he 'did not realise the fantastic cost of servants in America. The house in Beverly Hills had only four bedrooms and two acres but it was costing £100 a week in staff. I suddenly realised we were going bankrupt. Now we have a small, easy-to-run house with only two bedrooms and we're very happy.' This was the house that they had recently bought overlooking the San Fernando Valley. And 'the bad ambassador' charge? 'This all started when I said that Britain was swapping its pride for a packet of American dried eggs. Somebody changed that to "Britons have no pride", which I never said and would never say.' The reporter then brings up the accusation that Granger is offensive to stagehands and other studio staff, but Granger counters that by saying that if he irritates anyone, it's the upper strata. He is then asked whether he has ever offended the press in America and Granger replies, 'Well, when someone asked you for the third time whether it was true that Jean and I were being divorced, I told him to go to blazes and not to be so impertinent.' Asked if he was going to change his manner, Granger says he had no intention of changing anything about himself to please people who dream up scandal over a typewriter.

The questions are surprisingly hostile and it is perhaps little wonder that Granger seems rather tetchy in his replies. The reporter also brings up the 'fact' that after *King Solomon's Mines* Granger had been in three successive flops. The totality of the article suggests that Granger had got way too big for his boots, had overstretched himself financially, had failed to be successful in Hollywood after a promising start, was rude to those less important in the film world than himself and a lousy ambassador for his native country.

It was around this time that Granger suggested to MGM a remake of *Red Dust*, the 1932 movie starring Clark Gable, Jean Harlow and Mary Astor about a rubber plantation overseer in Indo-China torn between his attraction to an English lady and a woman of 'dubious virtue'. It all seemed set fair for Granger to star in the remake, which would now be called *Mogambo* and be set in Africa on a big-game safari park. However, one day he was called into the front office by Dore Schary, the head of production at MGM, and told 'the King' needed a big movie to boost his flagging career, and so Granger was no longer going to play the lead in that particular project. 'The King' was, of course, Clark Gable, who subsequently starred in *Mogambo*, with Grace Kelly and Ava Gardner in the Mary Astor and Jean Harlow parts respectively. The movie was a big success for Gable and for the studio. Granger was not very pleased about losing this plum role in a top MGM production, and he did not speak very warmly about Gable in his autobiography. According to Granger, one of the excuses Schary offered Granger for not giving him the part was he surely didn't want to be separated from 'that lovely little wife of yours'. Granger comments that, no, he didn't want to be separated from Simmons, but he certainly wanted to make this African picture.

This episode illustrates the kind of tensions and paradoxes inherent in a marriage of two ambitious movie stars. Yes, they wanted to be together as much as possible, but the reality was that important movies were often shot in locations far from Hollywood and so if you wanted to be a player in the movie-making game, then there were sacrifices to be made. Frequent long absences from one another were to be a feature of the Grangers' marriage; most marriages would feel the strain of such long separations, but when both partners were involved in the highly charged business of making major movies, and with all the temptations that were bound to surround them when they were absent from home, then it is hardly surprising that these separations gradually took their toll. Perhaps it is surprising that their marriage lasted as long as it did.

As compensation for losing out to Gable in *Mogambo*, MGM offered Granger *All the Brothers Were Valiant*, which Granger describes as a 'crappy melodrama about whaling, pearl-diving in the South Seas, mutiny and lust'. Most of the filming was to take place on location in Jamaica, which meant another long separation from his wife, who had just been cast opposite Richard Burton in the first Cinemascope movie, *The Robe*. This was clearly a very important role for Simmons because *The Robe*, however inferior a movie it turned out to be, was to be the Hollywood film of the year. Perhaps part of Granger's dissatisfaction with MGM was the contrast with his wife's then current project: *The Robe* was to be a huge production, but *All the Brothers Were Valiant* was perceived as just a potboiler.

His co-star was Robert Taylor, who had won the lead role in MGM's huge epic success *Quo Vadis*, which Granger had also wanted. This undoubtedly was another grouse Granger had with his employers, but he seemed to work well with Taylor, who had also suffered from the tag of 'pretty boy' in the film world. Some might consider that no one took him seriously because he could not act and his so-called good looks were irrelevant. However, Granger obviously had a fellow feeling for the insecure Taylor. Perhaps they even shared some political views, because Taylor had notoriously spearheaded the attack on so-called 'Hollywood commies' when the House Un-American Activities Committee hearings opened in Hollywood in 1947. Taylor's role in those persecutions may now be seen as indefensible, as it was his kind of testimony that had ruined the Hollywood careers of many workers in the industry. Nevertheless, Taylor was one of the few people whom he worked with of whom Granger expressed unreserved approval: 'He was such a nice guy, Bob, but he had even more hang-ups than I had.'

The setting of *All the Brothers Were Valiant* is the South Pacific in 1850, so once again Granger was appearing in a period film. He plays Mark Shore, the 'bad' brother to Robert Taylor's 'good' brother, Joel. Ann Blyth plays the romantic interest as the brothers inevitably vie for her affections and the loyalty of the ship's crew. *Variety* called it a 'regulation romance-adventure', which is a fair summation. The *Variety* critic also commented that 'the stars are competent, but the people they portray haven't enough depth or reality to come robustly alive'. Granger's character, after a sudden change of heart, helps his brother to quell a mutiny and dies heroically. Granger complained that his elongated death scene had been cut from the final version after the preview audience had howled with laughter at the length it took his character to expire after having been harpooned in the heart. 'What a waste of that tear-jerking performance,' Granger commented. Granger's director was again Richard Thorpe, who had worked with him on *The Prisoner of Zenda*.

One interesting incident in the making of this film is that while he was in Jamaica, Granger was offered an attractive stretch of land overlooking a beach, but he turned down the offer because he was worried by the prevalence of insects which had plagued him and his colleagues during the shoot. Later, the land Granger had been offered was sold for $5 million. 'Actors just aren't businessmen,' he ruefully commented.

All the Brothers Were Valiant would certainly not further Granger's Hollywood career or move him to a higher level of stardom. It was not an important film, although it did quite well at the box-office. Yet the reviews were mostly lukewarm and the film was seen as the programme-filler it indeed was. Bosley Crowther in the *New York Times* found 'the flip bravura of the dressed-up Hollywood stars a little hard to swallow'. He summed up the movie by describing it as 'a lot of pseudo-salty South Seas whoop-de-do put together with little distinction and without going off the studio lot'. Unless Granger's account of location shooting in Jamaica is highly exaggerated, it seems that Crowther got that wrong, but his summary of the movie is just. Incidentally, he described Granger's performance as 'downright operatic', which was not meant in a complimentary sense.

When MGM cast Granger in the title role of *Beau Brummell*, he was at first enthusiastic about the project. He claims even to have helped with the writing of scenes, but how much influence he had on the final script is impossible to judge. He had had pretensions to writing before, or at least working on storylines, so he was eager to break out of the straitjacket of romantic hero stardom. At this time in the 1950s, the British government had placed an embargo on Hollywood studios taking money earned in the United Kingdom out of the country in a move designed to encourage inward investment. MGM had a considerable amount of such 'blocked funds', which is partly why so many MGM movies were made in Britain during the decade. Granger's enthusiasm for the *Beau Brummell* project soon lapsed when he realised that MGM intended to film the production at the MGM Studios outside London. This would mean another long separation from his wife. Both pleaded with top MGM executives for the movie to be made in Hollywood, but such tearful arguments cut no ice with the hard-nosed brass of the studio, who included Benny Thau and Nicholas Schenck, the head of Loew's, the New York-based company that owned MGM. MGM may have propagated family values in their movies, but they were not about to change their minds about where an MGM movie was to be shot because a star husband-and-wife team didn't want to be separated. Business was business for MGM and there was money locked up in England, which they wanted to use.

So it was off to England for Granger, where he could spend some time with his children, while Simmons set to work on the turgid epic *The Egyptian*. If their marriage was already in trouble (according to Granger's own account), then another long separation like this was hardly likely to help matters. Neither *Beau Brummell* nor *The Egyptian* proved worthy of their sacrifice, at least in terms of artistic worth. However, in Hollywood terms, both were major productions and both headed the cast list, so their star status was reinforced, although *The Egyptian* was seen as risibly bad when it was released, putting paid to any hopes that the young lead, Edmund Purdom, had of achieving major stardom. *Beau Brummell,* on the other hand, was not risible, merely pedestrian and rather pointless.

Based on a nineteenth-century Clyde Fitch play, *Beau Brummell* is supposedly about the life of the elegant dandy who, at the beginning of the nineteenth century, became close friends of the Prince of Wales, the future George IV of England. Dispensing with historical accuracy, the movie never makes up its mind about how it should view the central character. Was Brummell an opportunist upstart who cultivated the Prince's friendship for his own advancement in society, or a patriot with only the good of the country at heart, who tried to influence the wayward prince with sage advice? As played by Granger, the film naturally veers towards the latter. George Brummell, the son of a valet, is represented as an adventurer, a gambler, with more than a touch of the womaniser about him and arrogant with it. A quintessential Stewart Granger part, in short, except there are no 'action' scenes.

The production values are sumptuous, and the movie, photographed by the distinguished lighting cameraman, Oswald Morris, looks good in that excessively glossy MGM style. Indeed, Bosley Crowther in his *New York Times* review positively enthused about its 'luscious pictorial display' and summed it up as 'a lovely film' with Beau Brummell as 'a blissfully beautiful gent'. According to Crowther, Granger played a 'death-bed scene that out-rattles the tubercular demise of Camille'.

Unfortunately, the death-bed emotions are not sufficiently earned, because of the shallowness of the representation of the character. This scene exactly typifies the sentimentalising approach to the characterisation of Brummell. It may say much about the movie's general approach that this death-bed scene, in which the Prince of Wales (played by Peter Ustinov) visits the penniless and dying Brummell in a Paris garret in order to make up with this former favourite, is not based on fact, as there was the little matter of the Prince having died in 1830 whereas Brummell lived on till 1840 and died at the age of sixty-two. Although Granger looks a trifle wan on his deathbed, he certainly does not appear to be in his sixties. Sundry historical characters such as Lord Byron (woefully miscast), William Pitt, George III and Burke are thrown into the unconvincing mix. Brummell is portrayed as defending the rights of the British monarchy against the parliamentarians, which about sums up the movie's reactionary agenda.

Granger in his autobiography complains about the 'unpredictable' Ustinov and the acting competition represented by Robert Morley. Frankly, he need not have worried. What is remembered from the film is not the acting (Elizabeth Taylor is also in the cast as the love interest – a part that is practically meaningless), but the visual splendour, costumes and settings. Granger wears period costume once more and, as usual, carries it off with elegance and panache. However, *Beau Brummell* is another instance of his being imprisoned in this kind of period film. He is once more playing an adventurer, a gambler, a man living off his wits. It was just another aspect of the Granger screen persona that was reflected in real life, and statements made by various characters in the movie to Granger/Brummell seem particularly apposite: 'You don't take kindly to discipline, you're a gambler, a non-conformist' and 'You're bitter because you feel inferior but does it make you feel any less inferior to be rude?' The movie may not have done Granger's career a great service, but perhaps unconsciously, he may have identified with the outsider who never feared to speak his mind and made his way in life through his wits and his charm.

Beau Brummell was chosen for the Royal Film Performance in London the following year. A devout monarchist, Granger was worried by this. He considered the film unsuitable for royal consumption because it portrayed an ancestor of the Queen (George III) as a lunatic. He clearly considered it chivalrous to 'protect' the Queen from anything that might be 'disagreeable', but his over-sensitivity on behalf of the monarchy seems overdone.

His role in his next film, *Green Fire*, again encapsulates in many ways the Granger screen persona. The film is what is called a 'romantic adventure', but in essence it is an extended male fantasy romp. Granger plays an Englishman in Colombia, determined to make his fortune by mining for emeralds, particularly in an old mine first developed by the Conquistadors at the end of the seventeenth century. Grace Kelly is the elegant American who owns and runs a nearby coffee plantation with her wayward brother.

Granger's partner (played by Paul Douglas) is a bluff American, whom Granger manipulates into investing in mining untold riches. There are lawless bandits at hand, led by one El Moro, who is determined to wrest control of the emerald mine away from Granger and his partner. There are betrayals, avalanches, encounters with leopards, romantic interludes, a Catholic priest on hand to remind us of 'true values' and the final redemption of the main character, who, when he has to choose between his mine and the coffee plantation, chooses to save the plantation, thereby winning the love of the beautiful lady. Before this, Granger virtually single-handedly vanquishes a horde of Colombian bandits. It is simply a Boy's Own adventure divorced from time and reality. There is a veneer of moralising splashed lightly over the action (voiced by the Catholic priest) whereby Granger has to learn that his money values are not so important as the values of hard work and devotion. This moralising is as bogus as only Hollywood religiosity can be.

At the end of the movie, the male fantasy is completed when the hero, having seemingly sacrificed his emerald mine for the sake of the community and the Grace Kelly character, is shown to have escaped from the buried mine with a few valuable emeralds. He has, despite everything, become rich and the fantasy is complete when the beautiful blonde, wealthy plantation-owning woman embraces him. They are destined for happy-ever-after land. The former womaniser (this is represented in the movie) is now supposedly to settle down in marriage. The gambler has won not only wealth but the perfect partner.

The film sidesteps any questions about the Americans and an Englishman exploiting local labour to make themselves rich. Indeed, the Colombians, apart from the rascally bandits, who are as clichéd a bunch of latino bandits as have ever graced the Hollywood screen, are shown to be eager to serve the interests of the foreign owning classes while they go about their rightful business of exploiting their country.

The movie opens and ends with a quite dreadful *Green Fire* song sung by a chorus, which presages the level of entertainment. As an adventure movie with major stars Granger and Kelly, it obviously hoped to reproduce the success of *King Solomon's Mines*. Within five minutes of the opening of the movie, Granger has had an encounter with a leopard and shot several bandits. He performs schoolboy heroics throughout the movie. He is shown to wager his last penny on a curious game of explosive quoits and laughs when he loses. It is one of Granger's most macho parts and he seems to revel in it, although he might well have been embarrassed when he saw the phoney heroics on screen. His character, Rian Mitchell, embodies a kind of male fantasy, but it is unconvincing and hollow.

The *ABC Film Review* of the time commented that as the 'the rugged adventurer, Mitchell, Stewart Granger has a role admirably suited to his lusty talents'. The *Monthly Film Bulletin*, however, thought the movie 'more pretentious in tone than seems justified by its material and lacks drive and conviction', which is another way of saying that its moralising tone is repugnant and the plot implausible and detached from reality. *Green Fire* is, in fact, not that bad a movie: it does have spectacular effects, the pace is sustained and some of the local environment is beautifully photographed, but it demands little of its intended audience. Indeed, it could fairly be called a 'no-brainer' of its time, the kind of Hollywood fare that is pure escapism, destined to be consumed and then quickly forgotten.

Thus, Granger had another major movie under his belt, but *Green Fire* could scarcely be described as advancing his career in any meaningful way. It certainly does not extend the range of roles he was attempting and audiences would have identified the movie and the part of Mitchell as standard Stewart Granger fare. But by then Granger was in his early forties. His greying temples were a reminder that his days as a romantic action hero were numbered. His career badly needed a new impetus if it were to have any kind of longevity with the status of major stardom. He had attempted no character parts and was closely identified with costume and action movies. If he were to survive at the very top of his career, he needed to diversify, but his employers at MGM seemed content to recycle him in familiar roles and movie plots.

Granger was a natural worrier; the duodenal ulcers that ended his army career and which would plague him all his life, were the result of his inability to match the devil-may-care attitudes of the characters he played on-screen in real life. The question is why he so seldom admitted to self-doubts and anxieties, at least in public, and seemed to feel the need to sustain a macho front at all times. The price of living out the male fantasy would be high in the years to come.

Chapter 7

GOODBYE TO MGM

'**B**RINGING UP CHILDREN is hell,' wrote Granger in his autobiography. However, when he acted with children on the screen, he had an easygoing interaction with them that went beyond the demands of the script. Examples of this are the scenes with the boy king in *Young Bess* and with Jon Whiteley in *Moonfleet*. He could act 'fatherly', just as he could act 'sincere', and be reasonably convincing while doing it. But the movies are not real life and children are not always as easy or as amenable as they are in a few short scenes in films.

The ill-health of Elspeth March, Granger's first wife, required long-term treatment in a nursing home in England, so Granger and Jean Simmons undertook to have his two children, James and Lindsay, stay with them in Hollywood while their mother recovered. Simmons was only in her mid-twenties herself at this time and Granger comments in his autobiography that when he saw her with his two youngsters, 'I often got the impression I was bringing up three children instead of two.' Granger was clearly very fond and proud of his kids and in many ways he must have been a terrific father to have, but parental responsibilities, like many other responsibilities and duties he faced, weighed heavily upon him. Nothing came easy for this man's man, the easygoing adventurer.

Granger dismisses the next film he made in one line in his autobiography as a 'dreary costume epic called *Moonfleet*'. However, this is rather unfair to the movie and to its director, Fritz Lang. The producer was John Houseman, former associate of Orson Welles and the producer of *Julius Caesar* and *The Bad and the Beautiful*. So the *Moonfleet* production and Granger were in the hands of accomplished film-makers. The film was shot in Cinemascope and Lang's main interest is to use the wide-screen frame and fill it with striking images. The story is adapted from J. Meade Falkner's adventure novel and has Granger again cast as an adventurer in Dorset, Jeremy Fox, who rules a gang of cut-throat smugglers with a fist of iron until he is softened by contact with a ten-year-old boy who hero-worships him and believes only the best of him. The boy is the son of the woman whom Granger/Fox had loved in his youth and whose powerful Mohune family had married her off to a rich cousin. Granger/Fox had been banished to the colonies where he had made his fortune before returning to live in the derelict Mohune mansion. Granger/Fox pursues a life of dissipation and criminality, but has a change of heart at the end of the movie and sacrifices himself to save the boy. Shot mainly on the studio backlot, Lang makes much of the gothic sets and uses impressive point-of-views shots to communicate the fears of the young boy. Even at this late stage in his career, it is clear that the director of *Metropolis*, *M* and *The Testament of Dr Mabuse* still had more innate directing talent than many supposedly more successful Hollywood directors.

Granger has some fine moments in this movie, notably in the scenes with the boy. It is another costume movie (the setting is Dorset in 1757) and, as usual, he looks elegant and assured in well-cut clothes. It is, in essence, another 'male fantasy' role: living the good life from the proceeds of crime, being the love object of competing beautiful women, imposing his authority over other males and gambling with danger in the pursuit of wealth.

However, the movie does not have a happy ending as Granger's character is fatally wounded in his attempt to return to the boy after trying to escape the clutches of the law.

It is interesting that the perhaps over-earnest French film critics of the time rated this movie highly, mainly because Fritz Lang had directed it. Lang was a revered figure to such critics and directors as Jean-Luc Godard and François Truffaut because of his early expressionist film masterpieces in 1920s German cinema, but also because of his underrated American movies, such as *Woman in the Window*, *The Big Heat* and *While the City Sleeps*. What these French critics liked in *Moonfleet* was its purely cinematic qualities, particularly the use of space within the screen frame. To them, style was meaning, and the meaning of a movie such as *Moonfleet* is in the style imposed on the conventional thematic material by Lang.

Moonfleet is definitely one of Granger's most underestimated films. David Shipman, the author of *The Great Movie Stars*, rates *Moonfleet* as by far the best movie Granger ever made. Actors are often not the best judges of something they have done, and perhaps the fact of being forced to star in what he considered to be yet another adventure romp meant that Granger was rather jaded by this time. But it is a much better picture than *Green Fire* and many critics prefer it to *King Solomon's Mines* and *The Prisoner of Zenda*, because it is evident from every frame that an artist is in control of the filming.

Granger recounts an anecdote about being visited on the set of *Moonfleet* by Dore Schary, by then head of production at MGM. With Schary was a young actor who had just made sensational starring appearances in *Rebel Without a Cause* and *East of Eden*. It was clear that MGM were courting this new star, but Granger was as unimpressed with James Dean as Dean seemed to be with Granger. Granger appears rather hurt that Dean did not return the compliment when Granger said how much he had liked his last movie. Granger almost inevitably comments on Dean's unkempt appearance ('unpressed trousers and sneakers'). This was a brief encounter between the old-fashioned romantic hero of the movies and a prime representative of the new kind of male Hollywood star that would make Granger's appeal almost obsolete. In his brief career, Dean would embody the sensitive, introspective and tortured young male on screen, showing a vulnerability and 'weakness' that romantic hero stars such as Granger could never afford to display. Dean also represented something else that was important to the Hollywood industry: he was in his twenties and the producers now knew that the majority of cinema-goers were under twenty-five, so they needed young stars who would appeal to this changed audience demography. The older generation were mostly stuck in front of their television sets and would only venture to the cinemas for big events like *The Robe* or *Ben Hur*. Whether Granger realised it or not at the time of this encounter, Dean symbolised the kind of change in taste and audiences that would bring about the end of Granger's career at the very top of the Hollywood tree. Perhaps Granger did realise it; it might partly explain his antagonism to Dean.

The Grangers were anxious to work in England again so that they could see family members and friends. Equally MGM needed to use up frozen funds that were locked in Europe and so *Footsteps in the Fog* became their next starring venture together. This movie was a creaky melodrama adapted from a novel by W.W. Jacobs set in Victorian England. Granger plays an adventurer, Stephen Lowry, who poisons his rich wife in order to inherit her wealth and leave him free to marry the daughter of his business partner. Jean Simmons plays the cockney housemaid who finds out that Lowry has murdered his wife, but uses this knowledge to blackmail him into becoming her lover and then, she hopes, her husband. Granger concocts an elaborate plan that involves taking poison himself, which is meant to show to the police that it is the housemaid who had poisoned his wife and who is now attempting to murder him. The plot backfires and Granger expires. It is the stuff of theatrical matinées and most of the action takes place in the house of Stephen Lowry. There are some scenes in fog-bound London streets, but the action is mainly confined effectively to the drawing room of the palatial house.

Granger describes the direction of Arthur Lubin as 'mulish', Lubin being one of a long list of directors who failed to win his approval. In fact, there is not much to direct. The camera is pointed at the action and the narrative winds its way to its extremely melodramatic climax. There is a winning score by Benjamin Frankel, which catches the poignancy of the adoration lavished on the unworthy Lowry/Granger by the lovesick housemaid. Jean Simmons is rather effective as the maid and Granger is thoroughly convincing as the manipulative and ruthless Lowry.

If the parts actors choose (and Granger claims to have actively campaigned for this particular project for Simmons and himself and to have worked on the script) reveal something about themselves, then what can be said about the roles he and Simmons played in *Footsteps in the Fog*? Once again, Granger is playing the authoritative role and Simmons the underling. Once again, as in *Young Bess*, he is the love object over whom two beautiful women are vying (the other woman, his fiancée, is played by Belinda Lee, who would die in a car crash a few years later). Yet again Granger plays a cad, a womaniser, a cold manipulator and a man who wants to become wealthy and established in society by less than honourable means. Some characters in the movie are impressed by his confidence and good looks; others distrust him and suspect he has been up to no good. This scenario could be said to reflect something of the Granger–Simmons relationship, and how Granger himself was viewed by many people. Inevitably, he had been initially the dominant partner in their relationship, but before too many years would pass, this would change and Simmons would fully assert herself, just as the maid in the film does. And Granger himself aroused love and antipathy in almost equal measures among the people who encountered him.

Footsteps in the Fog is no movie masterpiece, but it is an entertaining enough piece of melodrama. It has a certain atmosphere to it, despite Lubin's supposed mulish direction, and it never looks anything less than striking because of the talents of the British technicians who worked on the movie. It was not a big budget movie, but it extended the Granger–Simmons starring combination, which was now firmly established in the consciousness of the cinema-going public. It would be, however, the last time that the husband-and-wife team would appear in a movie together. Perhaps the machinations of the two characters they played in *Footsteps in the Fog* did indeed reflect the changing power relations within their marriage.

Long separations were now a constant feature of the marriage between this 'golden couple' of the film world. Such enforced separation from one another came with the territory of their both being top movie stars in a Hollywood film industry that more or less took for granted such sacrifices from their highly paid actors. Stars such as Granger and Simmons might well bring the customers in, but to the MGM executives, they were mere employees, albeit very important ones.

The MGM archives now lodged in the library of the film department of the University of Southern California in Los Angeles include the 'time cards' of major stars such as Astaire, Gene Kelly and other major MGM stars when they were making those wonderful MGM movies. Every minute of every hour that they were on the lot was accounted for, and their activities were logged in minute detail. The time at which they arrived in make-up, how long they were there, when exactly they reported to the set of the movie they were making, when they broke for lunch and returned to the set, how they spent their time on the set and the time they left the studio: all these activities were recorded by assistant producers in exact terms so that executives could check MGM was getting full value from these star employees. MGM was a factory, in essence, an industrial unit geared towards making a substantial number of movies every year, and it still required a 'factory-type' structure if they were to maintain the desired level of production. There was much propaganda about the glamour attached to being a top MGM star, but the reality was that even the stars at the studio had to clock in and clock off like lowly employees.

By the mid-fifties, MGM was busily divesting itself of unnecessary overheads as a reaction to the vastly changed market conditions. Famous MGM stars such as Joan Crawford had long gone and soon Clark Gable,

Elizabeth Taylor, Greer Garson and others would leave the studio as MGM decided that it did not a require a permanent roster of highly paid stars for whom they had to find film vehicles that would produce adequate box-office returns. Gene Kelly, that most MGM of stars, the star and director of the greatest MGM musicals, would shortly make his last musical for the studio (*Les Girls*) and be released from his contract. It was a whole new ball game out there and the upcoming stars such as Paul Newman and established stars such as Burt Lancaster were entering the production stakes in an attempt to create their own work and control the product in which they appeared. The power structure had tilted away from the studios towards the top talent agencies and the independent producers, many of whom were stars themselves.

Stewart Granger would not follow that star trend and become a film producer, but he had other business aspirations in mind to diversify his interests and perhaps provide a safety net in case his film star career stalled. He must have been acutely aware by the mid-fifties, as he himself approached his mid-forties, that the writing was on the wall for the old studio system. However much he chafed against the bonds of studio serfdom, MGM did provide almost constant employment and as long as they picked up his option every six months, he knew he would continue to enjoy the fruits of stardom. However, by his own admission, he had always been spendthrift and aspired to a standard of living that he could scarcely afford. He had had problems with the expense of the first house he had bought in Hollywood and now, at this stage in his life, he would use his capital in risky ventures that would bring him more problems and add to his anxieties. Granger was living out some kind of male fantasy of freedom, gambling and acquisitiveness, but found it difficult to cope with the real-life worries that such gambles brought with them.

According to his own testimony, it was Granger who recommended *Bhowani Junction* to MGM as a movie adaptation. John Masters's novel was about colonial India on the verge of obtaining independence during the last days of the British Raj. It would be shot on location in Pakistan. Therefore, the four-month absence from Jean Simmons that the filming schedule would entail can be fairly laid at his own door. Granger states that he intended bringing Simmons with him for the duration of the location shooting in Pakistan, but then out of the blue she was offered the part of the Salvation Army girl in *Guys and Dolls*, which was to co-star Marlon Brando and Frank Sinatra, a part she could not afford to turn down. How realistic it was for Granger to believe that Simmons could sacrifice her career for such a length of time in order to accompany him while he made a film is difficult to gauge. How sincere he was in his avowals that he never wanted to be separated from her is equally hard to measure. If people really want desperately to be with one another constantly, they surely arrange their lives in order that this should happen. Here, in both their cases, ambition and the need to stay 'on top' meant they made the decision to have this long separation. It could not have helped their marriage, which was already suffering.

Granger was frank about his worries over his wife working with Brando and Sinatra, two of the most sought-after men in Hollywood. He was also worried about the director of *Guys and Dolls*, Joseph L. Mankiewicz, who had had a string of affairs with his female stars, including Judy Garland. Granger worried about the competition that this trio of alpha males would pose, and that by comparison he would appear less fascinating to her. 'Never give a woman a chance to make comparisons,' Granger wrote in his misogynist mode, 'or you'll come up with the short end of the stick.' Many of Granger's statements about relationships seem to reflect his need to 'own' women against the competing attentions of other men. It does not seem too far-fetched an explanation to point to the experience of his parents. Granger had vowed never to let the 'emasculation' of his father happen to him.

Granger had had a falling out with George Cukor over *A Star Is Born*, but it was Cukor who was assigned to direct *Bhowani Junction*. Nevertheless, their relationship while shooting the movie seemed to be reasonable and Granger wrote some admiring words about Cukor's directing skills in *Sparks Fly Upward*. Cukor's high reputation among many critics is surely ripe for re-examination, however. He had directed *The Philadelphia Story* with Hepburn, Grant and Stewart, but that material with the actors he had was almost director-proof. He was known to be good with female stars, but it is hard to pin down what constitutes Cukor's personal contribution to any of 'his' movies. However, Cukor clearly did not annoy his star much during the making of this film, one of the few directors who managed that feat.

Granger plays Colonel Savage of the Indian Army, assigned to protect the railways at Bhowani Junction against the attacks of Communist guerrillas, who are seeking to plunge the country into chaos on the eve of its independence. The Communists are very much the villains of the piece and their representation in the movie is par for the course for many Hollywood movies of the 1950s, as the Cold War intensified and America passed through its McCarthyite persecution period. Ava Gardner plays an Anglo-Indian soldier, Victoria Jones, who is caught between the two worlds of the British colonials and the Indians, not knowing who she really is and to which 'side' she owes her loyalties. She tries to embrace her Indian roots when she becomes engaged to a Sikh, but soon she discovers she is really in love with the Granger/Savage character and helps to foil a dastardly plot by the Communists to kill Gandhi.

Bhowani Junction could have been an interesting study of colonial prejudices and racial tensions, but the film is not much more than a routine thriller set against the background of the last days of British colonial rule. Its values seem firmly on the side of the 'decent' British Raj, portrayed as generally misunderstood and trying simply to keep the peace between warring factions. The representation of the Congress Party is deeply reactionary and, all in all, it takes an essentially conservative standpoint on the issue of Indian independence.

Gardner is deeply unconvincing as Victoria Jones, and Bill Travers as her brother is as atrocious as he was in Granger's previous movie, *Footsteps in the Fog*. The climax of the film is a melodramatic chase to head off the dynamiting of a railway tunnel by the fiendish Communists, their attempt to assassinate Gandhi, but the tension all seems rather trumped up. At the end of the movie, Granger/Savage is seen on his way back to Britain but the audience is left with the impression that he will resign his commission in order to return to India to marry the Anglo-Indian heroine. The requisite happy Hollywood ending is therefore somewhat unconvincingly created. The crowd scenes are quite well staged and there is a general impression of the tensions igniting the rival communities in India at that time, but the movie settles for melodrama and conventional plot structures. The timidity with which MGM approached the subject of 'miscegenation' is revealed in the change of ending imposed on director Cukor by the MGM executives. In the original version, Gardner as the Anglo-Indian heroine chooses to marry her Sikh lover as a gesture of identifying herself with her Indian roots. However, when MGM sneak-previewed the movie in San Francisco, the audience objected to Gardner marrying a 'black' so MGM ordered Cukor to re-shoot the ending, which implies that Gardner will end up with the Granger character. Cukor at first refused to comply, but when the threat was made that if he did not cooperate he would never make another MGM movie, he caved in and duly re-shot the ending. So much for Cukor's integrity as a director. Granger, for once, is not in period costume and the film is set almost in contemporary times (1947), but he wears an army uniform throughout the movie. There is very little opportunity for Granger to be anything other than the straightforward, decent British officer type Savage is meant to represent. *Variety* considered that Granger 'cuts a manly and restrained figure', which is fair comment and reflects how little he had to do. Bosley Crowther in the *New York Times*, however, saw the movie as 'an exciting and picturesque trip into a land that is torn with the different races and nationalities'.

Granger enjoyed the military aspect of his role, however. Cukor had arranged for a battalion of Indian soldiers to be at Granger's disposal so that he could get 'the feel of the part'. This offended Granger – obviously 'the stupid sod' had forgotten that he (Granger) had been an officer in the Black Watch. No one need teach him how to drill and salute! Granger admits to enjoying the experience of taking the salute at a march past and claimed that 'no colonel ever stood more stiffly to attention or flashed such a snappy salute'. Clearly some important part of Granger still regretted the demise of his army career and his failure to replicate his father's military prowess. He knew all this play-acting in Lahore, Pakistan, was just pretence, but it is interesting that he took to it with such enthusiasm. He saw it as an expression of his manliness and associated India with his father, who had served for many years in the Indian Army. 'I could understand his unhappiness at having to leave it all and it wasn't only my mother's behaviour that had saddened him,' Granger wrote.

According to Granger, he had to resist the many attempts of Ava Gardner to get him into bed while they were on this long location shoot. Much as he was attracted to the beautiful ex-wife of Frank Sinatra, he resisted on the grounds that he wanted to remain faithful to Jean Simmons. Just as with his account of Hedy Lamarr's attempts to have an affair with him, Granger seems more interested in 'didn't kiss and tell' anecdotes rather than the more orthodox variety of gossip. It undoubtedly pleased his vanity that beautiful women such as Lamarr and Gardner made a play for him, even though he turned them down. However, he continued to worry about what Jean Simmons was, or was not, getting up to in Hollywood with Sinatra, Brando and Mankiewicz.

Granger found another means to express his manliness when he was granted a short break from filming. As he did when he had been on location for *King Solomon's Mines* in East Africa, he chose to go big-game hunting, this time in the jungles of Nani Tal, which James Corbett had made famous in his books about man-eating tigers. On this particular expedition, Granger shot a marauding tiger dead; it had been terrorising a local village, a fact used by Granger to excuse the killing. Even allowing for historical perspective, however, Granger does appear too eager to kill animals to express his courage and experience some real-life thrills as opposed to the mock heroics he enacted in screen.

By coincidence, Granger's next film was about hunting, buffalo-hunting in this case. *The Last Hunt* again co-starred Granger with Robert Taylor, but this time Taylor played the baddie and Granger the hero, Sandy McKenzie.

The film was shot on location in Custer National Park and the Badlands of South Dakota. Jean Simmons accompanied Granger on the location shoot. Once again, he was to be directed by Richard Brooks, about whom he has little that is commendatory to say. This, of course, may well be because Richard Brooks was to marry Jean Simmons shortly after the Grangers' divorce in 1960.

Brooks fancied himself as a tough Hemingwayesque character, and *The Last Hunt* in part reflects his interests and persona. It is a brutal, macho western with actual scenes of buffalo killing. Nowadays, film-makers would not be able to shoot these animals, but at this time there was an annual cull of buffalo to control their numbers, a cull that gave the opportunity to those who gained pleasure from that kind of thing to shoot them under licence from the National Parks of America. MGM bought up all the available licences and so Brooks was able to include realistic scenes in his gritty western of buffaloes being slaughtered. The Forest Rangers did the actual shooting, which Granger was apparently relieved about, because he did not consider shooting buffalo as 'fair game', unlike the killing of big cats in the jungle, which involved putting your life on the line.

Shortly after Granger and Simmons returned from the location work on *The Last Hunt*, Simmons became pregnant. The couple were delighted. This coming event galvanised Granger into taking an irrevocable step about his nationality status. 'What I like about America,' Granger opined in a newspaper interview given in 1957 to the *Sunday Graphic*, 'is that I don't feel guilty about being a success.' He went on to make a comparison between the US and Britain: 'Over here [Britain] it makes you feel awful. The gulf between the working man and people who are a success is too big for the man who is a success to feel easy.' Robert Robinson, the interviewer, comments rather tartly, 'I judge that Mr Granger will manage to stifle his guilt and continue, while he is with us, to ride about in dirty big shiny cars.' Later the article mentions the shiny new Rolls that Granger and Jean Simmons drove round London and how they had stopped it at an ordinary fish and chip shop so that Granger could indulge in one of the things he missed about England. Granger clearly enjoyed displaying the wealth he had accrued in the classic male fashion of expensive cars and fancy houses. He was almost certainly over-compensating for his youthful years, when he was by no stretch of the imagination poor, but had to deny himself certain things and opportunities because of the limitations of his family's means. The general impression Granger gave in his public statements about his attitude towards his native country and the United States is that the former symbolised restrictions, petty jealousies and socialist bureaucracy, and the latter freedom, lack of envy and economic opportunities.

Given these general attitudes, then, it is hardly surprising that Granger and his wife, around the end of 1955, started studying for their citizenship examinations so that they could become fully fledged American citizens and thereby the American parents of their expected child, although it should also be noted that Granger had always enthusiastically expressed his patriotism: he was proud to be British and proud especially of his Scottish ancestry, although some journalists had noted his increasingly mid-Atlantic accent, which can certainly be detected in his later films. The citizenship examinations involved them in a fairly serious amount of study, but both Granger and Simmons passed with flying colours. The *Daily Sketch* wrote up the story with the headline 'The Grangers Are No Longer British', which was surely calculated to raise a few hackles in their home country. The article comments that Brits in Hollywood had tended to cling to their British rights 'like clams'. It attempts to stir the pot further by quoting Jean Simmons's mother to the effect that the news was a 'bombshell' and Elspeth March, Granger's first wife, is reported as saying she had been surprised by the news. After all, Stewart Granger had been the heart-throb of the British cinema and now he had deliberately chosen to turn himself into a Yank. In those days especially, some British people would have seen his action as a kind of betrayal.

Thus, Jimmy Stewart from the Old Brompton Road had become Stewart Granger, the star of British movies, then an international star through his appearances in big-budget American movies, and now he was Stewart Granger, American citizen. He had outwardly divested himself of a lot of baggage, but he was, in an important sense, still that Jimmy Stewart who was wrestling with the same problems that had given him anxieties all those years ago. He was still aspiring, gambling, taking risks and wrestling with those childhood demons. And having become an official American citizen, he was now to aspire to become that most American of things: a real-life cowboy and ranch-owner. He had just finished a grim western and now he was to embark on a venture in the real modern West that would also have its grim side and add to his anxieties.

Having fallen in love with the open spaces of South Dakota and other western locations he had visited, Granger had become fascinated with the idea of owning a ranch in the real American West. It is not difficult to understand the fascination that the western states held for this guy from central London. Very few people can resist the appeal of the vast desert ranges of places like Monument Valley, where John Ford shot so many of his westerns, and the empty prairies like the one in South Dakota where Custer's Battle of the Little Big Horn took place. A state such as Wyoming, for example, has a total population of well under a million and yet it is the size of the British Isles. For anyone who wants peace and seclusion, the American West offers the promise of that with the very important added bonus of being surrounded by breathtaking scenery that has remained untouched for millions of years.

One of the wranglers employed by MGM to look after the buffalo that were an essential part of *The Last Hunt* had been a man called Elmer Black. Granger now commissioned Black to find him a ranch that would enable the film star to indulge his interest in horses and bull-breeding, and Black recommended a vast ranch in New Mexico. It had an extent of 66,000 acres, about a hundred square miles. It was true that only 3,000 acres of this was deeded land, but there was a permit to run 1,500 cattle on the rest of the area. Eventually, Granger paid $225,000 for the property, putting down a deposit of only $25,000, as he explained to the seller that he had a large income but little capital. He undertook to pay off the rest over a period of five years at a favourable rate of interest to the seller.

Although movie stars in those times did not earn a fraction of the money made by major stars nowadays, it is perhaps surprising that Granger had so little capital to hand, even though, by his own testimony, he was a spend-thrift. The burden of paying the interest on the debt and the expenses in maintaining this vast spread, plus the problems he had with the manage-ment of the ranch, were to cause him and Simmons great anxiety over the next few years and almost certainly contributed to the break-up of their marriage.

When Granger had 'made it' in the British film industry, he had over-stretched himself in buying the Elizabethan manor house and his venture into pheasant-breeding. Now that he had lived in America for seven years and had become an American citizen, his aspirations had taken a decidedly American turn. The central myth of the United States is of the pioneer taming the West, a story of bold adventurers braving privations and danger from Native American tribes to cultivate the often harsh landscape and establish small communities in the midst of vast ranges and empty deserts. The nation still sustains itself on the back of these myths, however de-romanticised they have become as historians discover more and more about the reality behind the legends. Western movies have for years helped to reinforce the legends of the American West, although not even Hollywood has been able to withstand the weight of evidence about the genocide of the Native Americans and the brutality and exploitation involved in much of the opening up of the West. In the 1950s, however, that rewriting of the West's history had scarcely begun. Apart from falling in love with the western landscape, perhaps Granger was also buying into the legends of the West as represented in the films he had starred in. As a man who liked to exhibit his manliness at every opportunity, he no doubt fancied himself in this new real-life role of cowboy and rancher. Unlike a vocation as an actor, no one could accuse those vocations as being 'pansy'. Had Granger still been a British citizen and had Britain not been at that period of history divesting itself of its empire, it is likely that Granger might have cast his eyes to the colonies for potential business ventures, as so many others of his social class had done in the decades before, but here he was in America and it had an 'empire' right on his doorstep there for the taking, if you had enough money to buy up a sizeable chunk of it. The former aspiring English squire had become the potential cattle baron.

The British press seized with glee on the story that the former number one British movie star, now an American citizen, had 'gone Yank' and become a cowboy. The *Daily Express* article reporting the news had the headline 'I've Roped My First Steer – says Stewart Granger'. Granger went on to explain: 'The nearest town is forty miles away. I have not yet sold my Los Angeles house. Jean is staying there at the moment, but I think the wide open spaces life is going to be great.' The reporter asks the question how much time film star Granger will have to be ranch-owner Granger. 'So far I have not had much chance to spend much time on the ranch, but I hope I shall be there quite a lot,' Granger replies. But he was to find that he did not have enough time to look after both projects properly. Romance would soon clash with reality, as the expense and difficulty involved in running such an enterprise from a distance had to be faced.

Granger's next film would turn out to be one of the worst in his career. *The Little Hut* is a dreary, unfunny and sexist so-called sex comedy that was adapted from a French stage farce and 'cleaned up' according to the then current juvenile Hollywood standards of sexual mores and Eisenhower's America. Basically, it is a desert island movie with Granger playing a neglectful husband stranded on the island after his yacht is sunk. His wife is played by Ava Gardner and his best friend by David Niven. The movie then plays with the possibility that the wife has previously had an affair with the best friend and will go to bed with him on the desert island with the husband being banished to the 'little hut' of the title, but this being 1957 and *The Little Hut* being an American movie typical of its time, naturally no adultery takes place or has taken place and it is much ado about absolutely nothing.

It is a forerunner to those Doris Day/Rock Hudson comedies of the 1960s, although compared with *The Little Hut*, those movies – such as *Pillow Talk* and *Send Me No Flowers* – are positive masterpieces. Granger's aspirations in real life are granted to his character, as he plays a wealthy English aristocrat who is much more interested in worldly affairs and his dog, Nelson, than his beautiful wife, who, on the desert island, sets out to make him jealous and more attentive by pretending that Niven has been having an affair with her for the last six years. There is a cameo appearance by the Italian comedy actor, Walter Chiari, who plays the chef on Granger's yacht. Chiari, unbelievably and insultingly, dresses up as a 'native' and terrorises the two men in the hope of enjoying Gardner's sexual favours. *The Little Hut* pretends to a kind of sophistication about sex, but betrays its suburban, puritanical standpoint at every turn. It is simply woeful.

During the shoot, Chiari and Gardner became an 'item' and Gardner got into the habit of having long lunches with her lover, which held up the afternoon schedule. Despite their friendship with Gardner, according to Graham Lord's biography of David Niven, Granger and Niven decided to complain to the producers about this behaviour. As Granger approached the powers that be on the set, he realised that Niven had melted away, which Granger considered typical: 'He never liked making trouble if he could get somebody else to make it for him.' Granger, on the other hand, seemed to look for trouble, but he seemed to envy Niven's ability to make himself popular: ' I was always rather jealous about the way that everybody seemed to love David. He had an enviable knack of seeming to be happy and people liked that.' The contrast with Granger could not have been starker. Niven may have been a rather bland and superficially jolly person with the ability to ingratiate himself, but Granger seemed to have an uncanny knack of appearing miserable and grumpy and upsetting most of the people he worked with. At times, his lack of popularity got to him.

Granger was never very effective in comedy parts because he would insist on acting 'funny'. A good comedy actor never strains for comic effect, eschews mugging and over-emphasis, and acts in comedy rather than acting comically. Cary Grant was an expert at that kind of role, for example, but unfortunately Granger wasn't. His performance is painful to watch, as he overacts and pulls faces and generally remains profoundly unfunny. David Niven is a better comedy actor than Granger but he too could do nothing with his part. The whole film is a total disaster and it scarcely could have done Granger's cause much good in Hollywood circles. However, Niven and Gardner were still big stars at the time and they also suffered from the lukewarm reception that the critics and the public gave to the film. It would be another decade or more before Hollywood treated sex in a mature way. *The Little Hut* pretends to be adult fare, but with its coyness and silly double entendres it only succeeds in appearing juvenile and dated.

The movie was largely shot at the Cinecittà Studios in Rome, which was then fast becoming the hub of European film-making and where many Hollywood productions would be shot over the next decade as the American film industry sought to avoid paying the high wages demanded by the technicians' guilds in the States. The temperature on the set sometimes reached 140°F so it made for a very uncomfortable shoot. A few sequences were shot in Jamaica.

The film involved the Grangers in another long separation and this at a time when Simmons was pregnant, but, according to Granger, she insisted that he should fulfil this filming obligation, as she did not want him to see her ballooning as her pregnancy progressed. It does seem odd, however, that a couple who professed such devotion to each other managed to be separated as often as they were. Meanwhile, the vultures of the entertainment press were poised to spread any disreputable rumour they could get their hands on or make up. The March 1957 issue of the scurrilous magazine *Confidential*, for example, purported to tell of 'the ants in Stewart Granger's pantry', an account of the supposed goings-on one weekend at 12 Charles Street in London where Granger was 'entertaining in very bachelor fashion'.

Shortly after he returned from completing *The Little Hut*, Jean Simmons gave birth to a daughter, Tracy, in the Cedars of Lebanon Hospital in Los Angeles. The Grangers had named their baby after their good friend

Spencer Tracy, who became the child's godfather. Thus, Granger, at the age of forty-four, had become a father for the third time, to the first and only child of his second marriage. He had bought an expensive second property hundreds of miles from L.A., which would need a great deal of attention if it were to prosper, and now he had this new responsibility. Meanwhile, he and Jean had to keep ahead of the game if they were to maintain their status in Hollywood. Granger never made things easy for himself. Indeed, it was almost as though he went out of his way to put more and more pressure on himself.

It was 1957 and Granger's seven-year contract with MGM was just about due to end. According to Granger in his autobiography, MGM offered him another seven-year contract. It is difficult to see why MGM would make such an offer at this stage in their history and in Granger's career. MGM had been divesting itself of most of its contract stars. Almost all of the big MGM stars had gone and the studio was certainly no longer able to maintain its proud boast that it had more stars than there were in heaven. Not only had the star actors been released but many of the long-serving directors, cameramen, art directors and technicians had also been cut from the payroll. MGM no longer required so many long-term employees because their movie production schedule had been drastically cut, as had the output of all the major Hollywood studios. The harsh economic facts were that half Hollywood's audience had vanished over the last decade. Why, then, would the studio offer Granger a new seven-year contract? It was obvious that Granger's career had peaked several years previously. He was now forty-four, an advanced age for any swashbuckling hero. He had not moved into character parts, which might have helped to prolong his days at the top. Whether this was an omission on his part, reflecting an unwillingness to face up to the reality of the passing years, or the result of the studio's desire to milk his romantic hero persona to its last drop, is difficult to gauge, but because he had not broadened his range, it was going to be increasingly hard to find suitable vehicles for this star whose movies had already produced very diminished box-office returns. In all these circumstances, the question has to be posed: how real was this offer? Granger had, in addition, been a 'pain in the ass' to the MGM executives, so it does not seem very likely that they would enthusiastically seek to prolong their relationship with this grumbling and ageing star. Perhaps Granger's recollection of this offer of a new MGM contract needs to be taken with a pinch of salt, a defensive reaction to his changed circumstances and to the sad fact that MGM did not want him any longer. Perhaps MGM did indeed make him an offer of renewal, but with terms attached that were much less favourable than his first contract and which Granger, in his pride, was bound to refuse. It is possible that MGM banked on his refusing these terms.

Whether it was coincidence or the result of Granger's then obsession with being a cowboy in real life, his next film featured him as a retired gunslinger and gambler, Tom Earley, returning to his home town to find his abandoned wife has died in the intervening years and that his teenage son hates him. It is a familiar western story of redemption, as the ageing ex-gunslinger atones for his sins by saving the township from the tyranny of a dastardly cattle baron who is determined to drive his herd through the town and destroy the livelihoods of the homesteaders. It has echoes of westerns such as *The Gunfighter*, which had starred Gregory Peck in 1950, and the wonderful *Shane* with Alan Ladd in 1953. However, *Gun Glory* is nowhere near in the class of those two films and Granger's aspirations to being a screen cowboy are sadly disappointed. He never really convinces as the ex-gunfighter and his mid-Atlantic accent grates. The storyline never veers from the clichéd and the conventional, with Granger single-handedly taking on the cattle baron and his henchmen. The family situation that he had destroyed by leaving his wife and son is reconstituted as he is supplied with a ready-made successor in the person of Rhonda Fleming, and his son forgives him for his past sins.

The ageing Lothario figure that Granger had played hitherto was now being trimmed back somewhat. His character is shown to be anxious to atone for youthful misdeeds and to re-create the family that he had so callously abandoned in the pursuit of adventure, a macho reputation and wealth. The gunfighter has to come out of retirement, as it were, but only temporarily so that order can be restored in the community and he can take his proper place in the patriarchal structure. By the end of the film, Earley/Granger is set fair to become a respectable husband and father once more, a veritable pillar of the community. At the end of *Shane*, by comparison, Alan Ladd as the gunslinger has to move on, leaving behind the community he has saved and the 'family' he loves, because he chose his path years before and has to pay for that choice. *Gun Glory* offers a more suburban conclusion, albeit much less romantic: the hero is subsumed by the values of the small town and cloaks himself in respectability. It is a long way from *Scaramouche*; the devil-may-care adventurer with a glint in his eye has at last settled down.

Granger had very caustic comments to make about the movie's producer, director and the young actor who played his son. Their appointments to the roles he ascribes wholly to Hollywood nepotism. He admits that he should have turned down the movie and accepted a suspension for the last year of his MGM contract, but the pressure of paying for the New Mexico ranch forced his hand. But this had been the story ever since he had first become a movie star in Britain. There were always pressing reasons why he had to go on making films he did not want to do and they were almost always financial. Granger had made yet another rod for his own back by impulsively buying his New Mexico ranch.

Gun Glory is an inglorious affair all round. It appears to have been made as double-bill fodder. By no means was this a top-budget movie and, as this was what MGM was offering Granger now, it must have been apparent that the studio had no further grandiose plans for their one-time major star. *Green Fire* had not taken off in box-office terms and had been unmemorable as a movie (to say the least), *Moonfleet* had been a commercial flop, *Footsteps in the Fog* and *The Last Hunt* had been received reasonably well, but *Bhowani Junction* had largely failed, while *The Little Hut* and *Gun Glory* had bombed. The prognosis for Granger's Hollywood career was not good and his seven-year contract with MGM was now coming to an end. Perhaps it was not the best time to have bought an expensive property in New Mexico and to add to his problems by taking another expensive decision, but that was exactly what Granger now contemplated.

It seems that most of his energy at this time was focused on the New Mexico ranch. What he remembered most about *Gun Glory* was his pride in the fact that for the scene where the hero has to separate a calf from its mother, he used a horse from his own ranch with the Granger brand 'T-4-J', the 'T' standing for his new daughter, Tracy, and the '4' and the 'J' standing for Jean, Jimmy, Jamie (his son by Elspeth March) and Lindsay (his daughter whose second name was Jean). It was as close as he would get to the coat-of-arms to which he probably aspired in his heart.

The rancher who had supplied MGM with the five hundred cattle that were required for the climactic stampede in *Gun Glory* came from Nogales in Arizona and this was where Granger would make his second investment in ranching. This time it would involve even more money. It was 10,000 acres with a large house, a swimming pool and a beautiful garden. This property was much closer to Los Angeles (about ninety minutes by plane to Tuscon, then an hour's drive to Nogales) and this was obviously a factor in the decision to buy it. The Grangers paid $500,000 for the ranch, the price including a herd of Santa Gertrudis cattle. They had to pay $75,000 as a first payment and the balance over the next five years. This would put increasing pressure on their marriage and careers. It does seem odd that Granger, and he appears to have been the prime mover in all of these deals, would enter into this new costly venture when he had not sold either his Hollywood home or the ranch in New Mexico. This was a man who wanted, it seems, to put himself and others round him under enormous strain in his quest to reach the perhaps hazy goals he had unconsciously set himself. He was Scaramouche adrift in a mad world, trying to stabilise things by investing in something solid – land and property.

However much he hated the press intruding into his private life, Granger did at times seem to court the newspapers when he wanted to project a favourable image of himself and his ventures. Typical of this is an article written in May 1958 by David Lewin, who had been invited by Granger to spend two days on the Nogales ranch. The article opens, 'The sign by the desert road out of Nogales, the Mexican frontier town, reads: "Yerba Buena Ranch. Owners J. and S. Granger". This is the new home of Jean Simmons and Stewart Granger . . . a home on the range with 10,000 acres, 350 head of cattle and a ranch house complete with swimming pool.' Lewin reports that Granger had taken two key decisions that week: first, to sack his manager and to take direct running of the ranch himself; and, two, to sell his New Mexico ranch. Granger is quoted as saying that every penny Jean and he possessed was invested in the ranch and that he lay awake at night worrying about the mortgage. Every time he made a movie, he said, he put the money he earned straight into the ranch. The impression created is that their marriage is very strong and that Jean Simmons is happy to be down home on the ranch: 'The drive to be an actress, to stay a star is being replaced,' said Jean Simmons. 'I don't want for anything now, I am very lucky.' She goes on to say that she would quit filming tomorrow but 'Jimmy' says we need the money to build up the ranch. 'Just so long as the old boy is happy, that is the main thing,' she concluded.

The article creates a very happy picture of this golden couple, devoted to one another, and living a dream life in the wonderful surroundings of the Arizona open range. But, with hindsight, we can interpret the reality behind the gush. Granger was clearly burdened by the debts he had accrued and it was fairly obvious that both of them had to continue to work as film stars in order to maintain the ranch. Two years after this article was published, Granger and Simmons would divorce. The anxieties connected with Granger's investments in ranches and cattle-breeding would almost certainly have much to do with their break-up. Marriages usually flounder over money or sex, or a combination of the two. The extreme worries that Granger had brought upon himself made him increasingly difficult to live with and this would prove fatal to their relationship.

Not only had Granger paid a considerable amount of money for the ranch and the property, but he followed that up by paying $250,00 for a

Charolais herd of cattle. He would pay $50,000 at the end of each of the five years after he acquired them. Granger did not do things by halves and he had set his heart upon this particular breed of cattle, so he had to have them.

Granger was soon in the running to be cast as Ben Hur in the remake that MGM planned of their 1920s epic. However, as he had 'refused' a new contract, MGM were unlikely to hand such a plum part to one of their departing and ageing stars, however much the producer Sam Zimbalist seemed to want him. He was then offered the second male lead, Messala, eventually played by Stephen Boyd, and Granger agreed to do that if Marlon Brando was playing Ben Hur. When Charlton Heston was finally cast as the hero, Granger turned down Messala, citing his agent's dictum that he would not allow him to play second fiddle to someone like Heston, who was at that time not the major star he became as a result of this movie. If his agent Bert Allenberg did advise Granger to turn this role down, it seems a very curious piece of advice to give to a client who was clearly desperately in need of a major role in a major film, which *Ben Hur* manifestly was going to be. What actually happened is lost in the mists of time, but it seems odd that a man like Granger, who always prided himself on being his own man and on making his own decisions, should so meekly accept his agent's advice, although Allenberg was one of the few men in the business whom he really respected. If he had gone against his agent's advice and played Messala, it would have undoubtedly kept Granger in the big league longer; the role certainly did Stephen Boyd's career no harm.

Ben Hur is one of a number of major films that Granger almost starred in but for various reasons he lost out on. Others included *Quo Vadis*, *Ivanhoe*, *The Adventures of Quentin Durward*, *A Star Is Born* and *Mogambo*. Six major features at least that Granger could have added to his curriculum vitae. He would have certainly been more effective than the wooden Robert Taylor in *Quo Vadis* and the two adaptations of the Sir Walter Scott novels; he might have been just as effective as Clark Gable opposite Grace Kelly and Ava Gardner in *Mogambo*. Only in *A Star Is Born* would Granger have suffered in comparison with James Mason, who made the part of the alcoholic, self-destructive and ageing movie star his own. Granger 'lost' these films as a result of a mixture of pigheadedness, insensitivity, star pecking order and sheer lack of judgement. In the latter part of his life, he often expressed his regrets that he had not fulfilled his talent and lamented his lost opportunities. Every single individual can contemplate his or her life and rue wrong turnings and thwarted hopes. Granger had a lot of those to think about in his latter years.

Thus, instead of *Ben Hur*, Granger was now contracted to appear in two low-budget movies to be made for Romulus Films, a British production company that had made the highly successful *Room at the Top*. After that, he was to don his safari gear again as he was off to India to shoot *Harry Black and the Tiger*. His role as Quatermain in *King Solomon's Mines* had identified him with safari movies and his liking for hunting big game was probably also a factor in his accepting the part. His MGM days were over: he was now a freelance star and was returning to the country of his birth to make what was little more than a second feature. The glory days were in the past and his box-office clout had vanished. For all MGM's talk about the studio being one big happy family, when push came to shove it was all about business and who could make you money. In that sense, GM was no different from any other large corporation. It was considered that Granger could no longer cut the mustard and he had been cast aside, whatever the circumstances of the parting may have been. If MGM had really wanted to keep Granger on a long-term contract, they would have made him an offer he could not have refused. As it was, he was now adrift in the film-making ocean and friendly ports were few and far between. For a worrier like Granger, he must have been anxious that his best years were behind him, especially as he had made things difficult financially for himself just at the time when his future was at its most uncertain. Whatever Granger said publicly about hating being a movie star, it was his status in the film business that had brought him fame, attention, wealth and constant employment. It must have been very difficult to contemplate all of that vanishing, but he was going to have to get used to the fact that his career would produce ever-diminishing returns over the next thirty years of his life. For those who disliked him, and there were more than a few of them around, the idea that the arrogant Stewart Granger was becoming a has-been must have been sweet music in their ears.

Chapter 8

DIVORCE AND DECLINE

WHEN GRANGER RETURNED to London to shoot *The Whole Truth*, he felt like a stranger in his own country. He enjoyed catching up with his friends and his first wife and his children, but it is clear that, having taken the step of becoming an American citizen, he no longer felt quite at home in Britain. Some people never feel at home wherever they end up, however, and Granger may have been such a type. Part of the swashbuckler ideal is, of course, never to settle down, to keep moving on and to live a free and unfettered existence. Some significant part of Stewart Granger yearned for that freedom, but another enduring side of him longed for intimacy and closeness as well. Perhaps in that, he was no different to millions of other men and many women dealing with the conflicting needs of independence and interdependence.

If the rationale behind turning down the part of Messala in *Ben Hur* had indeed been that his agent did not want him to play a supporting role to Charlton Heston, then, when the movies Granger did instead of *Ben Hur* are weighed in the balance, the validity and sense of that advice have to be queried. *Ben Hur* would go on to become one of the all-time grossers in Hollywood history and Granger would have certainly made a greater impact as the second male lead in that one movie than in all the movies he made in the couple of years following that curious decision. As it was, his first movie after his contract ended at MGM was *The Whole Truth*, a modest whodunit adapted from a stage play by Philip Mackie. With a running time of eighty-four minutes and limited production values, the movie was clearly destined to be double-bill fodder and that was indeed how it was treated by the distributors when it was released in 1958.

Granger plays an American film producer, Max Poulton, who is accused of the murder of a film actress with whom he has had an affair. As George Sanders is on hand as a smooth villain, the audience needed to be extremely stupid not to pick out the real murderer. Donna Reed played Granger's wife and the film was directed by John Guillermin, who would later direct *Waltz of the Toreadors*, *The Blue Max* and the 1976 remake of *King Kong*. Guillermin joined the long list of directors with whom Granger had difficulties, Granger describing him as 'peculiarly lacking in charm, to say the least'.

The truth behind *The Whole Truth* is that this film marked the start of the real decline in Granger's stock as a high-ranking movie star. His career had been in decline for a number of years, but with this 'banishment' to his native country to make a routine cheapie and quickie, it must have been obvious to people in the industry, and probably to Granger himself, that the decline was now terminal. He had not really done much to stave off the inevitable day when his currency as a romantic hero would lose almost its total value. If we compare him with, say, Gregory Peck, another heart-throb and romantic hero of roughly the same age as Granger, we can see that Peck had managed to land some parts that identified him as an actor with a broader range than westerns or adventure movies. He had played Captain Ahab in *Moby Dick* and had been ridiculed in many quarters because of it, but at least he had that role under his belt. He had taken straight dramatic roles in films such as *The Snows of Kilimanjaro* and *The Man in the Grey Flannel Suit*, so he was well placed in his late forties to make the transition from romantic leading man to dramatic actor. He had a total triumph in the 1962 *To Kill a Mockingbird* playing the lawyer Atticus Finch. Granger's career at the top would not be similarly prolonged partly because he had not moved on from the standard Stewart Granger part, so producers were unwilling to take a chance on an actor whom audiences so closely identified as a swashbuckling icon.

When Granger returned to America after making *The Whole Truth*, he had a short turn-round before he had to head off to India for three months to shoot *Harry Black and the Tiger*. It would be another long separation from his wife and child and, according to Granger, Simmons took it very badly. For a time, their marriage seemed to teeter on the edge of break-up, as Granger explained to the 'hysterical' Simmons that they had taken the pledge to make as many movies as they could so they could pay for the ranch. 'Miserably, I drove to the airport,' Granger wrote, 'thinking I'd probably blown my marriage and cursing myself for risking everything for that bloody ranch, which would mean nothing if we couldn't all be together to enjoy it.'

Husband and wife were reconciled, but it was a presage of what was to come shortly. It appears that Granger had got on a treadmill and he couldn't get off. His priorities seem confused to the outsider: on the one hand he was protesting that his marriage and family were the most important things in his life, but on the other hand he was piling more and more responsibilities and pressure on himself, burdens that could only in time gnaw away at the security of his personal life and which meant he had to go on making whatever movie was offered to him, thereby initiating the long separations between husband and wife that must have eventually contributed to the break-up of their marriage.

An interview he had given the *Sunday Express* newspaper in October 1957 had laid it on the line: 'Work I Must, Says Granger – It's the Mortgage'. Yet again, a newspaper article about Granger starts with a comment about how disliked the star was: 'Until the other day, I always placed Stewart Granger high on my list of arrogant, mirror-worshipping, self-centred, critic-hating egotists,' wrote the reporter. 'I make awful films,' Granger is reported as saying. 'I do it because I need money to pay off the mortgage on my 10,000 acre Arizona ranch.' When he is asked about his 'arrogance', he replies that he still has plenty of that, but he preferred to think of it as 'big personality'. His comments in this article smack of defensiveness. Reading between the lines, however, his sense of hurt, his sensitivity to the criticism he received and the charge that he was arrogant can be deduced. Again, he falls back on the excuse that journalists hated him because he had married 'their darling Jean', for which they had never forgiven him.

Harry Black and the Tiger scarcely seems worth the sacrifice of Granger separating himself from his wife for the three months of shooting on location in India. Part of the attraction of the movie for him may have been the fact it might give him the opportunity to hunt big game again. However, the producer, John Brabourne, forbade him to join in a tiger hunt because the insurers for the movie would not stand for the star endangering himself unnecessarily in his own time. So Granger had reluctantly to abide by this ruling. Another disappointment was that 20th Century Fox had refused to release his old friend, Deborah Kerr, to co-star with him. Apart from their abiding friendship, another reason for his chagrin at having Barbara Rush take Kerr's place may have been the lost opportunity of replicating the Granger–Kerr screen partnership from *King Solomon's Mines*. Clearly, the producers hoped to reproduce some of the success of that movie, but they were to be disappointed.

Leonard Maltin describes *Harry Black and the Tiger* as a 'mouldy jungle film tangled in the underbrush' and it is hard to disagree with this verdict. Granger plays a famous tiger hunter who is in love with his best friend's wife. The Indian locations look impressive and there is the required tiger hunt sequence, but the whole enterprise is a damp squib. *King Solomon's Mines* may not be one of the all-time classics of the cinema, but *Harry Black* by comparison is dire indeed. It is all the sadder because it evokes memories of Granger in his prime and at the peak of his career. The film looks like a rather pathetic attempt to re-create past glories. Certainly, it was received tepidly, at best, and with derision at worst. This was not the kind of movie that was likely to rescue Granger's fortunes and it was for this farce that he had left his disenchanted wife for three whole months.

The June 1958 edition of the *ABC Film Review* devoted its regular feature 'Star Interview' to Granger. The interview took place on the set of *Harry Black*. It starts with the almost regulation reference to Granger's 'awkward customer' reputation – 'I'd heard that Stewart Granger was brusque, arrogant, hard to get' – yet the interviewer, Norman Taylor, is won over and finds that the star is 'one of the most charming, sympathetic, friendly stars of the screen that I have ever met'. Now that Granger's career was decidedly on the wane, he seemed to become more co-operative with the press, perhaps feeling that he needed all the good publicity he could get at that juncture of his career. During the interview, Granger states that he would like nothing better right then than to be at home with his wife and children. He rhapsodises about his Arizona ranch, but mentions that they are thinking of moving to Colorado because there the climate was better. It seems odd that he should already be contemplating selling the Arizona ranch and buying yet another property. He discusses the planned movie he is scheduled to make with Jean Simmons, an adaptation of Eric Ambler's novel *The Night Comers* (the movie was never made). 'Now here, I'm glad to say,' wrote Taylor rather piously, 'was a film star husband who obviously adored and admired his film star wife.' As was usual when Granger gave interviews during his marriage to Simmons, he makes frequent loving and admiring references to her. The impression is given that she was a kind of talisman for him, a yardstick of his success, attractiveness and fame. With hindsight, this lightweight interview in that most lightweight of movie magazines appears rather sad now, given that two years later their marriage would be over.

The following few months must have been among the worst in Granger's life. In his autobiography, he writes about how difficult it was for him to cope with the troubles over his ranches. Although he does not go into minute detail, it seems clear that he teetered on the edge of breakdown during this period: 'I was obviously suffering a nervous reaction to all the troubles I'd been having. I hadn't really got over the strain of the Hughes years.' The Hughes case had been seven years previously, so clearly he had not come to terms with the anxieties that contretemps had caused, and now he was brooding over his clash with his former ranch foreman, whom he claimed had been cheating him. Beyond that particular issue, he had to wrestle with his prevailing sense of betrayal and paranoia. By his own admission, he had become unloving and irritable. He was burdened with the sense that he had taken on too many commitments and that he had to go on working to pay the bills. Money worries plus the ghosts that haunted him from the past were beginning to erode his marriage further and making him a miserable human being in the process.

At this low point, he then had to absorb the blow of the second film that he had contracted to do for Romulus being cancelled. This was *The Night Comers*. It left him with no film roles on the horizon and the difficulty of quickly finding another movie to fill this gap. It must have been all the more galling because he could have been playing Messala in *Ben Hur* at that time. However, his wife was able to earn immediate money when she took the part of the evangelist in *Elmer Gantry* opposite Burt Lancaster. They desperately needed money at this point so Simmons had to go to work. *Elmer Gantry* was to be directed by Richard Brooks, whom Granger had not warmed to in their previous professional association. Brooks was to play a significant part in both their lives in a very short time.

While Granger was wrestling with his emotional, financial, professional and marital problems, he was dealt a double blow with the deaths of two of his closest friends and associates, Sam Zimbalist, the producer, who had wanted him to play Messala, and Bert Allenberg, Granger's agent, who had advised him not to play Messala. Both deaths were sudden and it is clear from what Granger wrote about both these men that he was very upset. Granger did not give his trust easily to people, but these two people had won his confidence. Their deaths could scarcely have come at a worst time for him.

Jean Simmons left to make *Elmer Gantry* in Hollywood, while Granger stayed alone on his Arizona ranch. When he visited her in Los Angeles, he found it difficult to listen to her tales about the making of the movie and the people she was making it with. Granger felt left out and there may have been a strong element of competition in his attitude. In his autobiography, he states that he had made eighteen Hollywood films to her twelve and that he had been the main breadwinner. Now the tables seemed to have been reversed: he had no film in his immediate schedule and had been shorn of his major star status; she, by contrast, was starring in a plum role in an important movie opposite one of the biggest stars in Hollywood and was being directed by the 'detested' Richard Brooks. As Granger almost certainly had perceived himself as her mentor and guide in her professional and personal life, it may have been difficult for him to come to terms with the fact that his wife was now by far the bigger star and was showing her independence from him. The thought must have been present in his mind that she had outgrown him. For a man as insecure as Granger, this must have been a shattering insight.

Granger claims that the issue that forced the final breakdown in their marriage was Simmons's commitment to work for five extra days on *Elmer Gantry* for free. He exploded with anger when she announced this to him on the telephone, arguing that they were desperately in need of money at that stage so why should she work for nothing? Simmons asked for a divorce there and then, and angrily he said she could have one if that's what she wanted. Pride no doubt played a part in his response to this situation. He was now in the less powerful position, but he was not the kind of man who could acknowledge that. His anger about the extra five days' work seems exaggerated and it was almost certainly a symptom of his feeling of loneliness and powerlessness. He may also have suspected that there was a burgeoning relationship between Richard Brooks and his wife. His career and his life in general must have appeared to be slipping away from him. But he could not show his panic and vulnerability, even to his wife. He was, after all, a man of courage and of independent attitudes – on screen, that was.

That Christmas of 1959 was not a happy period. Granger and Simmons had invited Laurence Olivier to stay with them over the festive period and they agreed to act as though there were nothing wrong with their marriage, not just for appearances' sake, but because Olivier himself was going through a personal crisis at that time. He was trying to decide whether he ought to divorce his wife Vivien Leigh and marry his new love, Joan Plowright, who was considerably younger than himself. Olivier and Vivien Leigh had been the 'golden couple' of the 1940s and it could be said that Granger and Simmons had been their equivalent in the 1950s, but, ironically, here were the three of them spending Christmas together at the end of the decade with the Grangers on the edge of divorce and Olivier wrestling with his guilt about 'abandoning' Leigh, who had had numerous breakdowns in the course of their marriage and whose deteriorating mental health was driving Olivier to distraction.

By the end of his visit, Olivier had firmly decided that he must divorce Leigh, even though he would feel badly about deserting her. Simmons supported him in this move, whilst Granger advised against divorce, citing what this would do to Leigh. Simmons's advocacy (according to Granger's version of events) upset Granger because he sensed that she identified with Olivier's situation, although she had denied to him that there was anyone else in her life. Olivier inadvertently rubbed salt in their wounds by stating that it was seeing the two of them together and how much they loved one another that had made him finally decide to take the step because he wanted that kind of happiness in his life, too. Either Olivier was so self-absorbed with his own dilemmas during this visit that he did not sense the real state of their marriage or the Grangers must have acted out in a most convincing manner that they were still the same loving golden couple they had been a decade previously.

After Christmas, Simmons returned to Los Angeles with Tracy, their daughter, and Granger remained on the Arizona ranch, whereupon he managed to injure himself quite seriously while trying to rope a steer. This is one of the numerous injuries that Granger managed to sustain while playing his self-imposed 'manly role' both on and off the screen. He had already damaged his right knee when he had been filming *Scaramouche*, so now the doctor advised a cartilage operation. Granger suffered a serious reaction as a result of an infected catheter, a condition made worse by the antibiotics he was subsequently given. He lost nearly two stone within a week. He was looked after by Simmons in the rented house they had taken in Beverly Hills, but his condition deteriorated and he was rushed back to hospital. The doctors managed to save him, but it had been a close call.

It is difficult not to interpret these serious health problems, which culminated in a crisis that could have caused his death, as an unconscious cry for help on Granger's part. Like many men of his generation, he was, almost certainly, not a man who could easily own up to his vulnerability, emotional needs or sense of abandonment. All his emotional training in life, from his early family experiences, his schooldays, his short-lived army career and the cut-throat milieu of the British and Hollywood film industry, would have taught him that men had to be tough and not show their deepest emotions, that they had to 'play the man', accept hard knocks and just get on with life. Whining was for wimps or for those men who were not manly at all and therefore 'suspect'. He had deliberately set out to play the hero on screen and act the manly role off screen. But now he was faced with one of the most significant emotional crises of his life: his beloved young wife wanted a divorce. His sense of hurt and yes, perhaps betrayal, must have been profound, and this was happening at a time when his professional life was definitely on the slide while hers seemed to be still on the up.

So what outlet had a man like Granger for his feelings? He had always been an angry man, an eternal grumbler, but that anger and grumbling were only symptoms of a deep, unresolved emotional insecurity. One does not need to be a complete believer in the mind–body cause-and-effect theory of physical illness to wonder about the timing of this brush with death. It was Granger's unconscious *cri-de-coeur*; he was expressing his distress in one of the few ways he would allow himself, almost total physical breakdown, an illness during which he would be tended in part by the very person whose imminent 'departure' from his life had forced the crisis in the first place.

Simmons then left for England to make *The Grass Is Greener* with Robert Mitchum, Cary Grant and Deborah Kerr. While she was there, she announced that she was seeking a divorce. The case was filed in Nogales, Arizona on 7 July, and the divorce was granted on 12 August 1960 on the grounds of 'outrageous cruelty'. Jean Simmons asked for custody of their daughter, Tracy, but the agreement over joint property seemed to cause no problems. It is clear that they still cared about one another, despite the claims of 'outrageous cruelty', and neither wanted to cause any additional stress to the other party. They would remain on good terms and Granger would often publicly refer to Simmons in interviews with great affection, giving the strong impression that he had never really come to terms with the break-up of the marriage. He decided he did not want to stay in Hollywood to make films because their paths might cross, and the Arizona ranch was no longer a place where he wanted to be without his wife and children. His two children by Elspeth March now returned to England to live with their mother, with whom Granger also remained on good terms with for the rest of his life. The ranch was put up for sale, but it would not be sold till 1966, when it fetched $2 million. The venture that Granger had embarked upon with such great enthusiasm a few years previously had lost its attraction for him. It was an example of another initiative that somehow he did not follow through. This was another of the 'incomplete' aspects of his life along with his army career, his film star career, his other business ventures and, yes, his marriages as well. He was a man of sudden enthusiasms and seemed capable of walking away from things that he had started. He had a low threshold of boredom, a characteristic of gamblers who need constant excitement in their lives, and a lifelong dissatisfaction that gnawed away inside him.

Only the two people involved in the break-up of a marriage can ever truly know why their relationship ended. Outsiders can only surmise. Granger was in his mid-thirties and Simmons was only a teenager when they started a relationship. She had, of course, been around in the film world for several years and had undoubtedly a maturity beyond her years. However, an age gap of sixteen years is an important factor, especially when one of the partners is so young. There must have been a strong element of father–daughter or mentor–pupil about their relationship and, because they were both actors, manager and client. When they divorced in 1960, Granger was forty-seven and Simmons thirty-one. The power equation in their marriage had swung towards Simmons. Her career was still vibrant with all kinds of possibilities, while his was clearly on the way down. The man she had fallen in love with as a teenager, that romantic, handsome, happy-go-lucky fellow, had been shown to have feet of clay. He was in fact an obsessive worrier, an eternal grump, a man who was more often than not in conflict with colleagues and business associates, a driven individual who had piled pressure after pressure onto them until it had become almost unbearable and untenable. Then there had been the long separations during the course of their ten-year marriage and the temptations that working in Hollywood and loneliness would throw up. Granger had been possessive of his young and beautiful wife, and, by his own admission, prone to jealousy. With his mood swings, anger, combative nature, indulgence in alcohol and tobacco, spendthrift ways and insensitivity, he could not have been an easy husband. Yet he had loved her in his own way, although perhaps he found it difficult to fully commit himself to any relationship with a woman, given his own emotional blockages. Although he clearly regretted the divorce, some part of him, the Scaramouche side, probably relished a renewal of his male freedoms. That is in no way to diminish the hurt that he must have felt as his marriage folded, because he had not been the initiator of the break-up. His version of the story, however, certainly points to the fact that he did not battle to hold on to Simmons.

Granger's sense of hurt must have been intensified when Jean Simmons married her director on *Elmer Gantry*, Richard Brooks, on 1 November 1960, only a few months after the granting of their divorce. Brooks had directed Granger in *The Light Touch* and *The Last Hunt* and it is clear there was little love lost between the two men. Brooks was a tough guy of Hollywood, strong-willed and domineering. It is worthy of note that he was a year older than Granger so Simmons swapped one much older man for another much older man. The marriage would last for sixteen years until it ended in divorce in 1977. Granger's successor was Hollywood's idea of an intellectual and, indeed, Brooks was more a writer than a director of movies. Scaramouche had given way to a cut-price Hemingway.

The fact that Jean Simmons remarried so quickly after their divorce, and to a man who was so different to him and so disliked by him, must have made the bitter pill of their divorce even harder for Granger to swallow. 'I don't mind Jean leaving me,' he said some time after. 'It's like a child leaving an over-protective parent. But it's the guy she chose – that's what got me. Can you imagine anyone wanting to marry Richard Brooks?' The implication is that Simmons had traded in an Adonis for someone far less attractive, but in describing himself as an over-protective parent, he does show some self-knowledge. 'The trouble is that I did everything for Jean in our marriage. I taught her how to read, how to walk, how to carry herself. She was such a child. Our entire relationship was like *Pygmalion*.' There is more than the occasional bitter remark about women, and specifically about Simmons, in his autobiography and in some of his later interviews, so his latent misogyny could only have been stoked by the divorce and the circumstances surrounding it.

It is telling that Granger's autobiography ends in 1960, the year of the divorce and his departure from Hollywood. As the book was published in 1981, it seems odd that he should end the story of his life at that juncture. It is almost as though he is saying that nothing that had happened to him since then was worthy of the tale. It could be that he planned a second part to his autobiography which would cover the later years of his life, but, if that was the idea, then it never happened. I think it is a safe conclusion to make that he considered 1960 as some kind of closure, the ending of the really important Stewart Granger story, which culminated in his divorce from Jean Simmons and his last Hollywood movie. And yet he would live for another thirty-three years, would be involved in making numerous films and in other business ventures, and would marry again and start yet another family. Somehow, despite this, it would appear that, in his mind, 1960 was the turning-point in his life.

It is in fact difficult to disagree with that assessment, although thirty-three years of someone's life cannot be summarily dismissed. But Stewart Granger, the world-famous movie star, would no longer be nearly as famous, and none of the films he would make in the next two decades would make anywhere near the impact of *The Man in Grey*, *King Solomon's Mines* or *Scaramouche*. He had to come to terms with the harsh reality that many people would soon forget him and that new generations would scarcely know who he was at all. Yes, his old movies would turn up repeatedly on television and cable channels, but the films he would be making post-Hollywood would largely go unnoticed. For a man who had been as famous as Granger, it must suddenly have been a different ball game. If he wasn't Stewart Granger any longer, who was he? Jimmy Stewart from the Old Brompton Road?

Granger had been no ten-day wonder, but his rise to the top and his tenure there were comparatively short-lived. From nowhere, he had become an overnight star in 1943 as a result of *The Man in Grey*. He had been a top British star until 1949 when he went to Hollywood. Even by 1952, there were signs that his status as a top Hollywood box-office draw was beginning to weaken. So as a really important international star, he had no more than three or four years at the very top. Thereafter, he was trading on his past, and towards the end of his Hollywood years the decline was very rapid. Nevertheless, very few British stars have maintained a top star status Hollywood career over a period of many years: Chaplin, Ronald Colman, Cary Grant, Deborah Kerr, David Niven, Julie Andrews to a degree, Richard Burton perhaps when he was married to Elizabeth Taylor. Others such as Laurence Olivier, James Mason, Albert Finney and Michael Caine have had their successes in Hollywood, but none can be counted as truly consistent top box-office draws. Granger was, for a short period, exactly that. But it did not last, partly because his kind of swashbuckling, romantic hero was rapidly going out of fashion, and partly because he was thirty-seven when he made his first Hollywood movie and Hollywood can forgive anything in their heart-throbs other than the ageing process. Then there had been the reputation of a troublemaker and a grumbler that Granger had acquired, and some strange decisions about the movies he made. The truth is that time had caught up with Stewart Granger and the greying temples of this devil-may-care adventurer told their own tale. He had never really grown up on screen, but he could no longer play the eternal adolescent male.

Before Granger started work on the last Hollywood movie he made, he returned to Britain, announcing that he wanted to come home. A *Daily Express* reporter described him as looking fit, relaxed and tanned despite his recent divorce. Granger tells the readers that he wants to see London again and be near his mother in Cornwall, now that she was seventy-seven. He refers to the fact that he was selling the Arizona ranch, but that the money he would get for it would not go far because he had wives and children to support. He had already moved from the ranch to an apartment on the Sunset Strip in Hollywood. In the article Granger praises his first wife, Elspeth March, for her support during his divorce from Simmons. He states that he is going to be an actor once again and not a rancher. There is not only the Hollywood film in his schedule, but he has signed to do a British movie *Sleeping Partners* (eventually made with the title *The Secret Partner*) and two Italian movies. He is to give himself three years as a film star and hopes to have big parts and earn big money, then he wants to give up acting and direct instead. He acknowledges that Jean Simmons still has a highly successful career in Hollywood, but that, for him, there was nothing to hold him there. The interview gives the impression of a man whistling in the dark, expressing aspirations for the future and yet somehow conveying the impression that he knows the game is up. He appears to be looking to the future, but so much of what he says is about the past. How he was feeling inside is hard to gauge, but a fair assessment would be that he was a worried man. He may have felt that his gambler's luck had almost run out.

North to Alaska was a John Wayne movie, and that about sums it up. A couple of years previously, Allenberg, Granger's agent, had not wanted his client playing second fiddle to Charlton Heston in *Ben Hur*. Now here was Granger playing third fiddle at least to John Wayne in a routine actioner, a movie, which, if it was to be remembered at all, would be marked down as another mindless Wayne flick. As the title intimates, it is set in Alaska (in 1890) and concerns gold-prospecting. It is a brawling comedy western that no doubt pleased Wayne fans, but did little to enhance the art of the cinema or the status of the western genre. Granger plays Wayne's partner and sidekick, and others involved in this vulgar effort include Ernie Kovacs, the elegant Capucine and Fabian, a then-teenage sensation who sings a perfectly dreadful song in the course of the action. There is also a lamentable title song sung under the opening titles by one Tommy Horton. It is that kind of movie. Granger himself dismisses it as 'slapstick comedy' and subtle it certainly is not.

The director was Henry Hathaway, a notoriously tough bully of a director, who was added to the long list disliked by Granger. Granger was very nervous at the beginning of the shoot and drank alcohol to give himself the confidence to get through the scenes with Wayne. His anxiety must surely have had to do with what he had been through in recent months and his fear that he could no longer cut it in Hollywood. It is not difficult to feel sympathy for him in these circumstances, and the fact that he had to deal with the ultra-macho Hathaway and the equally insensitive Wayne could only have added to his problems. He must have been conscious that he was not the star of the movie and that his part was little more than an enlarged sidekick role. It was a less than glorious ending to his Hollywood career and he knew it. However, it seems he soon recovered his self-esteem enough to show his anger at Hathaway's directing methods. At one point in the shoot, he grabbed Hathaway and told him in very direct terms that if he did not stop treating him in the way he was, he would 'break his fucking jaw'. Hathaway was a kind of cut-price John Ford and *North to Alaska* has all the hallmarks of the knockabout, crude, macho aspect of Ford. (Ford's health was seriously ailing by this time and Hathaway was probably a substitute director.) Five minutes into the film, there is a comic bar-room brawl, which is always a bad sign for any movie. It ends with another bar-room brawl, which is portrayed as great male fun and in which no one really gets hurt. A gauge of how secondary Granger's role is in the film is how little screen time he is allowed. He is in the opening Alaskan section, then disappears from the film for almost an hour, as the action moves with Wayne to Seattle and back to Alaska. Not only that, for the first time since *Waterloo Road*, Granger fails to get the girl in the end. Wayne/McCord brings Capucine/Angel back from Seattle to console Granger/George, whose fiancée has already dumped him, but she has only got eyes for Wayne, and Granger has to play cupid for the rest of the film, bringing the two together for the regulation happy ending. Thus, the great romantic swashbuckler loses the girl to an ageing and broadening Wayne. Naturally, the two stars have to fight one another at some point in the movie and Wayne inevitably wins that one, too. The writing was finally on the Hollywood wall for Granger as a romantic leading man. He was now the second lead who loses the girl, a sort of more macho Gig Young, and he even has to lose punch-ups as well.

North to Alaska, then, was the last Hollywood movie Granger made and the last really major movie he appeared in that gave him star billing. His next film, *The Secret Partner*, would bring him down to earth with a bump. This production was Poverty Row stuff, destined to be a programme-filler at best. To call it a modest thriller would be to exaggerate its worth. It resembles those Scotland Yard Edgar Lustgarten shorts familiar to British film-goers in the 1950s and 1960s, especially in terms of the production values and the feebleness of the plot and presentation.

Granger plays the owner of a shipping business, John Brent, who carries out the robbery of a large amount of money from his own premises and deliberately frames himself for the crime in the process. This elaborate plan then involves him in escaping from police custody in order for him to prove to the police that he has been framed by a man in a mask who has used blackmail, drugs and violence to set it up to look as though Granger/Brent has carried out the robbery, which, in fact, he has. The man in the mask, however, is Granger/Brent himself, but he convinces the police that he is innocent. His wife has been his accomplice in all of this, but at the end of the movie she tells him she is leaving him because she is so disenchanted with him. Thereupon, our 'hero' has a change of heart, and hands the money back to the police saying that it was left on his doorstep. Although the police realise that he has been the mastermind behind the caper, they decide to let it go as the money has been safely returned.

Thrillers are quite often implausible, but *The Secret Partner* takes implausibility to new heights. The plotting is full of holes and highly unlikely twists and turns. It is the kind of movie, like the Edgar Lustgarten series, destined to provoke shrieks of disbelieving laughter from audiences. It is the cinematic equivalent of those dire thrillers that repertory companies in summer seasons at seaside resorts would produce in order to woo customers in from rain-soaked beaches. The red herrings are blatant, the motivations paper-thin and the police as dim as any that ever graced the silver screen. From the credits on, this film screeches 'B-movie'. The musical soundtrack is of the jarring-chords-at-moments-of-high-drama type. *The Secret Partner* was dated when it was first shown in 1961. Now it has acquired a certain period charm if you are in a very indulgent mood, because it is so genuinely bad.

Granger maintains a cheerful front through all of this and radiates energy and that familiar 'breeziness', but he must have known he was starring in a dismal movie. Others involved in the preposterous plot are Bernard Lee, as a Scotland Yard detective on the eve of retirement, Haya Harareet as Granger's wife and Hugh Burden as his dislikeable business partner, whom the movie makes number one suspect until Granger appears in his mask and takes it off with a flourish. Granger as Scaramouche had worn a mask, which he removed at the climax of the movie to reveal his real identity. In this film, the taking off of the mask reveals no more than the silliness of the whole story.

At the end of *The Secret Partner*, the lonely Granger/Brent is shown wandering alone over a London bridge, having been abandoned by his wife and with all his plans in pieces. Moody music underscores the character's melancholy. The intention is to make you feel sympathy for the character, which the movie signally fails to do. However, in some ways, this scene at the close of this dreadful movie reflects some of the reality of Granger's life at that time. His wife had divorced him and he was on his own in life once again. Financial worries had helped to create divisions between the two of them, just as Granger/Brent's machinations had finally alienated his otherwise loyal wife from him. It seems that bad art was imitating life in rather an uncanny way and this is another example of how Granger's screen roles, whether by unconscious design or sheer accident, seem to reflect his own aspirations and defeats.

Granger had been an international star in the true sense of the term when he was at his peak during his MGM contract, but now he was a peripatetic 'international star' in the sense that he hopped from country to country making movies wherever he could earn a crust and have a starring role. Italy was a hotbed of film production in the 1960s and it was to that country that Granger now sped to make two Italian movies almost back-to-back, one a swashbuckler, *The Swordsman of Siena,* and the other a cut-price epic, *Sodom and Gomorrah.* It would have been some consolation to Granger that he was the only major star in either of these productions and his presence in both was intended to be an attraction to the US and wider European markets. They also no doubt earned him some real money, although it is likely that by this stage in his career, his services came far cheaper than in his glory days. However, he was still working and if he was suffering emotionally from the aftermath of his divorce, which he clearly was, then at least he had the work to keep him busy and to stop him from feeling too sorry for himself.

The Swordsman of Siena in some ways resembles those minor swash-bucklers that Errol Flynn made in Europe in his declining years, such as *The Adventures of Captain Fabian* and *Crossed Swords*. Swashbuckling stars have a relatively short shelf life and their 'sell-by date' rapidly approaches by the time they are in their forties. Flynn was well into his forties by the time he made his last swashbucklers, but because he had indulged in all kinds of excesses, on screen in these movies he looked older and more dissipated than his years. It is rather a sad spectacle watching the once athletically handsome Flynn in these third-rate movies try to reproduce the screen antics of his much younger self. Granger, by comparison, was almost fifty by the time he made *Siena* and frankly it shows. It is not so much that he has his lost physical fitness along the way; it is more a matter of the inappro-priateness of this clearly middle-aged man behaving like a retarded adolescent and enacting Boy's Own adventures of the 'and-with-one-bound-the-hero-escapes' ilk. There is a time when the screen swashbuckler has to call a halt to such high jinks and say enough is enough. Sadly, Granger needed the pay day too much to heed the inner voice that must have been telling him he was too old for this kind of nonsense.

Nevertheless, *The Swordsman of Siena* was a fairly elaborate production in Cinemascope and colour, so it was something of a step up from *The Secret Partner*. Yet the movie was destined to be released in English-speaking countries in a dreadful dubbed version. Granger's voice was obviously his own, but the mainly Italian cast were badly dubbed, which constantly undermines any pretensions the movie might have. Granger plays an Englishman in Tuscany in the seventeenth century employed by the Spanish governor as a bodyguard to the Italian woman he is due to marry in an attempt to woo the local populace and reconcile them to foreign oppression. Needless to say, the adventurer Stanswood/Granger eventually discards his generally cynical and mercenary attitude to life in general and throws his lot in with the local subversives, leading them to the overthrow of their Spanish oppressors, after he has carried their colours in the famous horse race round the square and streets of Siena. After the usual combative hero–heroine relationship characteristic of Granger's on-screen love-life, he wins the heart of the intended bride of the rascally Spaniard. After all, Granger almost always got the girl in the end, even though he may have to renounce his love for the purposes of the plot.

Granger plays the hero with his tongue firmly in his cheek. He is particularly irritating in his scenes with the two women he is represented as being interested in (played by Sylva Koscina and Christine Kaufmann). The manner he uses is that familiar arrogant, teasing and patronising tone that so often characterised his on-screen treatment of women. It is the kind of vain, undermining behaviour calculated to provoke extreme irritation among women of even mildly feminist leanings. It must have appeared insulting to women even forty years ago, now it just seems rather pathetic. It is doubly dislikeable because Granger was beginning to show his age, but is still behaving on-screen as though he were in his twenties and convinced of his ability to 'conquer' any woman who comes into his orbit. Apart from that, Granger plays the fencing sequences almost for laughs and, in addition, he talks to himself, making facetious little comments at various stages in the movie. How much this approach and these lines stemmed from himself is impossible to gauge; a reasonable guess, however, is that they were probably his own contributions. It is almost as though he knows he is involved in something farcical and is telling the audience out there that he knows he is too old to be playing this part, so he is just having some fun. It is a get-out clause for the ageing actor. Yes, I know this is ridiculous, the sub-text seems to say, and that I may appear ridiculous by playing this swashbuckler role at my age, but, hell, it is only a movie and an Italian cheapie at that, so let's not take it too seriously and don't hold it against me because I know it's worthless.

The Swordsman of Siena is, in fact, not that atrocious a movie. It is just second-rate, a pale imitation of swashbucklers such as *Scaramouche* and *The Prisoner of Zenda*. The acting is poor, the direction pedestrian and the plot and characterisations trite and conventional. However, the action sequences are reasonably well staged, including the climactic horse race which leads to the downfall of the bad guys. But the movie falls between the stools of melodrama and facetiousness, aided by the 'playfulness' of Granger. Whereas it can be argued that you care about the characters in *Scaramouche*, it is really difficult to care a jot about any character in *Siena*. The purpose of the movie is to provide spectacle and highly unlikely heroics, and in these aims, the movie succeeds within its own very narrow limitations. Nevertheless, it is an entirely forgettable film, the last swashbuckler Granger would grace with his presence. His performance is perhaps his way of saying a swan song to his swashbuckler screen persona, an acknowledgement that he could no longer take himself seriously in that kind of role and that he did not expect audiences to either.

Granger was at least busy, even though the movies he was starring in now were not top-budget Hollywood extravaganzas. However, if he felt he was slumming it in making cheapie Italian potboilers, he could console himself with the knowledge that numerous other American stars from Kirk Douglas to Rory Calhoun were finding their way over to Cinecittà Studios in Rome to pick up a pay cheque. And these movies must have primarily been about making a living for Granger, because their artistic merit and prestige value were negligible.

The next movie he was offered was a biblical epic, *Sodom and Gomorrah*. Granger's only other biblical epic had been *Salome* and that had been a disaster, and *Sodom and Gomorrah* is certainly an improvement on that. Curiously, it was directed by Robert Aldrich, who had made *Kiss Me Deadly*, one of the most interesting of the film noir movies made in Hollywood in the 1950s. Aldrich's career would be revived again when he made *The Dirty Dozen* later in the decade, but he could do little with the basic material of this sententious and meretricious production. *Sodom and Gomorrah* came at the fag end of the biblical epic era, a couple of years after *Ben Hur* and *Spartacus*. Perhaps the producers hoped to find some of the international audience that those far superior movies had attracted, but their labours are defeated by a combination of the inanities of the script, the uneven acting of its international cast, its partial dubbing and the sheer exhaustion of the biblical epic genre.

Granger plays Lot, the leader of the Hebrew people, whom Jehovah had commanded to lead his people to the Valley of the Jordan and whose wife (played by Pier Angeli) was famously turned into a pillar of salt. They come to the twin cities of Sodom and Gomorrah, 'cities of sin and unspeakable vice'. Lot strikes a deal with Queen Bera (Anouk Aimee), who wants to use the Hebrews as a buffer force against the Helamites, a nomadic tribe that seeks to conquer Sodom for its riches in salt. After various treacherous manoeuvres involving the Queen's evil brother (Stanley Baker), the Hebrews defeat the Helamites by sacrificing the dam they had built to irrigate the desert and drowning their army. Lot leads his people into Sodom for shelter, but he and his people are corrupted by Sodomite hedonism, until Jehovah points out the error of his ways, frees him from captivity, performs a few miracles on behalf of the Hebrews, destroys Sodom and Gomorrah and turns Lot's wife, who does not believe in this Jehovah, into a pillar of salt. A distraught Lot is comforted by his daughters and continues on his way to the Promised Land.

Sodom and Gomorrah is a very queasy mixture of odious religiosity and piety, scenes of sadistic torture and extremely tame orgies. It would appear that Jehovah destroyed the cities because of the merest hint of lesbianism (actual sodomy is not even hinted at), the suggestion of incest, very bad dance routines and hammy acting. 'Unspeakable vice' is vaguely hinted at, but the prevailing censorship of the times and the need to attract a family audience kept the sin quotient to a minimum. The film spouts platitudes about peace and goodwill, but spends most of its running time focused on battle scenes, gore and sex. In short, it is the familiar mix of biblical epics that Cecil B. De Mille and others had made profitable at the box office since the dawn of Hollywood. The major battle scene is reasonably well staged, but the destruction of Sodom and Gomorrah looks decidedly cheap with the model structure being all too apparent. Sergio Leone, who would soon find fame as the director of the Clint Eastwood spaghetti westerns (*A Fistful of Dollars*, *For A Few Dollars More* and *The Good, the Bad and the Ugly*), worked on the movie for eight weeks as the second-unit director. It took him two weeks to shoot the major battle sequence. The cavalry charge involved a thousand horsemen from the Moroccan army and others. According to Leone, Aldrich had announced that he wanted to make an ancient version of Fellini's *La Dolce Vita*, but this idea foundered because 'the extent of Aldrich's audacity was reached when the brother of the Queen sucked his sister's finger. For Aldrich, this was the epitome of perversion.'

For much of his screen time, Granger has to act piously as Lot, a characteristic not usually associated with him, and he does not do it very convincingly. However, in his defence, the script is festooned with Hollywood biblical speak and no actor, however accomplished, can survive that kind of inanity. The role of Lot resembles Charlton Heston's as Moses in De Mille's *The Ten Commandments* and, in truth, he fares no worse than Heston in that role. He is given the chance, despite his advanced years, to perform a few heroics in the battle scene and vanquishes Stanley Baker in a duel to the death sequence. Although *Sodom and Gomorrah* is not of the epic dimensions of *The Ten Commandments* or *Ben Hur*, it was still a major production and at the centre of it was Granger. It is the last major movie in which Granger led the cast list.

In Britain it was distributed by the Rank Organisation, his old and detested employers, who gave the movie its full publicity campaign on television, through London Transport advertising and press publicity. There was a vulgar but 'spectacular' premiere at the Odeon, Marble Arch in London, which Granger and other stars of the movies attended. The publicists laid on a setting of sand and palm trees (the movie had been partly shot in Morocco) and guests were greeted by a group of 'Sodomite' slave girls. The tastelessness of the movie itself was encapsulated in the vulgarity of the premiere. To top it all off, a cheetah and a leopard wandered through the foyer of the cinema to provide further talking points for the show business hacks who attended. What Granger thought about all this ballyhoo can only be imagined, but he was probably quite happy still to be at the centre of it all as the star of this ridiculous epic. However, his self-esteem could not have been notably enhanced by appearing in such excruciating fare.

After that, Granger found himself in another co-production, *Marcia o Crepa* (*March or Die*), distributed in English-language markets as *The Legion's Last Patrol*, a war movie in which he plays a French Foreign Legion soldier, Le Blanc, during the Algerian War. It is one of those war movies that sets out to show the farcical nature of war itself, but which represents most of the elements of the war movie genre in order to entertain the kind of audience that is attracted to this kind of violent fare. *March or Die* did not receive much of a distribution in either the USA or Britain. It rarely crops up even on cable channels these days and is one of the numerous movies Granger would make during the last twenty years of his career that very few people actually saw on its first release or remember now. Yet from his point of view, it was movies such as this that were helping him to pay his bills and keeping him busy.

Granger would have another thirty years of his life to live. He was facing what most people have to face in their lives at a certain stage: in terms of his chosen career, his best days were decidedly in the past and this was especially true for the kind of romantic hero movie star he had been. He was now entering his fifties and although he had not lost his looks and was still in good physical condition (apart from some chronic ailments), he could not expect to be handed the kind of roles that he had found so easy to handle a few short years before. In a sense, he would have to struggle with ageist attitudes that defined for actors the kind of roles they could or could not play. Female film stars have always had to contend with this age barrier, whereby a Hollywood star could be considered 'over the hill' by her mid-twenties. Male stars had a longer shelf life, by and large, because there was not the same pressure for their looks to be 'preserved in aspic' as there was for their female counterparts. However, Granger had never broken free from the romantic hero category and so his looks, his physicality, became more important to his status as a movie star than to the average male star. Granger at this period of life would have been feeling the inevitable pressures of the ageing process just shortly after he had had to face a divorce from his beloved Jean Simmons and his Hollywood career had come to an end. In addition, he had burdened himself with financial commitments that would have been a challenge to meet at the best of times. The last thirty years of his life would have many troughs and few, if any, triumphs, and his increasing bitterness and isolation would become more apparent.

Chapter 9

ALL GLORY IS FLEETING

L IKE ALL OF us, Granger would have had his hopes for the future and his regrets about the past. He would have felt the pressures of everyday life, the sense of time passing too quickly, and the worry about the ageing process and the decay of the body. Many people, if they thought about him at all, would merely have wondered what had happened to him after he ceased to make 'big' movies. Whereas millions of people across the globe would have seen the Hollywood movies he had starred in, the films he made during the last three decades of his life would be seen by only a fraction of these former millions. Many of the films he made would not even find a distributor in the US or Britain. So for many fans of the actor and those who may not have been such ardent followers of him, Granger essentially stopped being a major movie star after 1960, although movie stardom grants a kind of immortality to the really important stars so that they never lose that status, however much their careers may have slumped. For Granger himself, it is clear that he had many regrets about lost opportunities and the passing of 'glory' and youth. He always stated he hated being a film star, but in his latter years he seemed anxious that people would remember him for the major star he had been. It was as Stewart Granger he wanted to be remembered, rather than Jimmy Stewart, however caustic his public statements about his movies and his acting ability.

Granger had never really settled anywhere for any length of time. It was part of his restless nature to keep moving, as well as the role he had adopted of the eternal adventurer, risk-taker and free spirit. Yes, he had bemoaned the long separations from Jean Simmons during their marriage when he had been away on location, but part of him, a very essential part, had needed to roam, to escape the bounds of domesticity and familiar surroundings, to experience and test himself against new environments and challenges. His screen roles mostly reflected that perceived male need to explore and put his life on the line. It was part of the glamour of the swashbucklers like Flynn and Granger, this perpetual desire to sail over the next horizon and to face dangers and conquer their own fears, to test their masculinity to the limit and thereby protect their own idea of their maleness. With Flynn, it became a pattern of grotesque self-indulgence and ultimate self-destruction. Granger did not kill himself through excesses, although his health undoubtedly suffered in his latter years because of his smoking and, to a degree, alcohol, and from the injuries he had sustained when he had been rather too reckless in his desire to show that he could do his own swashbuckling stunts. But he appeared to slip into a kind of perpetual dissatisfaction and unhappiness with his own life that was in its own way quite self-destructive.

The 'rootless' Granger, having taken out American citizenship with his former wife in 1956, now in 1962 reverted to British nationality. No doubt there were cogent reasons for this decision, which might have included tax and employment considerations, family matters, the stark fact that he would not now be working in the States that often, and possibly other practical factors as well. However, from the biographer's viewpoint, it does seem significant that he made this decision two years after his divorce and the end of his Hollywood career. It seems as though he was, consciously or unconsciously, drawing a line under that phase of his life in the States, including his seven years under contract to MGM. Perhaps it was an attempt on his part to shake off the ties of the recent past and to move on. The decision to adopt American citizenship had been made when his marriage had seemed strong (although by his own confession, it had been under strain for some years), and when it appeared perhaps that his MGM career would continue into the foreseeable future. But those two pillars in the structure of his life had tumbled down, and so the imperative to remain an American had gone, too. Why not mark this new phase of his life by returning to his roots, his Britishness?

Yet over the next thirty years, Granger would spend relatively little time in his native country. He would at various times live in the South of France, Switzerland, Spain, London and California. Perhaps he was a man who never belonged anywhere very much and his constant restlessness was a symptom of that feeling rather than a cause. A characteristic of restless spirits is that they find difficulty in accommodating themselves to institutions and social groupings of one kind or another. Granger had come up against the demands of the family, school, the armed forces, Gainsborough and Rank Organisation executives, MGM, the legal system, the business world, and had been in conflict with all of them. It was not just that he was a 'difficult' man (it seems more than likely that he was), but that he was working out some emotional problems in his interactions with the groups and institutions he came into contact with, and that was why he could not settle for very long, finish things that he started or sustain amicable relationships with more than a few people.

Granger's next film would bring him back into contact with the Hollywood industry, as the producer of *The Secret Invasion* was Roger Corman, king of the low-budget, exploitation movie. As an actor, you either worked in a Corman movie on the way up or on the way down. Jack Nicholson and Bruce Dern, among others, had served their apprenticeship in Corman horror and biker movies before they became stars in more respectable movies. However, Corman also utilised fading stars such as Boris Karloff in his last years because they came cheaply by that time in their careers while supplying a 'name' above the title. Granger clearly belonged to the latter category and his co-stars in this war movie were Raf Vallone, Mickey Rooney (whose career had dwindled to grotesque supporting roles) and Henry Silva.

Granger plays Major Mace, charged with freeing an Italian general from the hands of the Germans in Dubrovnik. *The Secret Invasion* preceded *The Dirty Dozen* by a few years, and is a cut-price version of a similar tale but without the visceral impact of that violent Aldrich-directed caper. Corman himself directed, but the movie got little attention on its release. Granger may have enjoyed playing another army officer, given his unfulfilled aspirations to military glory.

Granger made two other movies in 1964: *The Crooked Road* and *Unter Geiern*, both with Yugoslavian finance behind them. In the former, Granger co-starred with Robert Ryan, who plays a South American dictator who has seized power in a coup. Granger is a reporter who exposes his undemocratic ways and whom the dictator tries to eliminate. In *Unter Geiern*, Granger supposedly returns to his old patch of New Mexico in this movie playing Old Surehand, the blood brother of Winnetou, a Native American, and between them they attempt to eliminate a band of marauders who are threatening to break the uncertain peace between the whites and the Indians. The name of Granger's character seemed to symbolise the passing of the years and his move into 'older' roles. He was now fifty-one. The movie was based on a story by Karl May, a German writer who wrote western novels and who has acquired a cult following in his native land, although, like the Old Surehand movies based on his stories, he was little known outside Germany. Lex Barker had played this role in an earlier film for the same production team, but for one reason or another could not reprise the role, so Granger was cast. Just as Granger seemed to like playing military roles, he seemed equally drawn to westerns, which reflected his love of the

American West and his business interests. The film was shot in Yugoslavia in CinemaScope and colour, but it received a limited release, which did not include the UK or the US.

This was an important year for Granger, however, because in June he married for the third time. Whereas a mere sixteen years had been the age gap between Granger and his second wife, now he was to embark on a third attempt at marriage with a woman who was more or less thirty years younger than himself. She was a former Miss Belgium beauty queen, Caroline Lecerf. They married in Geneva City Hall in a simple private ceremony with only a few guests attending. David Niven acted as Granger's witness and Jamie, Granger's son by Elspeth March, was also present.

Thus, four years after his divorce from Jean Simmons, Granger had taken the matrimonial plunge again with a much younger woman. The marriage, however, would not last long and they would divorce in 1969. Was Granger replaying in his life some of the earlier Granger–Simmons scenario when he had won the English beauty in his prime of life and when anything must have seemed possible for both of them? Certainly in interviews Lecerf was frank about her attraction to Granger: 'I fell in love with him when I was thirteen,' she told the readers of the *Daily Express*. 'I saw all of his films. I thought he was wonderful. At night I used to dream of him coming to carry me off.' That statement has a naive quality, which clearly did not augur well for the longevity of their marriage. Rita Hayworth once explained the failure of all her marriages on the fact that her various husbands – including, presumably, Orson Welles – married Gilda (one of her most famous vamp roles) and woke up the next morning next to the real Rita Hayworth with all her emotional problems. Perhaps Caroline Lecerf married Scaramouche or Allan Quatermain, and woke up to the reality that she had married Jimmy Stewart, with all his insecurities and bad temper and propensity to free himself of bonds.

In the same *Daily Express* feature Granger already gives a hint of the difficulties that marriage to a so much younger woman had brought him: 'She drives me mad, of course, but I suppose she keeps me young.' Anxious to dispel any Lolita-like associations, Granger also describes her as very mature and says that he had been very frank with her when they had first started a relationship by stating that he was very fond of her but he did not intend to marry her. Two years after they met, she had proposed to him, saying that marriage to her would be very good for him. He had consented. The impression is given that she had done the chasing in the relationship and he had been a somewhat reluctant partner in the whole arrangement. Then why had he taken this step? Presumably, he felt lonely and there was perhaps a strong element of vanity in his motivation. The adoration of a very young, former beauty queen probably flattered his ego and bolstered his sense of his own attractiveness. After all, he had lost one of the great beauties of the age only a few years previously and she had subsequently married a man who, by no stretch of the imagination, could be classed in the same league for male looks as Granger, and was even older than him. That, in itself, must have been a further blow to his vanity.

Granger might have described Lecerf as very mature, but he meant for her years and he must have known that her experience of life had been necessarily much more limited than his. Unconsciously, he may have thought she would be controllable and malleable. However, the fact is that he was not a man who took easily to marriage and its restrictions. In a television interview he gave Mavis Nicholson in 1981 when he was publicising his autobiography, he describes himself as 'rather a loner', a fact which women did not understand. He again mentions his mother and his shock at finding out the nature of her relationship with the man he thought of as his uncle. 'I don't trust women,' he told Nicholson, 'because they are so devious and complicated. Men are more honest. Women always justify what they have done.' Even for the early eighties, these statements seem extremely misogynist and regressive, but they do illustrate how much his mother's 'betrayal' had affected his attitudes to women. The statement about women always justifying what they have done seems to hint at marital infidelities, among other things. This is all, of course, the most arrant sexist nonsense and typical of the views he held on gender and social issues. He goes on to admit that in some ways he needed a partner, but equally he could not live with anyone. He mentions his dislike of someone sharing his bathroom and his kitchen.

What seems plain is that Granger feared real intimacy with people, not only with his wives and lovers. He was, indeed, by nature a loner, which made it more difficult for him to be a film star and therefore on display for a lot of the time. On the other hand, it is clear that he relished adoration and fame, but it had to be on his terms and that was by no means always possible in the sphere in which he moved. It does seem that his third marriage to this woman thirty years his junior was more or less doomed from the start, given his insecurity, his domineering nature, his need to be alone and to live his version of male freedom. He, in essence, had married a representative of his female fan base, a young woman, like many others, who had fallen in love with his screen persona. She reflected back to him that glamorous image that he publicly decried but perhaps secretly valued. But Scaramouche was now in his fifties, had a wonky knee, recurring stomach problems, was an inveterate worrier and a loner.

But it was his much younger partner who was to face serious health problems. Two years into the marriage, Lecerf had to undergo major hole-in-the-heart surgery. It must have put enormous strain on their marriage. Here he was, the ageing movie star who might have expected, given his patriarchal attitudes, that his every need would be catered for by his young wife, and who then found himself looking after her.

After her operation, Lecerf was more than ever determined to have a child, and shortly afterwards she gave birth to a daughter, Samantha. But the marriage did not last. Granger remained on good terms with Lecerf – as he had with both his previous wives – but he did not play an active role in the bringing up of his fourth child. It seems Granger was one of those men who seemed to get on better with his women once they had ended their sexual and romantic ties with him and resumed a kind of friendship. The fact that Elspeth March and Jean Simmons would remain close to Granger for the remainder of his life also suggests that, however much he feared real intimacy in his relationships with women, he was reluctant to move on and let them go.

His third marriage to the twenty-two-year-old Lecerf could only have increased his financial obligations and so he had to go on making movies, however mediocre, to help pay the bills. *Mission Hong Kong* (aka *Red Dragon*) is a Cold War thriller in which Granger plays an American secret agent (complete with that mid-Atlantic accent) trying to put an end to a ring of smugglers selling weapons to the dastardly communists. It was a German/ Italian co-production and suffered the fate of the vast majority of these cheaply made European co-productions with a euphemistically described 'international cast'. This was followed by two more outings for the character of Old Surehand that he had played in *Unter Geiern*: in *Der Olprinz* and *Old Surehand Part 1*, again from the same German/Yugoslavian producers. In the 1960s, the Italian 'spaghetti' western, especially those directed by Sergio Leone and starring Clint Eastwood, acquired a large cult reputation and catapulted Eastwood to major stardom. German westerns did not enjoy a similar surge in popularity, in the same way that the Spanish attempts at the genre died the death. Granger acquired a new following in Germany, however, partly from his participation in these movies, but they did nothing for his reputation internationally and indeed very few people outside of continental Europe ever saw the movies. But they provided pay days for the financially pressed actor, whose slightly reduced circumstances had not brought about a reformation in his extravagant spending habits. He was gambling on the fact that some movie would always be there to help him pay the bills.

In 1966, the year his new wife underwent hole-in-the-heart surgery, he made two more movies: an Austrian–Italian co-production, *Das Geheimnis der gelben Mönche* and an espionage thriller *Spy Against the World* (aka *Killer's Carnival*). In the first, Granger played another secret agent who is in love with an heiress whose uncle, a crime boss, is trying to kill her before her twenty-fifth birthday. The movie had a respectable cast which included Curd Jürgens, Klaus Kinski, Karin Dor and Adolfo Celi, but this could not prevent it from quickly sinking into obscurity. *Spy Against the World* was set in Vienna and reunited Granger with Pierre Brice, who had starred with him in the Old Surehand movies and whom Granger disliked intensely, and Karin Dor. Lex Barker, the ex-Tarzan from whom he had inherited the Old Surehand role, also co-starred. It tells the tale of a missing journalist and drug criminals, and it all has an over-familiar ring to it. After the success of the James Bond movies, every producer in town seemed to be trying to climb onto that particular band wagon and there was a positive rash of special agent thrillers in the mid- to late sixties, most of which should never have been made and have been long forgotten. These two movies come firmly into this category.

His next film brought Granger back to Britain. *The Trygon Factor* was adapted from an Edgar Wallace story and so had a reasonably respectable source. It co-starred Granger with Susan Hampshire and Robert Morley. Granger plays Chief Inspector Cooper Smith on the trail of bank robbers who dress up as nuns. He rescues Polly/Hampshire from their clutches and marries her at the end of the movie. Now in his mid-fifties, Granger was still getting the girl on screen, just as he had done in real life with his third marriage. While he was in London making *The Trygon Factor*, he talked to the press about becoming a father again; a month earlier Caroline Lecerf had given birth to Samantha. However, in an interview given to Roderick Mann of the *Sunday Express*, he admits that it had been his wife who had wanted the child. 'I was worried about having another child so late in life,' Granger told Mann. However, he also admitted in his autobiography that he had been irritated by his first wife's obsession with having children and that when his marriage to Simmons had broken up, he had decided he would not play a major role in the life of their daughter, Tracy. Granger in his attitude to fatherhood betrays the fact that he still had unresolved emotional problems connected with his own childhood. For the whole of his life, he would seek to fill that emotional vacuum he had experienced as a child in the Stewart family, and because of that quest, it seems he had not much emotional energy to spare.

In the same interview, Granger talks about getting older and his physical problems. It does sound like something of a whine from a middle-aged grumbler: 'They say you're as old as you feel and right now I feel bloody old. I am paying the price for all those stunts I did in my pictures, where I had to charge about with a sword. I now spend half my time at the osteopath. I'm an absolute cripple.' Given that his young wife had just recovered from hole-in-the-heart surgery, Granger's complaints about his ailments do seem rather overdone. 'In fact,' he added, 'I wouldn't feel that bad if it wasn't for my ricked back and my ruined knee and my nervous heart and my bronchitis and the fact that I'm losing my hair.' He also laments the fact that he has been away from his roots in England for so long, but makes it clear that he was living in his flat in Geneva with his wife for tax reasons. He was making less money than he had in his heyday in Hollywood, but at least he was keeping most of it, which would enable him to save for his old age. He states he had never really been happy in Hollywood and that he would prefer to live in Grosvenor Square than in Geneva. As for his films, he had never been a good enough actor to gain much satisfaction from the movies he made. It had always been a question of how much, how long and when does it start?

This article strongly reinforces Granger's reputation as an arch-grumbler, a moaner par excellence, a Victor Meldrew before his time, the ultimate grumpy old man. He clearly is not very happy with his lot, yet there he was with a new baby, married to a beautiful young wife, a man who had enjoyed fame and fortune and who was still starring in movies, albeit of reduced quality and prestige. Nothing, it appears, would make this man happy. Even if his career had taken a spectacular turn for the better and his current marriage had been a great success and his business dealings had led to new riches, we still get the impression that it would not have been good enough. Nothing could fill the emotional void at the heart of this man's life. And it was this knowledge, deep inside himself, that made Granger the grumbler that he was. He knew that things were not going to get that much better at this stage in his life.

Meanwhile, he continued to make cheapie secret agent movies on the back of the James Bond cult. His next movie was a German/Italian/Spanish co-production *Der Chef schickt seinen besten Mann*, in which he played a sub-Bond British agent grappling with a criminal organisation. He must have been able to do this kind of role in his sleep by this point. Once again, the movie was destined to be shown only in continental Europe and was, like most of these European co-productions he made in the 1960s, never dubbed or subtitled into English. As far as his British or American fans were concerned, Granger might as well have ceased making films by this time because they had no chance of seeing them.

However, his next movie was distributed by Paramount, was classed as a British movie and did obtain a fairly wide release. In *The Last Safari* Granger plays a big-game hunter, Miles Gilchrist, a role that must have been pretty close to his heart. The Paramount press book for *The Last Safari* has a feature on Granger, in which he expresses his feelings about big-game hunting. 'As Gilchrist, the hunter, I am given a particularly pertinent speech,' Granger says. 'Hunting helps balance nature and is not a menace to animal life. The trophies claimed by myself and most hunters are animals that are past their prime . . . What hurts animal life most and is of greatest danger to professional hunting is the influx of tourists, which is increasing rapidly. There was a time not so long ago when the hunter killed only for his life and his food. Not so long ago men had to be protected from the beasts – today the beasts must be protected from man.' This poacher-turned-gamekeeper attitude is rather like those aristocratic defenders of Venice who decry the damage to the city that mass tourism brings, while defending their own right to visit Venice as often as they like.

The movie was directed by the veteran Henry Hathaway whom Granger had so detested when making *North to Alaska* at the very end of his Hollywood career. Adapted from a novel by Gerald Hanley, *Gilligan's Last Elephant*, it tells the tale of an embittered white hunter in Kenya whose best friend has been killed by a rogue elephant, which he determines to kill on his last safari. He has to deal with a rich American playboy and his girlfriend who want to accompany him on the trek. Finally, Gilchrist/Granger chooses not to pull the trigger when he has the killer elephant in his sights. The film tries to have its both ways by representing the thrills of big-game hunting while making some unconvincing conservation point as well.

It could not have pleased Granger that he had to accept second billing to the largely unknown Kaz Garas whose first film this was. Paramount clearly was more interested in boosting the career of a new young star (he never achieved real stardom) than marketing the movie as a 'Stewart Granger' film. They frequently evoked *King Solomon's Mines* in their publicity for the film, however, but such comparisons only drew attention to the deficiencies of *The Last Safari*. The critic Leslie Halliwell describes the movie as a 'dullsville adventure story with good animal photography redeeming some of the clichés'. For Granger it was indeed a return to *King Solomon's Mines* territory, but this was seventeen years later and the gloss had gone from his career. *The Last Safari* attracted only minor attention when it was released. In terms of Granger's career, the movie is well named, as it was, in a sense, a last safari for him as the star of an English-speaking movie. Indeed, it would be another ten years before he made another movie that received a cinema release.

This year, 1969, was not a great year for Granger as his third marriage ended in divorce. Although he had only recently become a father for the fourth time, that was not enough to keep the marriage intact. He was now a three-time loser in the marriage stakes and given his lifestyle, his attitudes to women, the fact that he was 'difficult' and a self-confessed loner, it is perhaps scarcely surprising that he appeared to be incapable of sustaining long-term relationships. He never again ventured into marriage.

What do fading film stars do when they are no longer being offered parts and the public that once adored them are fast forgetting they still exist? They turn to television, of course, and that was what Granger now did, taking the initiative to seek out roles on American television to help him pay his bills and sustain the lifestyle to which he had become accustomed. Firstly, he landed the starring role in a film-for-television produced by Universal, *Any Second Now*, a routine thriller in which he played a playboy unfaithful to his wife whom he plots to murder when she asks for a divorce. Then, more unexpectedly, he was given one of the leading roles in *The Men from Shiloh*, a western series that was a spin-off of the highly successful *The Virginian* and which was aired on American television between September 1970 and September 1971 and then was withdrawn.

Granger headed the regular cast list, which also included Doug McClure, Lee Majors and James Drury. The producers used so-called 'guest stars' from old Hollywood for single episodes, such names as Katy Jurado, Desi Arnaz, Alan Hale, Phil Harris, Ann Sothern, Carolyn Jones, Edgar Buchanan and Bradford Dillman among others. The general tone of the series was semi-comic and seemed to aim to replicate Hollywood B-movie westerns in weekly episodes. Granger played Colonel Alan MacKenzie, an ex-Indian army major and a big-game hunter.

When the series began a run on the BBC, Granger told the *Radio Times* that he coped with this all-action part by showing that he could ride as well as his American co-stars and by doing his own stunts. That way he earned their respect, he stated. On the edge of sixty, he was still metaphorically displaying the hairs on his chest. However, it seems he did not earn their love, because he admitted that tempers were frayed during the series. 'If you've made seventy films over thirty-nine years, it's not easy to work with a man who's only done one thing in his life – play a television cowboy.' This may well have been a not-too-subtle dig at James Drury who had starred in the original *The Virginian* series between 1962 and 1969 and had been retained for the new series. Granger also lambasted the television executives who had pulled the series. The initial reasoning behind using Granger must have been that he had been an A-list Hollywood star and his name would attract attention among all the decidedly B- and C-list stars below him in the credits. As is the way with series like these, Granger did not appear at all in numerous episodes, but his name always appeared at the head of the credits whether or not he was in the particular episode of the series being shown. So age had not mellowed the opinionated Granger nor taught him a measure of tact or respect for his fellow toilers. The interviewer on the *Radio Times* feature finished with a question about his wives. 'I don't know which was the greater disaster, my career or my wives,' Granger airily replied. *The Men from Shiloh* was not exactly a disaster, but merely a rather tired coda to a career that was almost exhausted.

The television movie and the western series had brought him back to the attention of potential employers in the States and now he landed the unlikely role of Sherlock Holmes in a television film of Conan Doyle's most famous tale, *The Hound of the Baskervilles*. It was transmitted as the 'ABC Movie of the Week' on 12 February 1972. Holmes is a character who is highly cerebral, ascetic, artistic, with a talent for disguise. He is literature's most intelligent and intellectual detective, but he is also represented by Conan Doyle as a tortured man dependent on drugs. Stewart Granger and Sherlock Holmes: an example of obvious casting or the miscasting of all time? Perhaps the latter. Granger had never in all his many roles played any character that could remotely be described as an intellectual and for very good reasons. His talents, such as they were, lay elsewhere and it defies belief that even the executives at Universal convinced themselves that Granger could play Holmes with any credibility. In the event, his portrayal of the role had as much conviction as his Paganini in *The Magic Bow*.

However, these pay days helped him pursue his entrepreneurial interests. He had always been fascinated by Africa since those months he spent in Kenya shooting *King Solomon's Mines* and he had returned there numerous times for other films and to go on safaris. Now he bought a farm in Southern Rhodesia (as it was then), a country which had endured stormy times as the rule of the white settlers came to an end. There would be further turmoil under the dictatorship of Robert Mugabe, so it was not perhaps the best time to be buying land in a former colony of Britain. But that obviously did not deter Granger, who clearly saw any earnings he made from these inferior movies he was now making as providing badly needed capital to invest in land and business ventures. He also bought a villa in Marbella set in 300 acres. In 1975 he began the construction of a house on the Costa del Sol. He also bought land in the Sierra Nevada in Andalusia in Spain, on which a Country Club with holiday homes was constructed. His investment in these ventures amounted to a considerable sum, so Granger, now in his sixties, was still in search of the El Dorado, the cup of gold that would bring him a constant supply of money, but it was not to be. He was not an astute enough businessman, it seems, by his own admission, and once more, these impulsive schemes of his would bring their own problems – and some very unwelcome publicity.

One incident from his stay in Marbella illustrates Granger's contrary nature and his propensity for making enemies and bearing grudges. He managed to get himself banned from the 'in-place' in Marbella because of an altercation with his old sparring partner from *Scaramouche*, Mel Ferrer, who had once told the authors of *Jimmy*, a German publication about Granger, that 'my recollections of Stewart Granger are the warmest . . . We became friends during the filming of *Scaramouche*. Later he went to live in Spain where I was also living and we saw a good deal of each other.' On this particular occasion in the hot spot of Marbella, it seems the 'old friends' saw a little too much of each other. Granger's account of the incident was this: 'I had a stand-up argument with Mel Ferrer, whom I dislike intensely, over a petty parking problem there.' This incident smacks of old Hollywood scores being settled, but at least Granger's expression of his real feelings about Ferrer cuts through the usual superficial nonsense that actors normally trot out to satisfy journalists and authors.

For about six years, Granger busied himself with these business interests and to the general public, he seemed to have disappeared from the big and small screens. Then in 1978 he was cast in *The Wild Geese* as an unscrupulous newspaper baron. The writers may have had in mind someone like the late Tiny Rowland. The stars of the movie were Roger Moore, Richard Harris, Hardy Kruger and Richard Burton, an old friend of Granger's who had suggested him for the role. Granger was still a 'name', albeit from the past, and so the producers agreed with Burton and cast him. Sir Edward Matherson, Granger's role, is an unsympathetic man who gets his come-uppance at the hands of a mercenary (Burton) for having double-crossed the band of noble warriors in his quest to own African copper mines.

The Wild Geese is an unpleasant movie, violent, reactionary and a no-brainer. It pretends to be on the side of white and black Africa co-operating peacefully, but all the action sequences represent black soldiers being murdered by these white mercenaries (white, that is, apart from a token black). The audience is asked to swallow that all these mercenaries suddenly get a dose of conscience and genuinely try to save the noble African politician in the cause of helping his beleaguered country. The body count is horrendous and war is portrayed as an exciting adventure. At the heart of it is an excruciating sentimentality about the loyalty even cynical mercenaries show to their colleagues in times of danger and it boasts a truly spurious ending where the cynical leader of the gang (Burton) returns to take care of the young son of his friend (played by Richard Harris), whom he has had to shoot in the final scene to save him from the machetes of the black soldiers. The ageing stars probably knew they were lending their names to meretricious nonsense, but all of their careers had seen better days and no doubt the hefty pay days were very welcome. Burton, after years of alcoholism, looks wrecked, and Richard Harris not that much better. It strains credulity that broken-down specimens such as these could under-take such an audacious mission. By comparison, Granger, his hair now completely silvered, looks rather fit and spruce, although by this stage in his career his features have a rather fixed and bitter look, which actually helped him play the role convincingly. *The Wild Geese* brought Granger back into the public eye, but it was a small role in an undistinguished film.

Granger gave an interview to a German television channel in connection with the publicity for *The Wild Geese* in which he stated he did not want to play minor parts in movies, because, as he put it, 'Having been a star, I can't play Marlon Brando's uncle.' He had never aimed to create art in his films, but to make money. He hated being older than thirty-five, but if he did not look like a sixty-five-year-old, he put that down to the daily bottle of wine and the sixty cigarettes. Women had kept him young as well and having had three marriages, he now was expectant of a fourth. This was Granger acting Granger for the television cameras, full of bravado and immature comments. By his mid-sixties he did not seem to have acquired much more wisdom than he had started out with.

It was at this point that his business interests in Spain were to explode in his face and he would be dogged by scandal over the affair. It concerned the Rancho Verde, a picturesque stretch of land 30 miles north of Malaga. Hundreds of people had bought land on the understanding that planning permission would be available for them to build holiday homes, but that planning permission could not be granted. Under Spanish law, a building plot without a water supply (as these plots were) had to measure a minimum of 25,000sqm. The plots measured only 3,000sqm and were therefore ineligible for planning permission. Granger's name and face had been plastered all over the brochures that the German-owned company had distributed to entice individual buyers and developers to invest. At the time the scandal broke, only three houses had been built because of this impasse over planning permission. An officer of the Junta de Andalucía, the local authority responsible for the region and for the granting of planning permission, stated that if plots of land smaller than 25,000sqm had been sold on the basis that the buyers would be eligible for planning permission to build homes, then that had been clearly illegal. Another regional government official stated that the buyers had been the victims of a fraud.

This was an unsavoury business for Granger to be involved in. He furiously denied that he had done anything wrong. He told the *Daily Express* that he had been used by unscrupulous 'mealy-mouthed' profiteers. He had never owned the Rancho Verde, but had merely put his name to the business venture as a front man in return for a percentage. He stoutly defended his reputation for honesty whilst conceding that he had not always been wise in his choice of investments or his associates: 'I might have been a fool in the past, several times in my life, but I've never been dishonest.'

However, the scandal arose because a Spanish-registered company had sued Granger to recover a loan of £72,000, which the company had lent Granger when he had started the development. In the *Daily Express* article, the company spokesman claims that they had been very badly let down by Granger.

In essence, everybody was accusing everyone else for the debacle and the fraud, if that was what it was. In the middle of these legal squabbles were the unfortunate investors, many of whom were retired people who had sunk their money into the land in the hope that they would be able to enjoy a retirement home in the Spanish sun. It was one of many scandals connected with the building of retirement homes and time-share apartments that would be all too familiar as Spain became the number one target among British people who wanted affordable 'sunshine' homes either as a permanent residence or as a second home. The scandals associated with this 'racket' are legion, but sadly, Granger had got caught up in it. It is impossible to untangle the rights and wrongs of the whole tawdry affair. Everyone defended their own corner, blamed others and even disclaimed ownership of the Rancho Verde. There is no evidence that Granger was involved in anything deliberately shady or dishonest. He was eager to make some quick profits, but that had been a characteristic of his other ventures in America. However, he can be believed when he stated that he knew nothing about the impossibility of planning permission being granted to plots of land of the size the company sold. Nothing in his previous life pointed to the fact that Granger would become involved in something dishonest. However, some mud always sticks and the publicity about the 'sunshine homes' scandal must have hurt him. He was a proud, perhaps arrogant, man and for his name and reputation to be involved with something as unsavoury as cheating pensioners out of their savings in bogus land deals must have been very hard to swallow. In addition, he claimed to have been financially ruined by the whole debacle: 'My own stupidity and credulity have been my ruin. Yes, I am ruined. I haven't a single dollar left in my pocket and feel I have been stung.' If other people suffered from this affair, and they undoubtedly did, so did Granger because it does appear that his financial affairs never really recovered from this setback.

Spain was no longer attractive (or possible) for Granger, so he sold his Spanish house and moved to Los Angeles again, buying an apartment near to the Getty Museum. Perhaps financial need now drove him to start writing his autobiography, eventually called *Sparks Fly Upward*. The title is a quotation from the Bible, Job ch5, v7: 'Man is born unto trouble, as the sparks fly upward.' It is Granger's way of acknowledging that his life had been full of 'trouble' as, in a sense, everyone's life is, but that, as the verse implies, comes with the very essence of existence and one must accept it.

Sparks Fly Upward creates a picture of a man who, in his latter years, is full of bitterness, regrets, anger, unresolved conflicts, raw prejudices about women, race and social issues, reactionary attitudes and personal enmities. What it decidedly does not do is paint a portrait of Stewart Granger as a rounded, contented and fulfilled human being. If man is indeed born into trouble and remains troubled, then Granger's autobiography is a testimony to that. The devil-may-care screen swashbuckler with a glint in his eye was, in his own life, unable to cast off his problems and ease his way effortlessly out of trouble with a carefree shrug of his manly shoulders. Granger's autobiography places him permanently if not exactly in the middle of the Slough of Despond, then very close to it.

However, *Sparks Fly Upward* at least had the effect of bringing Granger very much back into the public eye for positive rather than negative reasons, as he made the rounds of the television and radio chat shows in Britain to advertise the book. The interview Mavis Nicholson conducted with him on her series *Mavis* was one of the more revealing he gave. Apart from what he said, it is interesting how he interacted with his interviewer, a rather matronly lady perhaps representative of the kind of viewer who regularly watched her programme in mid-afternoon on Thames Television. Having confessed that she and her friends had been 'mad about Stewart Granger' from *The Man in Grey* onwards, Nicholson had to deflect some rather heavy flirtatious behaviour from Granger as he commented on her eyes and stated that she was his favourite girl. Commenting on his own looks, he expressed his dislike of his bent nose and his ears that stuck out, and said that he could barely stand to look at himself on screen. Women, Granger said, were attracted to him because of the parts he had played, and that was why he had avoided making public appearances because in reality he would have proved such a disappointment to his fans. He mentions having seen *Scaramouche* shortly before and how it had saddened him because he had been good-looking and athletic and now he was old and decrepit. About his state of happiness, he confesses he was not happy: 'A successful man is a happy man. I'm not very happy.' He had been ashamed of being a film star and immediately he had signed a long-term contract, he had felt trapped. 'But you want a Cadillac and a swimming pool,' he explained.

It was a familiar refrain from Granger and many viewers must have asked themselves what exactly he had to complain about. He had had fame and fortune and had lived in ostensibly glamorous circumstances. Some of those viewers would have been consoled by the thought that wealth and fame need not necessarily bring happiness, as Granger's life seemed to prove. For many people who envy the lifestyles of the rich and famous, there is a definite satisfaction in hearing that celebrity does not always bring fulfilment.

For a man like Granger who always resented intrusions into his private life by the media and who hated, or so he professed endlessly, the notoriety surrounding being a film star, it seems strange that at that late stage in his life, he had written such a frank autobiography revealing family, marital and extra-marital affairs to the world at large. Yet when the financial imperatives imposed on him by his recent problems are considered, it may not seem strange at all. He had always chased the buck and now he had served up what he thought his publisher and the general public would want to hear. He revealed to the world the private matters of his mother and her relationship with his father and his 'uncle'. He dealt with some of his own love affairs and some of the reasons for the failure of his first two marriages, although I think it is fair to say, as he himself later admitted, that he had gone pretty easy on his first two wives in the account he gave of the marriages. He showed himself to be an inveterate worrier and a man who had more often than not been a fool unto himself. Unkind words are written about most of the people he worked with and some of his business associates, especially movie executives. Overall, he comes over as rather insensitive and prejudiced, a man who knew he had not learnt much from his experiences of triumph and disaster.

Tony Sloman, the film producer and director, tells an interesting anecdote when Granger was signing copies of *Sparks Fly Upward* one day in Harrods. There was a queue of people and eventually a small, elderly lady arrived at Granger's table and handed over the book for him to sign. Granger looked up and said in astonishment, 'Ava! It's you! You didn't have to queue, for God's sake!' The diminutive elderly lady was indeed Ava Gardner, his glamorous co-star from *Bhowani Junction* and *The Little Hut*. Gardner, who was by then living permanently in London, had queued like any member of the public to have her copy autographed. The two ex-stars, according to Sloman, fell all over each other and arranged to meet later that evening. This incident is a timely reminder of how fleeting is glory and how time gets to us all, the famous and the obscure. Ten years later, Gardner was to die in London, a virtual recluse.

Granger wrote most of his autobiography while he was staying in the upper half of a house in Fulham owned by his former wife, Elspeth March, a testimony to their continuing good relations despite the fact they had been divorced for over thirty years. Indeed, in the eyes of some people, Elspeth March was the love of Granger's life, not Jean Simmons. Valerie Hobson, his co-star in the 1947 *Blanche Fury*, who considered Granger 'not an easy actor to work with because he was a worrier and rather moody', was of the opinion that he 'was really devoted to his first wife, who was equally devoted to him'. Hobson, who met Granger in his latter years when he was clearly very ill, also paid tribute to Elspeth March's loving devotion to her ex-husband in the last days of his life.

It was in this Fulham flat that Granger gave some of the interviews to the press to publicise his autobiography. In one interview given to the *Sunday*

Express, he explained that despite all the problems that Britain faced, he wanted to return to his roots. He was tired of Spain, he explained, neglecting to mention the legal and financial problems he had had there. (Within a short time, however, Granger had lost that yearning for his British roots and had settled in Santa Monica, where he bought a flat.) However, he does confess in this interview that he had made a mess of his life and describes himself as a failure. The same tale of disappointment and failure was given to show business reporter Jack Tinker of the *Daily Mail*: 'I ruined my life by being plain greedy. I was always spending more money than I had and doing films I didn't want to do to pay off the debts.' When Tinker asks him why he had written his autobiography, Granger replies it was for the money. Coaxed by Tinker, he says that his wives perhaps had not been as perfect as he had painted them in the book, 'but I wrote lovingly about them because that's how I wanted my children to know it was.' He had never learned from his experience of life; having had one marriage to a much younger woman end in divorce, he had then married an even younger woman. On the subject of his perceived arrogance, he excuses himself by saying he couldn't stand having idiots around him and there had been an abundance of those in his life.

In publicising his autobiography, therefore, Granger indulged in a positive orgy of breast-beating, but at the same time, much of what he is quoted as saying still comes over as arrogant. While calling himself foolish and incapable of learning from his own mistakes, he continues to 'play' the public Stewart Granger that he had paraded for decades: the intemperate, tactless and somewhat insensitive movie star who still thought of himself as superior to most of his fellow human beings.

His next role, in 1982, would cast him as someone who has often been accused of being tactless and insensitive, the Duke of Edinburgh. Ungenerous souls, indeed, might have believed that Granger had found his perfect role playing the Queen's husband, in that Edinburgh's general views on life and politics, and his personality, were as close as one could get to Granger's own. The role of Edinburgh was in a glutinous television movie

The Royal Romance of Charles and Diana, a laughably bad exercise in royal hagiography. Now that we know exactly what the Charles and Diana marriage was like right from the start, the whole treatment given to this subject matter seems in retrospect even more repellent. In a *Guardian* interview given to publicise the television movie, Granger describes himself as 'too tall, too old, too fat and with orange dyed hair', so he was still communicating self-dislike. One of the self-deprecating anecdotes he had told on talk shows when he was publicising *Sparks Fly Upward* was an account of his being approached in Bond Street by an elderly lady, who asked, 'Didn't you used to be Stewart Granger?' He brings that one out again for the benefit of the *Guardian* interview. Granger describes himself as 'a devoted admirer' of Edinburgh and then he adds rather tactlessly, 'I knew him when he was a penniless Greek.' He was a royalist through and through, he confesses, and at the time of the royal wedding, although he had been ill, he had taped seven hours of television coverage and watched it with tears in his eyes. 'After Nixon and Vietnam and the recession, and income tax and Israel and the bloody Arabs, it was such a joyful day. Two beautiful people in a fairy story romance,' he gushed.

If playing the Duke of Edinburgh in a dreadful television movie was not sufficient to endanger his reputation, perhaps his appearance in a Shredded Wheat television advert threatened to be the final nail. As the *Daily Express* reported, 'Quite the most shocking sight on the telly recently has been Stewart Granger dressed up as a rather decrepit Superman promoting Shredded Wheat. The fifties' idol who swung rapier in hand from the chandeliers of our youth is seen encouraging a lad to eat the stuff.' When the reporter asked the advertising agency for a photograph of Granger as Superman, he was refused, the spokesman saying only that 'Mr Granger is a very private person.' Not that private a person to turn down a reputed £30,000 to appear as a geriatric Superman in a telly ad. 'Could this be the chap who thrilled me in *King Solomon's Mines* and *Scaramouche*?' asked the *Daily Express*. However, this low point in Granger's career is evidence of the financial pressure he was under after he had lost money in Spain. The self-dislike that more and more he expressed in interviews with the media is reflected in this kind of demeaning work: the Shredded Wheat ad and the ghastly Charles and Diana movie tell us that his self-esteem was perhaps at a low point. A less shaming pay day perhaps was provided when he was paid to push the virtues of Canada Dry on television.

There was a curious legal episode in 1987 when Granger was moved to litigation once more. He sued the writer and broadcaster Penny Junor and her publisher Sidgwick & Jackson for libel damages because Junor had stated in her biography of Richard Burton that Burton had seduced Jean Simmons in their home while Granger had slept in the next room and that, subsequently, Granger had given 'an untruthful and boastful account of a conversation between himself and Mr Burton'. Junor and her publishers accepted the fact that the statements which reflected on Granger and his wife had no basis in fact and they undertook to withdraw copies of the book from circulation and not to republish the book containing those passages. Granger won substantial undisclosed libel damages and costs. The British press reported the case with headlines such as 'Actor wins damages for sex slur over wife' (in the *Independent*). What exactly Granger's motives were in initiating this legal action with its subsequent rather sleazy non-revelations are unclear, but he felt strongly enough about it to take the trouble to instruct counsel and put up with the attendant publicity, publicity that throughout his life he claimed to detest. Whether the damages awarded to him made it worth his while is impossible to say. His marriage to Jean Simmons and her reputation were obviously still a matter of great concern to him. It is a very bizarre episode of his latter years.

Television was continuing to provide Granger with sporadic work. This included guest appearances in two episodes of a series *Hotel*, an episode of *Murder She Wrote*, an episode of the *Love Boat* series, a mini-series *Crossings* in three parts and a television movie *A Hazard of Hearts*. All these projects were the kind of mediocre fare that filled the network schedules night after night in America. All of it was instantly forgettable, but it kept the actor, now in his mid-seventies, working and solvent. However, it was the unlikely medium of the stage that would bring him most public attention in his latter years. He was offered a part in a production of Somerset Maugham's *The Circle* in which he would co-star with Rex Harrison and Glynis Johns. The production opened in the States 'out-of-town' then came to Broadway so, at the age of seventy-seven, Granger was making his Broadway debut.

Rex Harrison had always been a notoriously 'difficult' man, which is a euphemistic way of describing an arrogant, sometimes cruel and egomaniac individual. Granger had also been described as arrogant and bad-tempered so sparks were likely to fly upward when those two worked together. According to Granger, that is exactly what happened. The rather patrician Harrison clearly looked down on this swashbuckling ex-movie star and addressed him as Granger all the time they worked together. Just what justification Harrison had for taking this superior attitude to Granger is hard to understand, since he had never achieved much in the theatre or in film, for that matter, apart from his Professor Higgins in *My Fair Lady*. Despite the fact that Harrison was eighty-three by this time and had very impaired vision, he did not seem to have lost the art of upsetting people. One night during a performance in Carolina, Harrison deliberately sneezed over one of Granger's best lines, whereupon Granger, when they got off the stage, threatened Harrison with these words: 'If you ever do that again, you mother-fucker, I'll break your fucking leg.' The ridiculousness of these two geriatric actors almost squaring up to each other backstage, with Granger expressing his anger with the profanities he had habitually used throughout his career, must have forcibly struck any who witnessed the scene. Even in his late seventies, Granger was still playing macho, threatening physical retribution to those who crossed him, even if the guy happened to be eighty-three and almost blind.

The Circle ran at the Ambassador's Theatre in Manhattan for a total of 208 performances from 14 November 1988 to 20 May 1990. Granger played Clive Champion-Cheney to Harrison's aristocrat and for his efforts he won a Theatre World Special Award for the Most Outstanding Broadway Debut for 1988. At the age of seventy-seven, it could be said to have been quite a debut. The production also won the Tony for Best Revival. For a revival, it had a very respectable run. The production had been mounted round Rex Harrison, whom Broadway theatre-goers would have remembered from *My Fair Lady* on Broadway, and it had been intended to bring the play to London's West End, but Harrison died before the transfer could be made. Nevertheless, *The Circle* was revived and Harrison and Glynis Johns were replaced by Ian Carmichael and Rosemary Harris for the British tour. For the first time in almost fifty years, matinée idol Stewart Granger was returning to the British stage, but the production was not a resounding success and it did not make its way into the West End. 'I'm still not sure why I'm doing it,' Granger told the British press. 'All I want to be is an old fart living at home in Southern California.' Granger was soon granted his wish, after a short tour which included weeks at Guildford and Bradford.

The National Film Theatre in London mounted a short season of Granger's films in 1990 and Granger was invited to appear at a Screen *Guardian* event. Tony Sloman, the film producer and broadcaster, remembers it vividly. Sloman was a lifelong but not uncritical fan of Granger's and has described him as 'the greatest British movie star ever'. Sloman makes the distinction between actors in film (he cites Sean Connery and Michael Caine as British examples) and outright film stars of whom Granger is a prime example. At the *Guardian* event, Sloman had expected to interview Granger on stage, but Granger decided at the last minute to take the stage alone and just talk, asking Sloman to sit in the front row so that if he could not recall details about his movies, then he would turn to him. Granger rambled through a string of familiar anecdotes about the mishaps of filming and made a few swipes at MGM and movie executives in general. He harked back to the golden days of Hollywood and expressed the opinion that stars were really stars in those days. He quoted Errol Flynn as the greatest example of this. Contemporary stars such as Al Pacino were very good actors, but he queried whether they were real movie stars in the full sense of the term. For someone who had moaned about the tribulations and nonsense attached to being a movie star, it was a peculiar refrain for him to be expounding, but that was part of the contradiction of the man. Part of him despised film stardom, but another part of him loved it. At any rate, Granger charmed and enthralled his audience throughout his 'talk' and the evening was a success. It must have helped to make him feel he still had his fans out there. Despite all his protestations, he liked to be remembered. Tony Sloman recounts how shortly before Granger's death in 1993, he had been asked by the actor to visit him in his Santa Monica home where Granger promised to cook him his famous spaghetti. Sloman believes that by this time Granger was desperate to be with people who remembered him for who he had been. To his eternal regret, Sloman had to turn down the invitation because he was returning to England. Shortly afterwards Granger died.

In 1991, the *Sunday Times* magazine featured Granger in its 'A Life in the Day of' series. Granger talked about his health: 'It takes me about five minutes to get out of bed because I creak a bit and I'm short of breath. When they've taken out half a lung by mistake, you feel rather angry about it to start with and then suddenly you realise it's your fault because you smoked cigarettes. If I had a lung and a half it would be no problem but I haven't because I've got emphysema in what's left.' Although he made light of it in this feature, it is clear that Granger by this time was not at all a well man. He remembers details about his childhood holidays in Cornwall, talks about the humming birds he kept, the tennis he plays and the fact that he hasn't been to a restaurant in years: 'They charge too much, the service is usually lousy, the food is not that good and there's always a man smoking a cigar near me which absolutely kills me.' He mentions he's on his own in Los Angeles although the children from his various marriages come and visit him: 'I think what a mess I made of my life, because I never reached my potential. I should never have gone on being an actor; I should have been a producer.'

The ill-health that Granger describes worsened soon after the article was published. He was diagnosed as having prostate and bone cancer. There was no way back for the ageing swashbuckler now. Time had caught up with him and the body had finally given out. He was cared for by various members of his family and several of them were present when he died at St John's Hospital and Health Center in Santa Monica on 16 August 1993. As a cancer sufferer, it could not have been an easy departure for Granger, but he was surrounded by some of the people who loved him when he made his final exit.

The boy from the Old Brompton Road, that Jimmy Stewart, died thousands of miles away in California as Stewart Granger, but the two were one and the same. He had lived for eighty years and by the standards of many people, he had had a fascinating life. Whether or not he really believed that himself is open to question. 'Man is born unto trouble,' Granger had quoted in his autobiography, and it is significant that that is how he chose to summarise his life, rather than dwelling on his successes or any happiness he had experienced. But now his grumbles about life had finally ceased and he had been relieved of his burden of troubles. Death had caught up with Scaramouche.

Chapter 10

SOME KIND OF A MAN

Almost all of the obituaries published immediately after Granger's death highlighted his swashbuckling credentials. *The Times* obituary opened with these complimentary words: 'Smouldering good looks, a 6ft 2ins physique and a nimble athleticism brought Stewart Granger film stardom playing swashbuckling leads in a series of costume dramas.' But later on in the piece Granger is described as 'abrasive' and 'given to a devil-may-care outspokenness who never endeared himself to fellow-actors, directors or studio bosses'. The *Daily Telegraph* obituary compared him favourably with Errol Flynn and Douglas Fairbanks, but mentioned that Granger preferred to see himself as a classical English actor who had sold his soul to the movies. The 1949 stage production of Tolstoy's *The Power of Darkness*, however, in which Granger's acting had been 'embarrassing', had revealed his limitations as a stage actor. The same obituary quoted one critic's summation of Granger's Apollodorus in *Caesar and Cleopatra* as reminding him 'of Surbiton's lawn-tennis champion at his most dashing'. The obituary also quoted Granger's own opinion that he had been an extravagant fool and that he had messed up his life and marriages and thrown away the good chances that had come his way. *Stage and Television Today*, read by most people in the theatre and film world, loyally quoted Laurence Olivier's opinion that Granger was 'a superb actor, which most people don't realise. He makes acting look very easy, which it isn't.' Patrick Newley, the writer of this obituary, bucked the trend and described Granger as 'a great character on stage and off, and more's the pity that he wasn't given the chance to display his admirable talent in more suitable roles'. The *Observer* obituary was headlined 'King of Broken Hearts' and explained that Granger was a 'heartbreaker on screen and off, and wasn't much loved', although he possessed the screen presence of a true star. The *New York Times* quoted Granger's own quote about his acting abilities: 'Stewart Granger was quite a successful film star, but I don't think he was an actor's actor.' This obituary has Granger pointing with pride to his work on the English stage, but when he was asked whether he would like to return to the theatre, he stated he was too lazy because the theatre was hard work. Indeed, the *New York Times* piece is rather dismissive, seeming to damn with faint praise, an approach which is betrayed in its headline: 'Stewart Granger, 80, Film Actor Known for Swashbucking Roles'.

By and large, the batch of obituaries were generally cool in tone and although they mostly stressed how successful a swashbuckling star Granger had been in his heyday, they were largely ungenerous in their summation of his career and Granger as a man. Clearly, the man had ruffled many a feather during his long career and the obituary writers were aware of this. There is also a collective sense of the missed opportunities and unfulfilled ambitions of the man. The overall picture is of an individual who was dissatisfied with his life as a whole, as well as his career. After all, Granger had moaned about his lot so publicly and for so many years that it is hardly surprising the obituarists continued that refrain and painted the picture of a largely unhappy and self-deprecating man, who was at the same time capable of extreme arrogance and insensitivity.

Famous and successful individuals are undoubtedly the target of envy and rumour. That is one of the down sides of fame, something that Granger was acutely aware of. However, Granger gave hostages to fortune by appearing to be arrogant, cocksure of himself and downright rude at times, so these innate propensities gave those poised with their scalpels more reason to wound in retort. In fact, all the evidence points to the fact that Granger had a far thinner skin than he pretended to have. He covered up his insecurities and his hurt with a mask of bravado, just as Scaramouche's mask disguised André Moreau. He revealed some of his real self in his autobiography and no doubt to those closest to him, but in public, although he put himself and his career down many a time, it was always in that kind of 'here-goes-nothing' vein, as though none of it really mattered. But, of course, it did matter to him; it was his life, his pain, his disappointments, his choices.

Stewart Granger the film star was a phenomenon of the times. In the way of these things, he came from 'nowhere' and became a top box office star in the 1940s and then went onto become a true international star. No one has very seriously claimed that he was a great actor (we can safely dismiss Olivier's statement that Granger was one of the best actors he knew as an example of overt loyalty to a pal, as well as an example of a truly great actor praising someone whom he must have known was a not serious rival). To become such a major star, Granger must have represented some qualities and ideals that appealed to a mass audience. When he had his first hit in the 1943, *The Man in Grey*, Britain was still at war and Granger may have represented an ideal of British maleness – strong, courageous, handsome, decent. He radiated confidence in unconfident times and he became the idol of teenage girls and older women as well for his physical attractiveness and breezy manner. He promised a girl a good time and, by and large, she got it. But there also something rather caddish about him. He was not the dangerous type like James Mason, merely wayward and hard to pin down. He was destined to be a swashbuckling star, an icon of unreconstructed masculinity like Fairbanks and Flynn, going his own way, sometimes cheating his ladies and treating them badly, but always chivalrous and romantic in between. It is worthy of comment that nowadays when Hollywood makes a swashbuckler, it is done tongue-in-cheek with a heart-throb star such as Johnny Depp in on the joke. The devil-may-care adventurer and his masculine posturing can no longer be taken seriously.

Granger wasn't Leslie Howard or Dirk Bogarde or even John Mills, the family man. He wanted to live dangerously as he did on the screen and so he helped ruin his own health by not only performing too many of his own stunts that caused lasting injuries but also by drinking and, particularly, smoking too much, a habit that eventually caught up with him. Swashbucklers are gamblers by nature and in his business affairs, he was a gambler par excellence, looking for the quick gain and too often landing himself with financial difficulties. In his private life, he had three failed marriages, but for a romantic screen hero, he did not make women the centre of his life, even though he claimed to have loved his wives and his children. He preferred instead to be doing manly things such as hunting big game, sailing, gambling and running ranches and business projects.

However, there is something not entirely convincing about Granger in this ultra-masculine pose. Beneath the surface bravado, there lurked something gentler and more vulnerable, perhaps the real Jimmy Stewart. He had learned to conceal this gentler side because the world, it seemed to him, was a risky place, full of traps and hurdles and people who were only too quick to criticise or let you down or openly deceive you. Born into an emotionally frozen family situation with its secrets and unspoken alliances and alienations, with an isolated father figure, a loved uncle figure who turned out to be someone else entirely and with a mother who did not give freely of her love to her son, the young Granger had learned to hold back his tears, to swallow his hurt and go his own independent way, determined not to be like his emasculated father. A barrier to intimacy had been erected and perhaps it never really was lowered thereafter. But the world was a cruel place and there were bullies out there, at school, in the army, in his first days of employment, in the theatre and in the film studios so he had to adopt a strong pose, an armour of indifference, even arrogance, he had to play the 'man' and that meant swearing like the proverbial trooper and threatening to punch anyone who really crossed him. People were envious of good looks and success, they did not really wish you well, and if that was the way of the world, then he would play that game better than most and give back more than he received. If that meant he was not popular or that the general impression he gave was of being overbearing and arrogant, then so much the better because he would choose his own tight circle of friends and the devil take the rest. Anyway, most people he worked were, in his estimation, incompetents or idiots, especially the studio executives both in Britain and Hollywood, and if they weren't particularly incompetent, there was usually something else about them to annoy him.

But that defensive pose, the barriers that he felt he had to erect, the retreat from true intimacy, the Stewart Granger persona he donned came at a cost. It is a wearisome business being at odds with the world. It takes its toll, applies pressure and gets worse if you don't have an outlet for those feelings of resentment and grievance and injustice, other than bursts of anger, vituperation and obscenities. It affects your sense of well-being and finally your health begins to go. Granger seemed to be in a constant state of dissatisfaction with himself, other people and life itself. 'They say I am moody, but I don't like people and they don't like me,' he is quoted as saying late in life, justifying his loner status, his separation from the world. And yet, to many people, he had it all in the palm of his hand: fame, comparative wealth (at certain stages in his life), looks, talent, sex appeal, a job as a glamorous movie star, a glamorous and talented film star wife. For many millions of people, Granger would appear to have been blessed with too much. Why, then, we ask, couldn't he be happy? He had it all going for him, while the rest of humanity struggle in humdrum jobs trying to make ends meet, living in obscurity without the least trace of glamour, with worries about how we look and whether or not we are loved. So are we happy or sad when we learn that someone as apparently blessed with the good things in life turns out to have been just as dissatisfied as the majority of humanity?

Do we shake our heads complacently and lament lost opportunities, or do we feel a genuine sense of disappointment that with all those advantages, happiness in life still escaped him?

Movie stars encapsulate the yearnings and fantasies of the audiences who watch them on the giant screen. They embody values and a way of living life. We project on to them our own desires and ambitions. They live out a dream in a dream world. Swashbuckler stars are involved in living out on screen a particular kind of male fantasy of freedom, merriment, adventure, romance, glamour and physical prowess. For a swashbuckler there is always another adventure over the next horizon, another beautiful woman to be tamed and won, another pot of gold to be discovered, another villain to be vanquished and injustice to the righted. The swashbuckler is out there in the bright blue yonder with only his wits, his sword and his maleness to protect him. He faces danger always with courage and a quip on his lips. Other males are either loyal pals or inferiors, or they are sworn enemies who threaten not only his very existence but his concept of himself. Authority and respectability have to be flouted, but decency will always finally prevail because the true swashbuckler is not just a scavenging pirate, but a hero who is chivalrous, the defender of the poor and the infirm, the scourge of bullies and tyrants. The swashbuckler, in short, is a myth, an idealisation of the freebooting male and of the rootless and the unattached and the emotionally immature.

Errol Flynn lived the life of the swashbuckler to the full off-screen and although he doubtless had some fun along the way, his path was a self-destructive one. Stewart Granger was far less self-destructive, but even by his own estimation he was a fool unto himself. Off-screen, there was something of the swashbuckler about Granger, but the consequences of being a gambler, of living the 'male life' to the full, of striking out for the next horizon, were not always beneficial and did not result in lasting, or even fleeting, happiness. As his career as a movie swashbuckler was coming to an end, so was society's concept of maleness changing. The macho life came under closer and closer scrutiny and many men realised that being out there on your own in the wide blue yonder wasn't a very great place to be. But the changes in male behaviour and goals came too late for someone of Granger's generation and mindset. He would never change and because he couldn't change in real life, he found it impossible to change his screen persona, and so he went on playing variations of the Stewart Granger role on screen until he was too old to play it any longer.

Swashbucklers went badly out of fashion in the 1960s and have never really returned to favour. Male Hollywood stars showed their independence and freebooting ways in films like *Hud* and *The Hustler* (both Paul Newman) or in the Jack Nicholson movies *Five Easy Pieces* and *One Flew Over the Cuckoo's Nest*. The new breed of Hollywood star often didn't get the girl in the end, they were sometimes depicted as lonely and defeated, but, importantly, they were still free spirits, individualists bucking the trend, going against the grain, doing it 'their way', however isolating and self-destructive that path became. Or male role models became tougher and more psychopathic like Clint Eastwood in his spaghetti westerns or the Dirty Harry series. In many movies the new breed showed their vulnerabilities as well as their violent urges as with Robert De Niro in *Taxi Driver* and *Raging Bull*. Then there were the grotesque unreconstructed models of masculinity in the robot bully figures impersonated by Arnold Schwarzenegger, Sylvester Stallone, Vin Diesel, Chuck Norris and other worthies. The grace, the chivalry, the devil-may-care quality of the traditional swashbuckler now seemed hopelessly dated, belonging to a different age and an antique concept of maleness. Today's macho heroes play ruthless hitmen like Tom Cruise in *Collateral* or emotionally shutdown loners like Russell Crowe in *Gladiator*. Our notion of the male hero seems to have changed irrevocably.

So was Granger the last of the true swashbucklers? He was certainly among the last of the male stars who became permanently connected with swashbuckling roles. Swashbucklers as a movie genre have largely disappeared from movie screens except for the occasional rehash of Dumas classics such as *The Count of Monte Cristo* or a self-consciously ironic *Pirates of the Caribbean. The Mask of Zorro* (1998) with Antonio Banderas and Anthony Hopkins was more in the tradition of the genre, but that seemed largely a one-off effort. Perhaps the huge success of *Pirates of the Caribbean* may spawn a series of imitations (Hollywood pounces like a hungry vulture on anything successful that can be recycled), but irony and affectionate send-ups cannot really be repeated ad nauseam. Costume dramas will continue to be produced, but the unreconstructed swashbuckling hero is unlikely to dominate them. We no longer believe in heroes in a world full of distrust and paranoia and technological violence. Errol Flynn or Stewart Granger with his rapier at the ready to defend the defenceless seem irrelevant in a world where precision-targeting can destroy the enemy you never see or who never see you. We have lost our belief in even the flawed hero, because manifestly everyone is seriously flawed, especially our leaders who speak with forked tongues. In contemporary society that is becoming more and more controlled and authoritarian, there is no longer any space for the devil-may-care freebooter, unless he or she is an international entrepreneur, a master of the economic universe, a megaplayer in the global village, an arch-manipulator and profiteer of the unfettered process of so-called globalisation. In the first decade of the new millennium, the screen characters played by Flynn and Granger would be incorporated into the international corporate world and they would be employed to destroy the enemies that the global corporations would define and target.

Perhaps if we ever believed in the swashbuckler as a valid model of masculinity, it was a testimony to our own refusal to grow up. Carousing and wenching and duelling and sailing off into the blue yonder made an appealing cocktail for those who needed to fantasise about breaking the bonds of duty and responsibility. For people, men and women, stuck in domestic dullness or bored out of their minds in soul-destroying employment, the idea of the swashbuckler was undoubtedly attractive. These movie stars lived out their fantasies, allowing them to identify with a life that was not about household bills and worries about getting on in their job or a marriage that existed primarily to bring up the kids. No swashbuckler ever worried about promotion, was never tied down by paternal duties, was always in love with some beautiful woman and never seemed to worry about getting older. A swashbuckler just went on and on having fun and adventures. However, the screen swashbucklers, the male stars who embodied these fantasies, had to exist in the real world as well. Errol Flynn is the outstanding example of someone who found the divide between his screen life and real life impossible to balance. John Barrymore was another. And so was Stewart Granger. He wanted to be free in his own life, felt consistently fettered by circumstance, money, emotional ties and the conditions of his employment as a movie actor. He never resolved the difficulties he had with accepting a curtailment of his freedom as he chased fame and wealth. His freebooting life off-screen became increasingly less rewarding as he stumbled from one disastrous venture to another. He did not like people, he said frequently, but, more importantly, he did not appear to like himself much. And a swashbuckler who does not like himself is not much of a swashbuckler, finally, because he above all has to radiate self-belief and self-love. Stewart Granger may have appeared superficially to be confident and too fond of himself by half, but the reality was very different. He was a guy who found it hard to like the world and the people in it, and that included himself.

At the end of Orson Welles's classic film noir of 1958, *Touch of Evil*, Marlene Dietrich, who plays the ex-lover of the wholly corrupt Sheriff played by a gargantuan Welles himself, is asked her opinion of the Welles character who has been fatally shot: 'What can you say about people?' she says. 'He was some kind of a man.' Stewart Granger was some kind of a man. His life had its share of successes and failures, its triumphs and disasters, its happiness and its sadness. He was not an extraordinary human being and, like most film stars, was just like you or me, a man who happened to be an actor, struggling to make something meaningful of life, except he did it in the full glare of publicity most of the time because he was one of those we elect to be movie stars and that 'elevated' status brings its advantages and disadvantages, as Granger himself was all too ready to emphasise. He was some kind of a man who was never really able to enjoy what success came his way because it never seemed to be what he really wanted. As a star, he will be remembered as a swashbuckler. As a man, he will be remembered fondly by some, not so fondly by many others who knew him. But, then, in truth, that is the legacy most of us leave behind. Some kind of a man and some kind of a movie star. The two roles, the private and the public, intermingled, affecting his 'performance' as a human being and as an actor. He was both Scaramouche and Stewart Granger, and he was also Jimmy Stewart and Stewart Granger. Some of the problems he had in his life arose because he never clarified exactly who he was. Geographically, it was a long way from the Old Brompton Road to Hollywood, but the emotional distance was much shorter.

SOURCES

Chapter 1
Sparks Fly Upward, Stewart Granger, 1981
Photoplay magazine feature, 1953
The Swashbucklers, James Robert Parish and Don E. Slanke, 1976
Letters from the Reverend Wulstan Hibberd and Dr J. Cedric Jones

Chapter 2
The Celluloid Mistress, Rodney Ackland and Elspeth Grant, 1954
Once A Wicked Lady, Hilton Tims, 1993
Before I Forget, James Mason, 1981
Picture Show 1945 feature article
The Swashbucklers
Daily Mirror, 'He Doesn't Want to be a Heart-Throb', 10 August 1945
News Chronicle article
The Disciple and His Devil, Valerie Pascal, 1971
Sparks Fly Upward

Chapter 3
Once A Wicked Lady
Richard Burton: A Life, Melvyn Bragg, 1989
The Finest Years: British Cinema of the 1940s, Charles Drazin, 1992
Daily Mirror feature, July 1948
Various reviews: *Monthly Film Bulletin, New York Times, The People*
Picturegoer magazine, 'Are They Doing Alright by Our Jimmy?', 20
    November 1948
The Disciple and His Devil
Daily Express, 'Do You See All the Film?', 1 April 1949
Sparks Fly Upward

Chapter 4
The Swashbucklers
Daily Mirror, 'Smile Please!', 6 August 1952
Sparks Fly Upward

Chapter 5
BBC Radio feature, George Sidney, 5 September 1993, written and
    produced by Tony Sloman
The Swashbucklers
Guardian Screen Event at the NFT, September 1990
'Days in the Dream Factory', Kenneth Tynan, *Punch*, 1954.
Daily Mirror feature, Donald Zec, 1952
Picturegoer, 7 February 1953
Daily Mirror, 'Stewart Granger says I Love Jean', 12 October 1950

Chapter 6
Daily Mail, 'I Plotted to Murder Howard Hughes', Robin McGibbon, 4
    July 1953
Picturegoer, 'The Marriage They Said Wouldn't Last', Donovan Pedelty,
    1953
Picturegoer, 'Stewart Granger's Charm School', 24 January 1953
Evening Standard article, David Marlowe, November 1953
Charles Laughton: An Intimate Biography, Charles Higham, 1976
New York Times, 'Actors Settle Court Case', 1 September 1953
Sunday Express, 'Granger Hits Out at Critics', 9 January 1953
News Chronicle, 20 June 1952
The MGM Stock Company: The Golden Era, James Parish and Ronald
    Bowers, 1973

Chapter 7
Sunday Graphic article, Robert Robinson's Film Page, 20 October 1957
Daily Sketch, 'The Grangers Are No Longer British', 26 June 1956

MGM archival material, Film Department, University of Southern
   California, Los Angeles
Daily Express, 'I've Roped My First Steer', 3 July 1956
Confidential magazine, 1957
Niv: The Life of David Niven, Graham Lord, 2004
The Great Movie Stars: The International Years, David Shipman, 1994

Chapter 8
Sunday Express: 'Work I Must, Says Granger', October 1957
ABC Film Review, June 1958
Daily Express, 'We Stake All on the Range', 21 May 1958
Paramount Pictures press book for *Sodom and Gomorrah*
Sparks Fly Upward

Chapter 9
Granger television interview with Mavis Nicholson, 1981
Jimmy, Christos Tses and Dirk Bruderle, 1997
Sunday Express article, Roderick Mann, 9 October 1966
Paramount Pictures press book for *The Last Safari*
Radio Times feature, 7 October 1972
Daily Express, 'Star in Scandal over Sunshine Homes', 2 November 1984
Interview with director Tony Sloman, June 2004
Independent, 'Actor Wins Damages for Sex Slur', 11 March 1987
Evening Standard, 'Burton Never Slept With My Wife Jean', 10 March
   1987
The MGM Stock Company
Sunday Express, 'I Made a Mess of My Life', 22 June 1980
Daily Mail, 'Where I Went Wrong', 9 February 1987
Guardian, 'Return of the Lone Granger', 18 September 1982
Sunday Times, 'A Life in the Day of . . .', 17 February 1991

Chapter 10

Obituaries: *The Times, Daily Telegraph, Stage and Television Today, Observer, New York Times*

FILMOGRAPHY

The following is a list of all Stewart Granger's major films. Other, minor projects for film and TV included *Secret Mission, Convoy, So This is London, Under Secret Orders, I Spy, Give Her a Ring, Over the Garden Wall, A Southern Maid, Chameleons, Fine Gold, Erbe der Guldenburgs, A Hazard of Hearts, Crossings, The Royal Romance of Charles and Diana, The Hound of the Baskervilles, Any Second Now, Requiem for a Secret Agent.*

Thursday's Child: GB, ABPC, 1942, 81 mins. Director: Rodney Ackland. Screenplay: Donald Macardie and Rodney Ackland. Cast: Sally Ann Howes, Wilfrid Lawson, Kathleen O'Regan, Stewart Granger.

The Man in Grey: GB, Gainsborough, 1943, 122 mins. Director: Leslie Arliss. Screenplay: Margaret Kennedy, Leslie Arliss and Doreen Montgomery. Cast: James Mason, Margaret Lockwood, Phyllis Calvert, Stewart Granger, Nora Swinburne.

The Lamp Still Burns: GB, Two Cities, 1943, 90 mins. Director: Leslie Howard. Screenplay: Elizabeth Baron and Roland Pertwee. Cast: Rosamund John, Stewart Granger, Godfrey Tearle, John Laurie, Joyce Grenfell

Fanny by Gaslight: GB, Gainsborough, 1944, 98 mins. Director: Anthony Asquith. Screenplay: Doreen Montgomery and Aimee Stuart. Cast: James Mason, Phyllis Calvert, Stewart Granger, Wilfrid Lawson, John Laurie, Jean Kent.

Love Story: GB, Gainsborough/Rank, 1944, 113 mins. Director: Leslie Arliss. Screenplay: Leslie Arliss, Doreen Montgomery and Rodney Ackland. Cast: Margaret Lockwood, Stewart Granger, Patricia Roc, Tom Walls, Moira Lister.

Madonna of the Seven Moons, GB, Gainsborough/Rank, 1944, 110 mins. Director: Arthur Crabtree. Screenplay: Roland Pertwee and Brock

Williams. Cast: Phyllis Calvert, Stewart Granger, Patricia Roc, Peter Glenville, Jean Kent, John Stuart, Peter Murray-Hill.

Waterloo Road: GB, Gainsborough/Rank, 1945, 76 mins. Director: Sidney Gilliat. Screenplay: Sidney Gilliat. Cast: John Mills, Stewart Granger, Joy Shelton, Alastair Sim, Jean Kent.

Caesar and Cleopatra: GB, Rank, 1945, 139 mins. Director: Gabriel Pascal. Screenplay: Bernard Shaw. Cast: Claude Rains, Vivien Leigh, Cecil Parker, Stewart Granger, Flora Robson, Francis L. Sullivan, Jean Simmons.

Caravan: GB, Gainsborough/Rank, 1946, 105 mins. Director: Arthur Crabtreece. Screenplay: Roland Pertwee. Cast: Stewart Granger, Anne Crawford, Jean Kent, Robert Helpmann, Dennis Price.

The Magic Bow: GB, Gainsborough/Rank, 1946, 106 mins. Director: Bernard Knowles. Screenplay: Norman Ginsbury and Roland Pertwee. Cast: Stewart Granger, Jean Kent, Phyllis Calvert, Dennis Price, Cecil Parker, Felix Aylmer, Marie Lohr.

Captain Boycott: GB, GFD, 1947, 93 mins. Director: Frank Launder. Screenplay: Wolfgang Wilhelm, Frank Launder, Paul Vincent Carroll and Patrick Campbell. Cast: Stewart Granger, Kathleen Ryan, Alastair Sim, Robert Donat, Cecil Parker, Mervyn Johns, Noel Purcell, Niall MacGinnis.

Blanche Fury: GB, GFD/Cineguild, 1948, 95 mins. Director: Marc Allegret. Screenplay: Audrey Erskine-Lindop, Hugh Mills and Cecil McGivern. Cast: Stewart Granger, Valerie Hobson, Walter Fitzgerald, Michael Gough, Maurice Denham.

Saraband for Dead Lovers: GB, Ealing, 1948, 98 mins. Director: Basil Dearden and Michael Relph. Screenplay: John Dighton and Alexander MacKendrick. Cast: Stewart Granger, Joan Greenwood, Françoise Rosay, Flora Robson, Peter Bull.

Woman Hater: GB, GFD/Two Cities, 1948, 105 mins. Director: Terence Young. Screenplay: Robert Westerby and Nicholas Phipps. Cast: Stewart Granger, Edwige Feuillère, Ronald Squire, Mary Jerrold,

Jeanne de Casalis.

Adam and Evelyne: GB, Rank/Two Cities, 1949, 92 mins. Director: Harold
French. Screenplay: Noel Langley, Lesley Storm, George Barraud and
Nicholas Phipps. Cast: Stewart Granger, Jean Simmons, Helen Cherry,
Edwin Styles, Beatrice Varley, Wilfred Hyde-White.

King Solomon's Mines: US, MGM, 1950, 102 mins. Director: Compton
Bennett and Andrew Marton. Screenplay: Helen Deutsch. Cast: Stewart
Granger, Deborah Kerr, Richard Carlson, Hugo Haas.

Soldiers Three: US, MGM, 1951, 87 mins. Director: Tay Garnett.
Screenplay: Marguerite Roberts, Tom Reed and Malcolm Stuart
Boylan. Cast: Stewart Granger, David Niven, Robert Newton, Walter
Pidgeon, Cyril Cusack, Greta Gynt, Robert Coote.

The Light Touch: US, MGM, 1951, 107 mins. Director: Richard Brooks.
Screenplay: Richard Brooks. Cast: Stewart Granger, George Sanders,
Pier Angeli, Kurt Kasznar.

Scaramouche: US, MGM, 1952, 115 mins. Director: George Sidney.
Screenplay: Ronald Millar and George Froeschel. Cast: Stewart
Granger, Mel Ferrer, Eleanor Parker, Janet Leigh, Henry Wilcoxon,
Nina Foch, Lewis Stone, Robert Coote, Richard Anderson.

The Wild North: US, MGM, 1952, 97 mins. Director: Andrew Marton.
Screenplay: Frank Fenton. Cast: Stewart Granger, Wendell Corey, Cyd
Charisse.

The Prisoner of Zenda: US, MGM, 1952, 100 mins. Director: Richard
Thorpe. Screenplay: John Balderston and Noel Langley. Cast: Stewart
Granger, James Mason, Deborah Kerr, Louis Calhern, Jane Greer,
Robert Douglas, Lewis Stone.

Salome: US, Columbia, 1953, 103 mins. Director: William Dieterle.
Screenplay: Harry Kleiner and Jesse Lasky Jr. Cast: Rita Hayworth,
Stewart Granger, Charles Laughton, Judith Anderson, Cedric
Hardwicke, Alan Badel, Basil Sydney.

Young Bess: US, MGM, 1953, 112 mins. Director: George Sidney.
Screenplay: Arthur Wimperis and Jan Lustig. Cast: Jean Simmons,

Stewart Granger, Deborah Kerr, Charles Laughton, Kay Walsh, Guy Rolfe, Kathleen Byron, Cecil Kellaway.

All the Brothers Were Valiant: US, MGM, 1953, 94 mins. Director: Richard Thorpe. Screenplay: Harry Brown. Cast: Stewart Granger, Robert Taylor, Ann Blyth, Betta St John, Keenan Wynn, James Whitmore, Lewis Stone.

Beau Brummell: US, MGM, 1954, 112 mins. Director: Curtis Bernhardt. Screenplay: Karl Tunberg. Cast: Stewart Granger, Peter Ustinov, Elizabeth Taylor, Robert Morley, James Donald, James Hayter.

Green Fire: US, MGM, 1954, 100 mins. Director: Andrew Marton. Screenplay: Ivan Goff and Ben Roberts. Cast: Stewart Granger, Grace Kelly, Paul Douglas, John Ericson.

Moonfleet: US, MGM, 1955, 87 mins. Director: Fritz Lang. Screenplay: Margaret Fitts and Jan Lustig. Cast: Stewart Granger, Jon Whiteley, Joan Greenwood, George Sanders, Viveca Lindfors.

Footsteps in the Fog: GB, Columbia/Film Locations, 1955, 90 mins. Director: Arthur Lubin. Screenplay: Dorothy Reid and Lenore Coffee. Cast: Stewart Granger, Jean Simmons, Bill Travers, Ronald Squire, Finlay Currie, Peter Bull.

The Last Hunt: US, MGM, 1956, 103 mins. Director: Richard Brooks. Screenplay: Richard Brooks. Cast: Stewart Granger, Robert Taylor, Debra Paget, Lloyd Nolan, Russ Tamblyn.

Bhowani Junction: GB, MGM, 1956, 110 mins. Director: George Cukor. Screenplay: Sonya Levien and Ivan Moffatt. Cast: Stewart Granger, Ava Gardner, Bill Travers, Francis Matthews, Abraham Sofaer, Freda Jackson, Edward Chapman.

The Little Hut: US, MGM, 1957, 90 mins. Director: Mark Robson. Screenplay: F. Hugh Herbert. Cast: Stewart Granger, Ava Gardner, David Niven, Walter Chiari, Finlay Currie.

Gun Glory: US, MGM, 1957, 89 mins. Director: Roy Rowland. Screenplay: William Ludwig. Cast: Stewart Granger, Rhonda Fleming, Chill Wills, Steve Rowland, James Gregory.

The Whole Truth: GB, Columbia/Romulus, 1958, 84 mins. Director: John Guillermin and Dan Cohen. Screenplay: Jonathan Latimer. Cast: Stewart Granger, George Sanders, Donna Reed, Gianna Maria Canale.

Harry Black (aka *Harry Black and the Tiger*): GB, Mersham/Fox, 1958, 117 mins. Director: Hugo Fregonese. Screenplay: Sydney Boehm. Cast: Stewart Granger, Barbara Rush, Anthony Steel, I.S. Johar.

North to Alaska: US, Fox, 1960, 122 mins. Director: Henry Hathaway. Screenplay: John Lee Mahin, Martin Rackin and Claude Binyon. Cast: John Wayne, Stewart Granger, Fabian, Capucine, Ernie Kovacs.

The Secret Partner: GB, MGM, 1961, 91 mins. Director: Basil Dearden. Screenplay: David Pursall and Jack Seddon. Cast: Stewart Granger, Bernard Lee, Haya Harareet, Hugh Burden, Melissa Stribling.

The Swordsman of Siena: Italy/France, Mondiale/Monica/Artisques, 1961, 95 mins. Director: Etienne Perier. Cast: Stewart Granger, Sylva Koscina, Christine Kaufmann.

Sodom and Gomorrah: Italy/France, Titanus/Pathe/S.G.C., 1962, 165 mins. Director: Robert Aldrich and Sergio Leone. Cast: Stewart Granger, Pier Angeli, Stanley Baker, Anouk Aimee, Rossana Podesta, Rik Battaglia.

March or Die: Spain/Italy, Midega/Monachia/Tempo, 1962, 98 mins. Director: Frank Wisbar. Cast: Stewart Granger, Dorian Gray, Hans von Borsody, Dietmar Schönherr.

The Secret Invasion: US: Roger Corman/United Artists, 1964, 96 mins. Director: Roger Corman. Cast: Stewart Granger, Raf Vallone, Mickey Rooney, Henry Silva, Helmuth Schneider.

The Crooked Road: US/Yugoslavia, Seven Arts/Argo/Triglavfilm/Trident, 1964, 93 mins. Director: Don Chaffey. Cast: Stewart Granger, Nadia Gray, Robert Ryan, Marius Goring.

Unter Geiern: Germany/France/Yugoslavia, Rialto, 1964, 101 mins. Director: Alfred Vohrer. Cast: Stewart Granger, Pierre Brice, Götz George, Elke Sommer, Walter Barnes.

Mission Hong Kong/Red Dragon: Germany/Italy, Arca/Pea, 1965, 89 mins. Director: Ernst Hofbauer. Cast: Stewart Granger, Rossano Schiaffino,

Harld Juhnke, Margit Saad.

Der Olprinz: Germany/Yugoslavia, Rialto/Jadran, 1965, 91 mins. Director: Harald Philipp. Cast: Stewart Granger, Pierre Brice, Macha Meril, Walter Barnes.

Old Surehand: Germany/Yugoslavia, Rialto/Jadran, 1965, 90 mins. Director: Alfred Vohrer. Cast: Stewart Granger, Pierre Brice, Letítia Román, Larry Pennell.

Das Gehiemnis der gelben Mönche: Austria/Italy, Intercontinental/Pea, 1966, 102 mins. Director: Manfred Kohler. Cast: Stewart Granger, Karin Dor, Curd Jurgens, Adolfo Celi, Klaus Kinski, Rupert Davies

Spy Against the World/Killer's Carnival: Austria/Italy/France, Intercontinental/ Metheus/ inter, 1966, 94 mins. Directors: Sheldon Reynolds and Alberto Cordone. Cast: Stewart Granger, Lex Barker, Pierre Brice, Karin Dor, Margaret Lee, Walter Giller.

The Trygon Factor: GB, Rialto, 1967, 88 mins. Director: Cyril Frankel. Cast: Stewart Granger, Susan Hampshire, Robert Morley, Daniela Bianchi, Peter van Eyck.

The Last Safari: GB: Paramount, 1967, 110 mins. Director: Henry Hathaway. Cast: Stewart Granger, Kaz Garas, Gabriella Licudi, John Sekka, Liam Redmond.

The Wild Geese: GB, Richmond, 1978, 99 mins. Director: Andrew McLaglen. Cast: John Glen, Richard Burton, Richard Harris, Roger Moore, Hardy Kruger, Stewart Granger.

Rage to Kill: 1987, 95 mins, Director: Ernst von Theumer. Cast: Stewart Granger, Candice Daly, George Lazenby.

BIBLIOGRAPHY

Ackland, Rodney and Grant, Elspeth, *The Celluloid Mistress*, Alan Wingate, London 1954

Bragg, Melvyn, *Richard Burton: A Life*, Little, Brown and Co., New York 1989

Drazin, Charles, *British Cinema of the 1940s*, André Deutsch, London 1992

Granger, Stewart, *Sparks Fly Upward*, Granada Publishing, St Albans 1981

Higham, Charles, *Charles Laughton: An Intimate Biography*, W. H. Allen, London 1976

Lord, Graham, *Niv: The Life of David Niven*, St Martin's Press, New York 2004

Mason, James, *Before I Forget*, Hamish Hamilton, London 1981

Pascal, Valerie, *The Disciple and His Devil*, Michael Joseph, London 1971

Parish, James Robert and Bowers, Ronald L., *The MGM Stock Company: The Golden Era*, Ian Allan, Shepperton 1973

Parish, James Robert and Slanke, Don E., *The Swashbucklers*, Arlington House, New Rochelle 1976

Shipman, David, *The Great Movie Stars: The International Years*, Little Brown and Co., New York 1994

Tims, Hilton, *Once A Wicked Lady*, Ulverscroft, Anstey, Leics 1993

Tses, Christos and Bruderle, Dirk, *Jimmy*, Granlex PIV, 1997

The following newspapers and periodicals:
ABC Film Review, Confidential, Daily Express, Daily Mail, Daily Mirror, Daily Telegraph, Daily Sketch, Evening Standard, Guardian, Independent, Monthly Film Bulletin, New York Times, News Chronicle, Observer, The People, Photoplay, Picture Show, Picturegoer, Radio Times, Sunday Express, Sunday Graphic, Sunday Times, The Times

Paramount Pictures Press Books

MGM Studio archives in the Film Department of the University of
    Southern California, Los Angeles
British Film Institute Information Department, St Stephen Street, London

INDEX

This index is compiled on a word-by-word basis so that, for example, *Picture Parade* comes before *Picturegoer*.

Stewart Granger's films and his performances in other media are indexed under Granger, Stewart.